Early Mississippi Records

Volume #2

Washington *and* Issaquena Counties

- 1827-1900 -

Compiled by:
Katherine Clements Branton

Southern Historical Press, inc.
Greenville, South Carolina

This volume was reproduced
from a personal copy located in
the Publishers private library

Please direct all correspondence and book orders to:
SOUTHERN HISTORICAL PRESS, Inc.
1071 Park West Blvd.
Greenville, SC   29611

Originally printed Leland, MS 1983
ISBN #978-1-63914-324-5
Printed in the United States of America

EARLY RECORDS OF MISSISSIPPI
Issaquena County & Washington County
Vol.II

Washington County was formed,1827, out of Warren and Yazoo Counties, and is not to be confused with an earlier Washington County. The first Washington County covered an area along the Southern line between Mississippi and Alabama, and no longer exists.

The present Washington County borders on the Mississippi River and is situated on the rich,river-bottom lands. The first County Seat of this Washington County was New Mexico, which for various reasons was unsuitable. The next chosen spot was Princeton, but the Mighty River ate huge chunks of the banks away and it was moving time again. Another County Seat was laid off, and is referred to,now, as "Old" Greenville. Old Greenville served well as a suitable place, until the Yankees grew weary of being sniped at from the banks, and setting ashore, burned the whole town to the ground. Luckily, many of the records were salvaged, and when a courthouse was raised in "New" Greenville,after the War, the much traveled records found a home.

Naturally, some of the records were lost. The Deed Books seem to be intact, as are Will Books and Circuit Court records. The Packets, which furnish back-up information for Estates,Suits,etc. seem to have suffered most. Many are missing, and it is an almost impossible job to sort the ones that were saved into a comprehensive, chronological listing. All records since the Civil War are well kept and cared for.

Issaquena County was made from Washington County in 1844, and many of the early people have common records in both courthouses. Sharkey County was made from Washington, Issaquena,Warren Counties in 1876, so that, if you lived on lower Deer Creek it would be possible to have records in five counties.

The Courthouse records are on Microfilm in the Archives in Jackson, with the exception of the Packets. However, many volumes are unindexed, water-marked, and very faint. The Packets included in this Vol.II contain information not otherwise available. Collecting it is slow,dirty work.

K.B.

TABLE OF CONTENTS

EARLY MISSISSIPPI RECORDS
VOL.II

ISSAQUENA COUNTY:
Will Book "A", Abstracted;Feb.1846-Dec.1853...1 - 8
Index to Estate Packets........................9 - 14
Packet Gleanings: Abstracted 210 Packets
   1840 - 1900........................15 - 59
Index to Apprenticeships; 1867...............60

WASHINGTON COUNTY:
Original Patents: 1829 - 1840................61 - 66
Marriage Records: Circuit Court Records
   1854 - 1871........................67 - 75
Marriage Records from "The Greenville Times"
   1874 - 1889........................76 - 93
Death Notices from "The Greenville Times"
   1868 - 1889........................94 -120
Deaths From the Yellow Fever Epidemic,1878..121 -124
Will Book "1",(cont. from Vol.I)
   1880 - 1894........................125 -140
Packet Gleanings: Abstracted - 70 Packets
   1827 - 1868........................141 - 153
Index...154 - 191

WILL BOOK "A":Issa.Co.

P.1: **Est. of William White**,decd. Residence - Issa.Co.Ms.
Exec. Henrietta White,Mordecai Powell,Atty. Inventory;
28Feb.1846 before Judge John H.Farr,Probate Judge and Thos.
J.Leigh,J.P.bt Saml. Wells,George Joor,Jas.W.Robertson.
Total inv. - 17 slaves,$6,250. Adm. of Est. p.40/41;
Final a/c p.240,242 - Jan.4,1854.

P.2: **Est. of MarkH.Mayfield**: decd. Intestate: Res.Issa.Co.
Invent.16 June 1845, approved by R.J.Pettway,H.G.Martin,
J.Forbes.

P.2-3: **Est. of Joseph and Cynthia H.McQuillian**:Intestate,
Res.Issa.Co.Invent.3 Mar.1846 by N.H.Vick,Wm.Rushing,
Wm.Myers.Total - $3,300. Children - Joseph B.,C.J.,A.P.
all minors. Adm.a/c p.90-91.Exec. and Guard.Bd.p.143/144.
Wm.B.McQuillian app.Guard. of minor heirs.Guard.Bd.signed
by John Lane,Cynthia Jane Butler,Dec.1851. Hire of slaves
for 1846-1851 p.103-106,approved / Mordecai Powell,Wm.
Rushing,Green B.Long.

P.3: **Est. of Samuel N.Sullivan**:Res.Washington Co.Ms.Inv.
24 Apr.1846 names son - Oliver Goldsmith Sullivan and
dau.Susan Anne Sullivan,both minors.(pp.84-85)Adm.a/c
of Susan Ann made Jan 1850 for 7 yrs. by Guardian Wm.
Dodd and wife Nancy Y.Dodds. P.109 - Petition of Wm.Dodd
to sell land of his ward 24 Sept.1849,3/7th int. of Susan
Ann sold to Mrs. Mary Ann Farr,widow of John H.Farr. 377
acres,$7,500.States that Oliver Goldsmith Sullivan is now
deceased.

P.4-5: **Will of Homer V.M.Ledbetter:** Will dated 5 Apr.1846.
Filed 24 Aug.1846,Recorded 15 Sept.1846.Residence - Issa.
Co. Will states: Violet and her 3 younger children -
Daniel Boon,Elizabeth,and Laura are constituted "my legal
heirs:.Asks Exec.Wm.M.Deeson to carry Violet and her 3
children to a free state,purchase a small tract of land,
and to see that the children are educated. To sister-
Nancy Beard-3 negroes,which on her death to go to James
Beard and Eliza Ann Beard. "Idesire to be buried in the
family burying ground".(does not say where it is) Wit:R.W.
Pettway,John L.Fortson,H.G.Martin. P.9/10 Inv; P.11-15
Let. of Adm.Approved by R.Christmas,G.N.Parks,Elisha North,
J.R.Miller,R.B.Cammack. Final a/c by Pettway,Adm.,17 March
1849 p.46-48.

P.5-6: Will of Absolom H.Barrow:Res.Issa.Co.Ms. Will was
written 7 Oct.1846; Prob.18 Apr.1848. Names: Sister -
Frances A.Peace...4 negroes; Neice - Marinda L.Peace:To
negroe Sarah Smith,$25 per yr. for life from Estate to be
managed by brother-in-law Willis Peace;Brother - Joseph
J.Barrow; to Dr.Richard Pettway;Brother Wm.Barrow;Sister
Eliza G.Cole;Sister - Sarah J.Connelly; to son of Willis
Peace. Wit:Sam F.Bugg.Exec.Willis H.Peace.P.17-19 Inv.
and Appraisal 20 Apr.1848 by Elisha North,Elias Farr,Saml
L.Moore,F.E.Mayfield,R.Christmas.

Will Bk.A, Issa. Co.Ms.

P. 8-9: Est. of Stephen D.Howard: Res. Issa.Co. on Deer Creek. decd. Intestate. Inv. and Apprs. 24 Jan 1848 by D.T.Williams,A.H.Saunders,Thos.J.Shelby,Thomas M.Northam. Apr.18,1848, property co-owned with John M.Clark. (P.37-39) sale of personal prop. 15 July 1848 ..John H. Clark, buyer.Exec. Wm.Myers app. by court 13 June 1848. Adm a/c filed June 1849 (pgs. 56-57).

P.15-16: Est. of Thomas W.Hill: Res. Issa.Co. decd.Intest. Adm.Bd. 19 Oct.1846 by J.H.McCutchen,J.H.Woolfolk, John Shackleford, W.E.Crump,J.B.Dixon.(pgs. 44-45) Sale of prop. W.R.Hill bought ld.&slaves with A.P.Hill - 8 Jan. 1848. Exec. was John A.Hill and W.R.Hill (relationship unexpl.) Thomas W.Hill was a school teacher in Township School.

P.19-20: R.Williams, Est. of: Res. Issa.Co., decd.Intestate; Judge John H.Farr apps. Sheriff Geo.P.Johnston as adm. 19 June 1848. (p. 134) ADm.a/c Mar 1850. (p.242) Final a/c July 1853 made by E.W.Shelby, Sher.&Adm.

P.20: Est. of John H.Farr: Res. Issa.Co. Adm. Mary Ann Farr, widow 26 Sept. 1848. Inv. of personal prop.Oct. 1848 (pgs.48-49) by R.W.Pettway,F.E.Mayfield,R.B.Cammack. P.67 - Adm. details - Oct.1849, Elias Pharr show interest in adm. Est. Co-owner of Plt. was David Hunt. Buyers of Est. prop. Washington B.Farr,B.M.Sellers. (p.71-76) Pet. 12 Nov.1849 Adm Mary Ann Herring by husband B.F.Herring to sell all prop. New Appraisals Jan 1850 by John McLaurin Elisha North,Robt.Smith. Sale Mar 1850. P.86-89 sale.

p. 21-22: Will of Hiram Hagan: Res. Issa.Co.Ms. Will written 17 Feb.1847; Prob. 13 Nov.1848. Names: Wife - Martha; sons Stephen,John,Hiram; brother Henry Hagan; Exec. to be Martha Hagan and Henry Hagan. (All to sh. =) Wit: J.W.Barnete, E.Lowe,David Hagen.Court named Jas. W.Barnete, Ad. Nov.1848. Inventory & Apprs. Jan 1849 by J.J.White,H.B.Brickell,K.W.McKinney,John Stennis,Jeff J.Hughes.(Pgs. 99-100) Adm. a/c. Nov 1849.

P.21: Est. of George Joor: Evan W.Shelby named Guard.and exec. of minor John S.Joor, son of George Joor. 12 Oct. 1848. Guard. approv. 16 Nov 1848 (p.31); Inv. & Apprs. 15 Nov 1848 by Jos.W.Robertson, A.H.Sanders,J.P.Woolfolk, S.W.Wells,N.H.Vick. p. 35-36; Notice of sale posted on door of Col.R.P.Shelby on Deer Creek.Sale 50-53,65-66, Adm.a/c p.79 May 1850. Final a/c 13 Jan 1851, p.120.

P.24: Will of J.William Lowry:Res. Sharon, Madison Co. Ms. Copy of will p.28-30;Will written 3 May 1841; Rec. Madison Co.Ms 10 Apr.1843; Rec. Issa. 15 Nov.1848. Names: son William Thomas Lowry; daus. Agnes Eugenia Collins, Susanna Lusehia(?), Elizabeth Caroline Gwin, Lucia Cornelia (Marr. Jas.H.Hughes Apr.1849). Asks dau. Agnes Eugenia and son-in-law to remain on homeplace

Will Bk.A, Issa. Co.

and raise and ed. family. States the decd. originally came from Fairfield Dist. in S.C. Wit: Rich.Beard, Alexander Campbell,Wm.J.Austin. (p.94) June 1850 Final a/c in Madison Co. by Wm.Lowry (Jr.). Division of Prop. by request of heirs 25 Mar 1848 p.95; Pet. to close Est. signed by Lucia,Agnes,Wm.Thos. 12 Apr.1852 pgs.163-164.

P. 25-27: Will of Madison P.Deloach: Will written 26 July 1848, Issa. Co.; Prob. Sept. 1848. Will stated: "Wished burial Baptist Church Graveyard in Vicksburg". Left everything to D.J.Fore and Lorenzo B.Anderson, naming them exec. except for $100 to be divided among legal legatees by consanguinity. Inv.& Appr. Sept.1848 by Wm.W.Yandall, Stephan Gray,John Mallary; Wit to Will: Henry Hamblin,Albert McCall,Stephen Gray. Adm. a/c Dec.1849,1850 pgs.131-132. Final a/c Dec. 1851.

P. 31: Est. of Wm.Taylor: 16 Nov. 1848 Court appoints Geo.P.JOhnston Adm. Inv. and Appr. 13 Mar.1849 by Wm.T. Lowry,A.M.Gwin,T.Leatherman,John Colter,John Hester, p.55; Final a/c Oct.1850 p 125.

P.32: Est. of Melvin H.Shellis: decd.Intestate, Nov. 1848 Court app. Geo.P.Johnston Sher. Adm.

p. 33: Est. of William Barnard: Guard. Adm. Dec.1848, Wm.T.Barnard app. Guard. and Adm. for minor heir Henry C.Barnard, about 18 yrs.old, Issa. Co. Sons of William Barnard, decd. Wm.T.Barnard, home on Deer Creek, Issa. Henry C.Barnard, born on July 1830. On p.190-191, May 1852, closing and completing guard. of Henry C.Barnard, now 21 yrs. old appr. by T.J.Leigh, Judge of Probate.

P. 58: Will of Isaac Sellers: Let. of Adm. Court app.
62-64 Ann Hill exec. 2 July 1849, Res. Issa.Co.; Names
68-69 sons Henry C.,Jas.F,Elbert A,Edward B., Isaac F.;
102   daus Amelia A., Alice G. : Inv. & Appr. 28 Sept.
208   1849 by R.M.Smith,R.E.Cammack,E.Tidwell,Elias
247   Pharr,W.E.Edgar. Benj.M.Sellers, interested party.
Ann Hill app. Guard. of minor heirs 20 Nov.1850; Guard. a/c 1852,1853 by I.C.Hill, Agent. (Relat. of Ann Hill and decd. not expl.)

P.60: Est. of Peter M.Crouch: 9 Oct. 1849 Court apps. Wm.B.McQuillian of Issa.Co. to have inv. made of Est. P.117 - Inv. by Wm.Rushing, Green B.Long,Mordecai Powell. Pgs.206-207 Auction 14 June 1852; Exec. Evan Shelby, Sher.Issa. (Land on Sunflower River)

P.61: Est. of Wrenna B.Sellers: Res.Issa.Co. Sons Edwin R.,Thos.W.;dau. Emily C.Hill. Guard. Oct. 1849 Isaac Hill app. Guard. of Edwin R.& Thos.W.Sellers. P.93-94 Inv.&Appr. June 1850, prop. in Holmes Co.Ms inher. from Wm.Wright of Holmes Co. P. 248-249, Adm.a/c 1853 by Guard.

Will Bk.A, Issa.Co.Ms.

p.70: Est. of Stephen Gray: decd. Intestate: Res. Issa.
Let of Adm. to Geo.P.Johnston, Sherf.8 Feb.1850. Inv. &
Apprs. 10 June 1850 by Saml.Nelson,Geo.V.Parks..p.92-93;
Adm. a/c 1852, 1853 by E.W.Shelby p.168,243. Final a/c 18

P. 77: Will of James Swanson: Res. Tenn. Dated 1 Apr. 1850
80-83 Names: wife Minerva B.; Son Jas.Jr.; Exec. & Adm.
192 to James Swanson,Jr. and John W.Miller. Inv. & Appr.
198   11 Apr.1850 by Will Rushing,W.Robertson,Joseph J.
230   Sullivan,Rich.Rawls, John F.Chaney. Inv. made by
231   Wm.Myers, Geo.V.Parks,Saml.Nelson. Adm. a/c from
234   June 1850 to June 1852 approv. before Judge T.J.
       Leigh, Probate Judge. Adm. a/c 1853 approv. before
       G.W.N.Smith, Probate Judge. of Issa.
       Apr. 14, 1853, allots dower to widow, now Minerva
       B.Smith, 1/3 part of 652.03 acres.

P. 78:   Est. of Geo.Coalter, decd. Intestate; Res. Issa.
121-122 Co. on Miss. River. Let. of Adm. 14 May 1850 to
149   John Coalter (relat. unexpl). Inv. & Appr. 9 Dec.
200   1850 by A.M.Gwin,Wm.T.Lowry,G.Leatherman; Pet.
201   by John Coalter to sell all of personal Est.
         Filed for rec. 9 Feb.1852. Rep. of sale 5 Mar.
         1852

P. 95: Est. of John Hester: Res. of Miss. Lett Ad Coll-
igendum issued to Geo.P.Johnston, Sherf. of Issa.Co.,
dated 14 June 1850.

P. 96: Est. of Thomas C.Nelson: Res. Issa.Co. decd.Intes-
114   tate; Guard. issued to Saml.Nelson for minor Mary
115   L.L.Nelson, dau. of Thos.C.Nelson, 12 June 1850.
116   Rep. of sale by Saml.Nelson of land for ward Mary
223   L.L. 9 Dec.1850. David Hunt - buyer of 479 ac.
224   Adm. a/c Dec.1850,51, to Oct. 52. Final a/c 11
       Oct 1852 by Saml.Nelson to Court for minor Mary
       L.L. who is now wife of John C.McLemore.

P. 98: Est. of John F.Chaney:Res. Issa.Co. Let. of Adm.
128   25 Nov.1850 to Saml. W.Wells. Guard. 12 May
157   1851 issued to Saml.W.Wells for minor John F.
199   Chaney,Jr. Appr. of negroes for hire, Adm. a/c
202   1852,53. Let. of Adm. 15 Nov. 1853 by Wm.T.Bar-
239   nard app. adm by court, stating Saml.Wells decd.
257   in Aug. 1853.
259   Duplicate of p. 257.

P. 98: Will of Susan H.Chaney; Will dated 4 June, 1850;
126   Prob. 25 Nov.1850. Attested and appr. 10 Feb.
130   1851. Res. Issa. but temporarily residing at Miss.
187-   Springs, Hinds Co. when will was written. Names:
189   to my bros. & siss. of the whole blood (unnamed)
236   Exec. Wm.T.Barnard. Let of Adm. to Wm.T.Barnard
       Nov 1850.Wit: H.R.Austin,M.A.McComb,E.A.Austin.
       Final a/c May 1853.

Will Bk.A; Issa. Co.

P. 99: Est. of Joseph Steif: decd. Intestate. Res. Issa. Co. Let of Adm., 25 Nov.1850 to Morrell Hodgedon. Adm. a/c, pages 217-219, Bill presented to Court by M.Hodgedon who states he boarded and waited on Steif while sick, and also buried him. Accepted; 13 Sept. 1852. (No heirs named)

P.101: Est. of Samuel S.Moore: decd. Intestate, Res. Issa. Co. Let. of Adm. by widow Rachel Moore, 21 Oct. 1850; Inv. & Apprs., p.118-119, by R.W.Pettway, ___Leatherman, Elisha North, 2 Nov.1850. Adm. Report, July 14,1852 Pet. Court to declare Est. insolvent, p.209-210; Voucher #6 amt. due Wm.Franklin Moore by Est. $2,491, S.S.Moore Guard. as per probate voucher. (No relat. given). p.211-213, Report of Sale at public auction, Hinds Co.Ms. at the Raymond courthouse (there is also one at Jackson) states the land belonging to S.S.Moore was situated near Clinton,Ms. 28 June 1852. P.214-215 gives desc. of land sold.

P.113: Est. of Edmond Tidwell: Let. of Adm. 21 Jan.1851 to Evan W.Shelby. P. 140, E.W.Shelby reports he found a note among the effects of decd. from Z.H.Dorsey,W.W.Sutton, dated 17 Mar 1849, Lake Providence,La. for $1550 to be pd. to Thomas W.Deeson and endorsed by W.A.Deeson in favor of E.Tidwell. Doc. dated 5 May 1851. Final a/c Oct.1853.

P.127: Guardianship of Minors to Elias Pharr: (Pharr/Farr seem to be used interchangeably)Doc. dated 15 Apr.1851;
Heirs of Robt.Pharr:　　Heirs of Sarah Allen:
Margaret B.Pharr　　　　Margaret Allen
Henry N.Pharr　　　　　 Henry Allen
Saml. A.Pharr　　　　　 Mary Allen
Walter N. Pharr
Teresa I. Pharr　　　　 Heirs of Margaret M.Beavers:
　　　　　　　　　　　　 Henry Beavers
Heirs of James Pharr:　John Beavers
Mary Pharr　　　　　　　William Beavers
Sarah Pharr
Henry Pharr
Hester Pharr

P. 129: Est. of Sarah Barnard: decd.Intestate: Guard.Bd. by husband Wm.T.Barnard, for minor ch.- son-Wm.Bailey Barnard, dau.- Sarah Louise Barnard, dau.- Mary Jane Barnard.Doc. dated 12 May 1851.

P. 135: Est. of John Scott: Decd. Intestate; Res. Issa.
136　　Co. Let. of Adm. 8 Sept.1851 to J.J.Sullivan;
164　　Inv. 6 Mar 1852 by Mordacai Powell, Wm.Simmons,
165　　Thos.W.Robertson. Sale of prop. 12 Apr.1852.

P.136: Est. Walter McCoyin (sp.Cowyan): decd. Intestate;
137　　Res. Issa.Co. Let. of Adm to Thos.J.Leigh 8 Sept
139　　1851; Inv. & Apprs. 10 Oct 1851 by D.T.Williams,
　　　　Thos.Shelby,W.Mills.

Will Bk.A; Issa. Co.

P. 140: **Guard. of Melissa J.McQuillan**: Res. Issa. Co.
141   Pet. of Guard. by her father Wm.B.McQuillan
         for Melissa A. age 4, stating his wife left a
         small personal est. of $3,000. 8 Dec.1851.

P.141: **Est of John McLaurin** Decd. Intestate, Res. of Issa.
Pet of widow Sarah G.McLaurin for the Court to app. Isaac
C.Hill adm. Further states John decd 28 Sept.1851. Est.
probated 10 Dec.1851. Let of Adm. to Isaac C.Hill, bds.
N.B.Cammack; P.149-151, Inv. & Apprs. by R.M.Smith,Geo.
N.Parks,W.B.Farr,Wm.Myers,B.I.Chaney,E.North,John Coalter,
9 Feb.1852. P. 154,167,168,252; Pet. to sell personal
prop - 10 Feb 1852; Report of Sale - 10 Apr.1852;Final
Adm.a/c - Oct. 1853.

P.144,145,146: **Est. of Benjamin M.Sellers**: Decd. 20 Aug.
1851; Res. Issa.Co; Let. of Adm. filed by Anne Hill,
sister and next of kin to B.M.Sellers, pet. Court to
appoint her as Adm. I.C.Hill, R.M.Smith co-signed Atty.
bond. Pgs. 151,152,153; Inv. & Appras. 4 Feb.1852 at
home of Anne Hill, followed by Pet. to sell personal
prop, by Isaac C.Hill, her Atty. Pgs.166,167; Report of
sale - 20 Mar 1852.- Buyers were I.C.Hill,S.F.Green,
R.J.Turnbull,S.Tilman,M.J.Brooks,D.F.Castleman.

P.147: **Est. of G.P.Jones:** declared decd. by Court, Apr.
1851; Res. Issa.Co; Wife - Martha H.; Son-Charles H.;
Daus - Mary S.,Maria H.,Martha P.; Exec. Martha H.Jones.
(Feb.1852, Report of sale of personal prop. and undiv.½
interest in landed Est, subject to widows dower. Negroes
not sold. D.W.C.Bonham, agent, Atty for Adm. who reports
that a fire had destroyed a dwelling and many of the
items in the Inv. were gone. P.147,148, Martha, widow,
Pet. to work negroes on her plantation in Hinds Co.Ms.
for 1 yr. Jan 1852-53.Doc. was dated 9 Feb.1852: Dr.
Catchens,H.White,J.Reynold appr. their value. P.237,238,
Final a/c May 1853.

P.155: **Will of Anne S.Chaney** Will written 17 Dec.1850,
Probated 12 Apr.1852 Issa. Co. Names: Son - Wood S.
Chaney; Daus - Margaret A., minor more than 14; Dau.
Mrs. Evan W.Shelby. Bequest...everything to Wood and
Margaret. Pay $300 to Melissa C.Jackson, 2 yrs.after
date of Will. Exec; Mordacai Powell, brother of Anne
S.Chaney. Wit: John E.Butler, Wm.Myers,A.H.Powell.
Guard. of Wood and Margaret Chaney awarded to Mordacai
Powell by the Court. P.158, Apr.13,1852 - Margaret A.
Chaney pet. Court for change of Guard. from Mordacai
Powell to brother-in-law E.W.Shelby. Court agrees.
P.222, Aug. 1852, Margaret Chaney asks the court to re-
voke guard. of E.W.Shelby and reappoint her Uncle,
Mordacai Powell. So ordered and filed 13 Sept.1852.
Oct. 1852, Adm. reports no prop. in Issa. Co.; P.235
Apr.12,1853 - Division of slaves to Wood and Margaret,
equal shares. Rec. 13 May 1853

Will Bk.A; Issa.Co.

P.159: Est. of Thomas Nelson: Pet. by Nathan T.Nelson, and John N.Nelson for Guard. to be given their father, Samuel Nelson to protect their int. in the est. left to them by their grandfather, Thomas Nelson, who died in Rutherford Co.Tenn, sometimes in May 1852. The 2 boys are over 14 and by law allowed to choose their Guardian. Doc. dated 12 Apr. 1852.
P.159,160: Copy of Will of Thomas Nelson, of Rutherford Co. Tenn. Will written; 19 Feb.1850, Rec. 14 Apr.1852, (a copy filed in Issa.Co.) RutherfordCo.Tenn.
Names: sons - Samuel and wife Eunice R.; Thomas C.; John; Daus - Sarah Crichlow; Mary S.L.Walkin.
Grandchildren: ch. of Samuel's - NathanThomas,John N., Julia L.,Nelson, Pettway, Samuel, James, Francis L., Eunice Ann, Emma.
ch. of Thos.C.'s - Mary Louisa.
ch. of John's...does not name any.
" " Sarah Crichlow's ...does not name any.
" " Mary S.L.Walkin - Wm.S.Walkin.
Bequest: left 1/3 sh. of real est. to each son's ch. The slaves to be sold and the proceeds to be divided thus; Sarah Crichlow's ch. - 1/3 sh.
Thos.C.Nelson's ch.Mary Louisa - 1/10 part.
Wm.S.Walkin's dau. or son (who would be a gr.grand child) 1/10 part
One negroe slave to be given to his wife, unnamed, who was living at the time the Will was written.
Exec; Jointly - John Nelson,Arthur C.Edwards.
Wit: Thos.W.Miles,I.S.Payne.
P.160-162: Pet. for Guard. of his 7 minor ch.; 12 Apr. 1852,byS. Nelson.. So Granted.

P.169: Est of Barton Millsaps: Res. Issa.Co.; Court app. E.W.Shelby, Sherf. of Issa. Adm of Est. 5 Apr.1852.

P.170-171: Will of Samuel Varner: (Will of Samuel Vernen, of County of Okteluka Ms.) Of Oktibbeha Co.Ms., about 71 miles from Starkville where he lived at that time. Written - 18 July 1846, Rec. 14 Oct.1850 in Linden, Marengo Co.Ala. in Will Bk.A,p.291. Rec. in Issa.Co.Ms. 12 May 1852. Sworn to in Chickasaw Co.Ms 3 July 1848, by John H.Willingham,one of the wit. to the will.
Names: sons - Joseph'"deef and dumb", James, "deef and dumb", John; Daus. Sarah Varner Bevell, Martha Varner Lassater (Lassiter) Minerva Jane Varner Whitby (Whitely) Mahaley "deef and dumb". Son-in-law Decature Whitby(Whitely) and son John exec. and Guard. of 3 afflicted ch.
Wit: by Wm.Champion,John W.Willingham,Constine Gibson.
(stated his wife survived him, unnamed) Pages of litigation follow as daus. Sarah Bevell and Martha Lassater contest will's validity. Some doubt of actual death - some say 1847 - some 1850, one believed he died in La. 1847. No results of litagation shown.

Will Bk.A; Issa.Co.

P.183: Est. of James M.Briscoe: Res. Texas; sons - Mason, James, William, all residing in Texas, all under 20; daus Mary, Anne, both residing Jefferson Co.Ms. and under 20.
P.184: Pet. by Wm.Brisco, 11 May 1852. States there are no personal assets in Issa.Co. to pay $13,000 debts and request permission to sell a tract of land to pay debts. Signed joint notes - James Brisco,James Crane,R.Valentine.
P.185,186: Court apps. Wm.P.Brisco of Jefferson Co.Ms.Adm. Court app. Elias Pharr Guard. of minor ch.'s interest in sale of land, 11 May 1852. P.225-227 Court allows and approves sale, 11 Oct. 1852.

p.228:Est. of Elias Pharr, Res. Issa.Co, Let. of Adm. to R.M.Smith 11 Jan 1853. P.229, Ursilla M.Pharr app. Guard. of Elias's dau. Mary Eunice Pharr. P.231-233, Inv.& Apprs., 11 Jan 1853 by F.E.Mayfield,E.North,Jas. S.Mayfield,R.B.Cammack,R.W.Pettway.

P.244,245: Est. of Thomas J.Leigh: Res. Issa.Co. Appras. order, Apr.1853 to D.G.Williams,Lewis S.Dameron,Wm.Bradford. Apprs. filed 14 July 1853.

P.250: Est. of Robert Prince Shelby: Will Recorded in WBk.B,p.39. Let. of Adm. to Wm.T.Earnard and request him to have Inv. made, 10 Oct 1853.
P.250-251: Bond, 10 Oct.1853, Joint exec. and adm. are Wm.T.Barnard, Evan W.Shelby,Isaac C.Hill, Wm.Myers.

P.254: Est. of Joseph S.Barnard: Will Recorded in WBk.B, pgs.5,6. Res. Issa.Co.; Date of Will, 16 July 1853, rec. Issa. Co. Aug.1853: Names; wife- Rebecca F.Barnard;sons Henry, Joseph: Request that wife and 2 ch. share equally. Exec; Wm.T.Barnard, brother of decd; Wit, Saml.Wells, E. Jones Harvey, D.D.Jackson. Court Order for Inv. & Apprs. 8 Aug 1853 for personal est. to Wm.Rushing,D.D.Jackson, J.J.Sullivan,J.N.Jones. Inv. returned 5 Sept 1853, Apprv. Oct. 1853.

P.256: Est. of Samuel W Wells:Res.Issa.;Adm. to Martha A. Wells and E.J.Harvey,Nov.1853, Rec. Nov.15, 1853.

P.258: Est. of Sarah Foster: Res. Adams Co.Ms. Let.of Adm., 15 Nov.1853 issued to Wm.T.Barnard, plus making Inv.&Apprs. (Will recorded WBk.B.P1,2 Issa.)..

P. 260,261: Will of Alexander D.Duval: Res. Issa.Co.; Will written-23 July 1850; Prob. - 10 Mar 1851; Names: wife-Margaret; 3 youngest ch. Claiborne Alexander, Matilda, Gwinet S...all to receive a good ed.; other ch. Caroline Cook, Mary C.Duval, Elizabeth P.McNairy. Exec; wife Margaret; Wit: (1 signature, looks to be A.M.Gwin. Rec. 1 Dec.1853 by Probate Clk.W.B.Farr, Tallula, Ms.

INDEX TO ESTATES: Issa. Co.Ms.
Numbers following names are Packet numbers.

Alston, P.G. #126
Alexander, D.H. #36
" , Heirs of, #36
Adams,D.A. #121
Anderson,Alex #60
" , Ophelia #321-324
" , Harmon #18
Adams, Randall #210
Armstrong,Josephine L.#348
Aden, H.B. #77

Baker, Joseph #181
Brehur, J.H. #199
Bonley, Leila #222
Banks, Aaron #213
Brown, Charles #266
Birdsong, Frank #271
Brown, S.B. #339
Bland, Elizabeth #327
Barnes, Henry #330
Brown, Emma #332
Baskins, Frnak #334
Brown, Geo.H. #302
" , Lucy #302
Barlow, Frank #75
Barnard, Henry C. #6
Boyd, J.L. #10
" , A.P. #11
Buan, B. #18
Branch, Henry #19
Barnow, W.L. #20
Binney, Martha #28
Bennett, Minors #51
Brisco, Wm.P. #50
Blanton, Oliver #78
Barrett, J.E. #47
Bernstein, Elias #67
Beard, Benj. #122
Bell, J.S. #125
Banks, O.R. #158
Brehm, Rebecca #118
Brazil, Albert #140
Brum, Alex #183
Beaker, Minor heirs #201
Brown, Violet #240
Broma, Fleir(?) #245
Boyd, John W. #254
Binder, Leon #288
Blair, Mila Lachs #300
Bronson,Minie B. #306

Collins, Wm.A. #49

Christmas, H.H. #20
Chase, Alexander #79
Coffield, H.D. #74
" , Amanda #68
Chapman, John L. #109
Calhoun, John C. #112
Clark, J.S. ___
Chaney, Susan H. #32
" , Ann L. #46
" , John F. #34
" , Thos. Y. #18
" , Margaret #48
" , C.A.
Crouch, P.W. #23
Creath,M.B.A. & S. #3
Council, W.S. #10
Cullen,E.W. --
Cobb,Henry #80
Coker, John H. #--
Coalter, George #25
Coleman, Angelina #75
Conner, John A. #133
Converse, J.B. #134
Coursey, D. --
Cowan,T.B. #169
Cox, J.H. #182
Curd, Elizabeth --
Chilton, Mrs. Alice P.
  (Will) #198
Curd, David #148
Coleman, Nancy #212
Carter, Louisa #216
Coleman, Wesley #224
Cunningham,John #242
Carter, H.C. #235
Cheatham, John #241
Carter, R.T. #275
Chilton, St.John #318
Collins, Abe #357
Cook,G. #333
" ,Frank #361
" ,Mary Jane #345
Cullen, E.W. #21
Cohn,John W. #51
Chapman, Isabella #109
Chilton, H.R. #186

Davenport, Jos. #61
Dunn,Franklin #71
Duval,A.D. ---
Deloach, M.P. #12
Davis,Fielding --

INDEX TO ESTATES: Issa. Co.
Numbers following names are Packet numbers.

Doughtery,Belle,Nora,et al#78
Dickens, E.B. #190½
Dorsey,Mary #192
Davis, Winchester #208
Diggs,A.R. #278
  " , Alfred #268
Davis, Josephine #320
Dreyfus, Albert #354
Dean, James Ann #356
Davenport,E.V. #359
Duval,A.D. ---
Daniel, James W. #37
Deeson, A.G.& M.J. #87
Davis, Yancey #328

Elliott,J.S. #17
  " , S.C.,Minor #157
Eastman,R.F. #89
Eustis,H.S. ---
Everhart, M. #129
Elliott, Walter #95
  " , Mrs. Emma (Chas.)#96

Fox, Henry #82
Fowler,E. #124
Fischel,Lyon #45
  " , A.L.& M. #46
Fore, B.B. #12
  " , C.J. #16
Foster, Lelia A.& E.
    Minors #40
Foster,Sarah ---
Fulton, R.N. ---
Ferriss, Anna M. ---
Farr, Jno.H. ---
  " , W.B. ---
Fly, A.D. ---
Fore, Manly ---
Farish, Wm.S. #171
Fitz,John W. #155
Fowler,Sarah (Will)#184
Fleming,Nathaniel #220
Fore,Edna (Guard) ---
Farish,Jane L., H.P.
    (Guard) #217
Freshwater,Peter #256
Fields, Drury #243
Fleming,Kinworth #270
Foe, Henry #279
  " , " #188
Foster,Nannie E. #280
Farish,Robt.D.minor, #222
Farish, Thos.H.,minor #221
Farish,F.Powers 223
Ferguson,Gabrell #335

Freshwater, Peter #368
Farr,John & Robt.---
Furlow,Robt.N. ---
Ferriss, St.Clair ---
Foster,Nannie E. #280
Ford, West #365

(Ed. Many boxes unnumbered
Gray,Stephan ---
  " , John W. ---
  " , Saml.B. ---
Gregory, G.G. ---
  " , Peter ---
  " , Peter & Mary
    Minors #---
Garrett, Jacob ---
  " , M.R.,minor ---
Gwin,A.M. ---
Garner, H.C. ---
Griffin,Jno.& Mary ---
Green,E.H. #39
  " , Annie &Sarah
    #107 & 108
Grace,J.C. #80
  " , Eva & Louis #99
Gilkey, Ada L. #72
  " , Eva,Loyd,Laura #94
George;H.P. & Jas.M.
    Parks #24 (See Parks)
Grooms, Pane & Viney #35
Griffin, Alfred ---
Gamble,J.T.---
Grambling,(Heirs) #147
Grant, (Heirs) ---
Grace, Geo.C.,Minors #98
Goodwin, Jno.L. #151
Grant, Amos #138
  " , Mary #146
  " , Lenora #145
Green,Henry #161
  " ,Taylor #184
Grant, Lawrence H. #144
Green,L.S. #219
Gilkey,Mary E. #233
Green,---- #177
Gilkey, A.S.(Adm.)#229
Grant, Lenora (Guard.)#145
Gray,Jno.H. #238
Gubbs,W.G. #287
Gano,Robt. #329
Grant,Thos.J. #143
Green,Jolen #167
Grant,James ---
Goshea, Liz. #352
Graves, Geo. #353

INDEX TO ESTATES: Issa. Co.Ms.
Numbers following names are Packet numbers.

Harwood,Agnes E. #56
Hollberg, Robt. & Ida #27
Hays, Thos.W. #134
Hardin, Ira #57
Heyman,A. #69
Holmes,R.B. #50
Hester,C.A. #54
 " , Jno. --
Heath, Jno.W. #23
   Minor
Heath,Thos.& Jas. #22
Henderson,H. #18
Harris, J.R. --
Hennessy, Jno. #48
Hampton, Wade ---
Howard, S.D. ---
Hill,H.R.W. #65
 " , Isaac C. --
 " , Frank,B.G.,A.Lizzie,
   et al #67
Halloran, Jas. --
Hardin, Alma, & Ida --
Hamel, Kate & Wade H. --
Hogan,Wm.--
Hamel,Patrick --
Higgins,R.G. #137
Hicks, W.P. #135½
Hays,J.P. #138½
Harden,Nancy --
Heath, John #174
Hill, Henderson #200
Harris, John --
Holmes, Mackley #205
 "   , Chas.(Minor) #209
Henderson, Geo. #268½
Hennessy, Adaline #246
Holmes, Margaret Hughs #203
Howard,L. #252
Holland, Clara #244
Hart,Anna M. #316
Holmes,Angeline #326
Hailburton, Robt. #130

Irving, John #115

Jeans,Wm. --
Johnson,Jas. #59
 "   , Moses #84
Jackson,Andrew #42
Julienne, L. --

Joor, Geo. --
 " , John S.(Minor) --
Jones, Geo.P. --
Johnson,C.S. #18
Jeffords,Mrs. N.P. #228
Johnson,Henry #231
 "   , A.G. #225
Jones,L.J. #232
Jenkins, Geo. #250
Jones,Penella #230
Jackson, Matthew #247
Jinkins, Eliza @274
Jackson, Posey #337
Johnson,Sam #340
Jordan, York J. #312
Johnston,C. #166
Jones, Rachel #308
Johnson,Wesley #310
 "   , Wm. #349

Knight,Geo.& Mary #55
Keep,H.V. #106
 " , Anna L. --
Killian,Max #159
Kellog, M.B. #172
Killian,Va. #313
Keep,Mrs. Sallie B.#331,106

Luhm,A.G. #97
Lallien,John --
Leatherman,Saml. #9
Leighton,T.J. --
Ledbetter,H.V. --
Lax,Aaron & W. #34
Lynch, J.C. #138
Lucus,I. (Est. of I.
   Stretch) #173
Lucus, I. (App. Levee
   Comm.) --
Lynch,Jas.P. --
Lighes,Rial --
Lynch,Mattie T. --
Lynch,Ruby #138
Lawson,L.E. #257
Love,Dave #289
Larsen,Morris #303
Logan, Mary #360
Lee, A.N. #360
 " , Sam #185
Lypscomb. Ben #362
Lee,Lizzie B. #366

INDEX TO ESTATES: Issa.Co.Ms.
Numbers following names are Packet numbers.

McYoung,John(Est.of)#179
McClaud,Saml.(Est)#206
McGehee,Saml.(")#286
McDonald,J.A.(Est)#53
McDonald,John #13
McQuide,Jas.M.#66
McCown,---#190
Mayer,Henry L.(Est)#319
  (Mrs. M.B.Mayer,exec.)
Moore,Minerva M.(Est)#273
Morris,D.L.(Est)#307
Murchison,Amelia(Est)#322
Moore,Harry(Est)#269
Morrison,John(Guard.)#195
Morrison,John(Est)Shark.Co.
  Chanc.Crt.Pkt.#1582-Issa.
Maxey,Walter(unnumbd.file)
Merrill,Saml. "   "
Manning,Lucy #301
Maralis,A.(Est)#363
Murrell,Saml. #15
McDonald,J.A. #53
" ,John(unnumbd.file)
McQuillen,M.A. "   "
" ,Jos.R."   "
" ,J.& C."   "
" ,Melissa A. "
McQuillen,Jas.M."   "
McCoyan,Walter "   "
McLaurin,John "   "
Moore,Jesse #26
" ,Saml.L.(Unnumbd.file)
" ,Rachel "   "
" ,F.W.& E.N. "   "
Morton,Washington"   "
Moseley,J.H. "   "
" ,Eugenia & Lucy #14
Miller,Lewis(Unnumbd.file)
Maitland,Robt.L. "   "
Messinger,G.W.B. "   "
Millsaps,Barton #53
Myers,Francis S.(Unnumbd.F.)
Magee,Wm.   "
Myers,F.C.   "
Mayfield,T.E.   "
" ,M.H.   "
Meacham,Orville   "

Minor,Robt.#104
" ,Polly &Robt.(minors)
Mollison,Robt.(unbd.file)
Moore,C.(Est) #154
Meacham,Orville(Est)#105
Morrison,John #195
Moultri,Ed #162
Miller,John #149
Marshall,Henry #229
Mason,P.L. #226
Morris,W.J. #218
Moore,Abe #237
Murray,---#253
Nelson,S.S.#58(9?)
" ,Saml.#102
" ,Emma H. #101
" ,E.R. #21
" ,Sam.J.#103
" ,Howard J.#104
" ,Mary L.S. ---
Neibert,Jos.W.---
Nash,Hagan #117
Noble,Allen(Est)#141
Nunnalla,H.H.(Est)#178
Nichals,Marecy(Est)#236
Neal,Jas.#338 (Est)

O'Neal,Kitty(Est) #180

Preston,Lynas#120
Price,Jas.,Jacob,Annie
  Minors,#76,#89
Paddleford,W.B.#31
Pettway,R.W.#9
Parks,Jas.M.#24
" ,Geo.N.(Est)#22
" ,Geo.(Minors)#22
" ,Geo.P. #25
" ,M.E. #22
Pharr,Elias ---
Pharr,Eliz.A.(Minor)#10
Purnell,Wm.(Est)#164
Pending,---(Est) #48
" ,---(Est) #49
Passino,Edna Worthington
  (Minor)#62
Pheisfas(?)R.B.(Est)#255,#70
Porter,Clars(Est)#317,#71

INDEX TO ESTATES: Issa.Co.Ms.
Numbers following names are Packet numbers.

Peyton,L.M.&A.vsDiggs
  #293,(66)
Peace,Wm.H.#11
Price,Lucy#153
Pinkston,T.E.(Est)#234
Pinkney,Ned(Est)#343

Robertson,Leanah#1
" ,Ella C.(Minor)#99
" ,Alta C. " --
" ,J.H. " #10
" ,Lula C. " #98
" ,J.W. #14
Robinson,Geo.(Minor)#77
Rushing,Wm.#11
" ,Henry(Minor)#11
Riley,Nancy(Minor)#68
Ritter,Ida P.(Est)#281
Robinson,Talee(Est)#279
Rudy,W.H.(Est)B.F.Rudy,Adm.
  #314
Robertson,L.#96

Smith,R.M.,Sr.#62
" , Lawrence&Lovena
  (Minors) #63
" ,Preston H. & Lee
  (Minors)#64
" ,Stephen #110
" ,Wm.C. #3
Sink,Geo.B.#14
Spencer,Selden #70
Simmons,Jimmie #43
Shields,W.B.#119
Sullivan,J.J.---
" ,M.K.,M.A.,L.S.,E.C.
" ,Susan A.---
Steiff,Jos.---
Shoaf,Jacob---
Skinner,Jno.S.& Louisa---
Scott,John ---
Sanders,H.H.--
Sellers,B.M.---
" ,Isaac---
" ,T.W.& E.R.---
" ,H.C.& I.F. ---
Swanson,Jas.---
" ,Heirs(Minors---
Shillis,M.H.---
Shelby,R.P.---
Smithheart,O.E.(Est)#136
Slater,Chas.T.(Est)#127
" ,John D.(Est)#120½
Sellers,B.M.---

Sellers,Isaac---
" ,T.W.& E.R.--
" ,H.C.& I.F. ---
Swanson,James ---
" ,Heirs(Minors)---
Stern,Henry#123(Est)
Stout,W.F.& Mary Ellen,
  (Minors) #156
Smith,P.H.(Est)#142
Scott,H.P.(Est)--
Smith,Lee A.(Est) --
Stern,Jos.(Est)#189
Smith,P.H.(Est)---
Stokes,Macklin(Est)#160
Stewart,--#248
Scruggs,Lula(Est)#282
Stern,Cicie(Est)#196
Smith,Preston O.(Est)#277
Sessoins,Rich.(Est)#315
Smith,Catherine #311
Scudder,Marie Gertrude(Est)
  #341
Smith,----
Strechin,David(Est)#175
Sanford,C.C.#248(Est)
Smith,H.S.(Est)#336
Smith,Eunice W.(Est)#276
Sanford,C.C.(Est)#248
Skinner,J.S.(Est)#347
Starnes,Macklin(Est)#160
Scott,Henry P.(Est)#170
Simpson,O.P.(Est)#346

Turnbull,Dr.Robt.J.#93
" ,Chas.F. #7
" ,Lewis &Mary Rubin
  (Minors) #8
Toy,H.P.---
Travis,Ella---
Thomley,J.E.---
Tidwell,E.---
Taylor,Wm.---
" ,Benj.B.----
Tillman,Lewis ---
" ,Ann M.#91
" ,Heirs(Minors) --
Turner,Marshall(lunatic)#81
Tedo,Agnes L.& J.(Minors)#85
Thomas,Leannah(Est)--
" ,Sistella(Minor)#132
Turnbull,Robt.J.(Will)#187
Taelton,Chas.#163
Thames,T.M.#344

Utz,Lovell #113

INDEX TO ESTATES:Issa.Co.Ms.
Numbers following names are Packet numbers

Williams,Smith #30
"   ,R. ---
"   ,D.T. ---
"   ,M.C.(Minor)
"   ,Aaron(Apprntce)#29
"   ,Louisa(Lunatic)--
Wilson,Sam---
Wakefield,M.S.#38
Wedley,G.B.#33
Winslow,E.M.(Minor)#110½
"   ,R.P. " #111
Wells,S.W.---
"   ,J.J.(Minor)---
Wheeler,John#32
Whitehead,S.Y.---
White,Wm.E.---
Woolfolk,Jas.B.--
"   ,J.E.& V.T.(Minors)-
Wright,C.J.--
Watson,Louis C.#44
Welling,A.(Est) #92
Warburton,Rich.(Est)#130
Wilson,Susan#52
Watson,Pompey(Est.)#165
Walker,Fannie(Est)#176
Williams.John(Est)@214
Winston,Robt.L.#211

Williams,Chas.E.(Est)#239
Walker,Elen(Est)#193
Walten,Grey(Est)#204
Wesley,Robt.Sr.(Est)#284
"   ,Aaron E.(Est)#285
"   ,Indiana(Est)#305
"   ,Robt.Jr.(Est)#283
Walker,F.W.(Est)#323
Wade,L.T.(Est of Minor
        Children of)#191
Watson,Harriet #342
Wesley,Indiana & Robt.
        (Minors)#296
Wesley,Aaron E.,et al vs
        Steven Wesley #301
Winfield,Amelia #34
Wesley,Chas. #299
Williams,James #304
Wesley,Indiana(Est)#305
Wheeler,Wash.#325
Weightman,Minnie V.(Est)#355
Woods,Alfred(Est)#358
Wade,L.T.#364

Young,N.(Est)#184
Young,Grant(Est)#202

Ed.Note: The inclusion of the complete Index to Estates has been made even though there are many Packets missing and the numbers on several are incorrect. In some cases, the listing of the names is the only clue that a certain person was here. When the present Clerk,Mary A. VanDavender took office, the Packets were all jumbled in cardboard boxes. She and her staff have enclosed the existing ones in clean covers and tried to file them systematically, even though many had no file numbers. Because of these discrepencies, we, the editors, decided to include a large section of abstracted Packets, which follows this section. If the person you are seeking only shows in the Est. Index, then shift to other types of documents for further information. We have not copied Deed Books,Tax Books,etc. or their Indexes as they are on Microfilm in the Archives in Jackson.

Packet Gleanings: Issa. Co.
Probate Drw., Unnumbered File⚹ A-D

*These packets are filed Alphabetically in a series of "unnumbered file drawers". Some have numbers corresponding to Index to Est., but look as if these had been added since being filed. A few Chancery Cases are here, also. The numbers will not be in sequence, and the cases after 1890 are not abstracted here. Supplementary Information only.

Est. of J.H.Bolling: 1891

#20: Guard. of Henry C.Barnard: (See WBk.A, Pg.33,190,191, abst. in this Vol.II, & Prob. Pkt.#6) No addit. infor.

#50: Est. of James M.Briscoe, decd. (See WBk.A,p.183-186, this Vol.II) No Addit.Infor.

Est. of Demas Coursey: 1890

#25: Est. of Geo.Coalter: WBk.A,p.78,121,122,149,200,201, Abst. in this Vol.II. No add. infor.

#32: Est. of SusanH.Chaney: WBk.A,p130, this Vol.II. No Add.

#12: Est. of M.P.Deloach: WBk.A, P.25-27,131,132,216; this Vol.II, No Add.Infor.

Guard. by Wm.Dodds of Susan A.Sullivan: WBk.A. this Vol.II

Est. of Walter McCoyan:(misfiled),WBk.A. this Vol.II

#80: Henry Cobb, Est of: WBk.B,p.218,219.220, Oct. 10,1856. Let. of Adm. for her husbands Est. filed by Mary A.Cobb, and their minor ch.- Olivia Terrasa, Leonora Susan,Rosa Eulelia Cobb. No date of death, decd. in West Feliciana Parish, La.; No est. in Ms. but a prom. note from R.D.Gill, and I.S.Scott, residents of Issa.Co.Ms, Court apps. F.E. Mayfield, Sherf. of Issa., Adm. Oct Term 1856. Final a/c filed July 1859. Suit for collection unresolved.

#48:Guard. of Margaret A.Chaney, minor ch. of Ann S.Chaney. WBk.A,p/155, Abst. in this Vol.II. Addit. Information: By Jan.6,1855,Margaret is now Margaret A.Williams, wife of Sampson Williams; 8Apr.1853 Wood S. states he is over 21 and wishes a div. of prop. - 15 slaves.

#18: Est. of Thos. Y.Chaney: Pet. for div. of Est. by WM.J. Chaney, 4 Jan.1858. He states that his father, Thos.Y. Chaney decd. 22 yrs.ago. Mother now intermarried with Moricai Powell (Emily M.). Sister Sarah C. now Mrs. Littleton P.Franklin, Winchester Co.Md. Further states he has a bro. Thos.Y.Chaney. Pet. now wants div. Dismissed Apr. Term 1858 at cost of Pet.

Packet Gleanings: Issa.Co.
Probate Drw., Unnumbered File; A-D

#51: **Est. of John W.Cohn**:(sp. Cocoa,Coker inside) decd.
7 June 1852. John Hudson, creditor, files let. of Adm.
ad col. 27 July 1852. Pet withdrawn by order of Court
Aug.1852. Pet. of H.B.Coker, bro., granted & filed 9 Aug.185

#75:**Guard. of Angelina Coleman**: awarded to her grandfather,
Malekiah Bradford, with whom"she is living", 2 Oct.1854.Rec
Bk.B, of Wills,p.66, Filed 3 Oct.1854; States Angelina is
10 yrs.child of Thos.H.Coleman and Sarah Ann, both decd.
leaving prop. in La. under Adm. of W.H.Dameron, who has
settled Est. except for prop. in New Orleans, La. G.Bd.
$3,000, surety Wm.M.Bradford, filed 10 Nov.1854, Bk.of Bds.
pgs. 1 & 6.

#23: **Est. of Peter W.Crouch**: Rec. WBk.A,pgs.60,117,206,207,
Abst. in this Vol.II; new infor. descrp. of land to be sold
advertised 15 Apr.1852, all 112 acrs. on Sunflower River.
Sold, 12 July 1852, to John E.Butler (John M.Clark, sec.bd.)
Lots 1,4,5,in Sec.6,T13,R5W, for $30.

#34: **Guard. of John F.Chaney**: Minor, Rec.WBk.A, P.98, Guard.
to Saml.Wells. Pkt. also contains Adm of **Est. of John F.
Chaney**, his father,by Saml.Wells. Doc.states that John F.
Chaney (Sr.) decd. at home of Saml.Wells Aug.1850. Widow
C.A.Chaney is dau. of Saml.Wells.Another Guard.Bd. for John
F.,Jr. filed 6 Oct.1858 to Bailey I.Chaney, his step-father,
Rec.Bk.of Bds. p.33,34.Pet.filed WBk.B,pg.414 26 July 1861.
Div. of prop.between minor John F.Chaney and mother Catherin
A.Chaney filed 1 Apr.1861. Rec.Bk.of Inv.&Appr.282,233,234.
B.I(J?)Chaney asks relief in 1866.

#46: **Est. of Anne S.(L?)Chaney**: Will Rec.WBk.A, p.155.
New infor.: 1855 Doc. advertises final settlement cites
Wood S.(L?) Chaney of La. Copy of James J.Chaney's partit-
ion of Est.- dated 5 Feb.1840 West Feliciana Parish,La.
Partition between 1st and 2nd marriage heirs, and widow
Ann L.Chaney. Names the following heirs: Mrs.Martha A.
Whitten, Bailey D.Chaney,Mrs. Margaret Jones, Bailey J.
Chaney, John F.Chaney,Sarah E.Chaney,Mary Chaney,Susan
Chaney,Michael Chaney, Anne L.Chaney surviving widow and
her ch. Wood L.Chaney,Margaret Chaney, and Wm.Thos.Chaney.
Some of the slaves listed in this settlement are, later,
the one's inherited by Wood.S.& Marg.Chaney from their
Mother.

#10:**Est. of Washington S.Council**: decd.(sometimes referred
to as **William S.**)WBk.B;Inv. & Appr.-p.387; Final a/c by
Saml.Nelson, Adm. of R.W.Pettway, decd. filed 4 Oct.1859.
Oct. 1858, states Richard W.Pettway, 1st Adm. is now decd.
Widow of W.S.Council is Permelia Council,1 Nov.1859.
Guard. ad litem, by J.W.Prescott, of Mary Elizabeth Coun-
cil,Martha Ann Council,Frances EvalineCouncil,Serinia
Council,Franklin Singleton Council,minors, Jan.1860.
Pet. for Guard. filed 21 Feb.1860 for minor heirs of W.S.

Packet Gleanings: Issa.Co.
Probate Drw.,Unnumbered File; A-D

Est. of W.S.Council,(cont) Council by Mrs. Permelia Council
of Madison Co.Ms. She states that at the time of W.S.'s
death she was residing in Hinds Co.Ms. Inv. made 5 May 1858
states decd. left a widow and 6 ch., Inv. taken by D.M.
Birdsong,Geo.H.Robertson,W.F.Cdom.

Est. of Mary B.Creath: et al,minors;Guard. Bd. by D.F.
Blackburn for minors Mary B.Creath,Alberta Creath,Shalline
B.Creath - 3 Apr.1854 (he resigned 1858) secr. E.W.Shelby.
Est. of Alberta Creath: minor - 1st a/c by WM.T.Barnard,
Guard.Filed 1 Apr.1861(Rec.Bk.Inv.& App.243,244);15 Aug.
1861 Pet for G. by WM.T.Barnard, WBk.B.p.391;
minor heir of Mary B.Creath, decd. chooses Guard.; She is
also legatee of Robt.P.Shelby, decd.(5 Apr.1858 - date
of doc.) 1 Apr.1861 Doc. states: Alberta is one of 5 sole
surviving ch. of late Albert G.Creath, who dept. life
"several yrs. ago" in this state, leaving land in Wash.
Co.Ms. Other heirs are Mary B.Waddell,D.H.Creath,Shalline
Y.Creath of Madison Parish, La. and E.J.Barnard - wife of
your petitioner. Signed by W.T.Barnard. Final settlement
of Mary B.Creath by Guard.Blackburn - Apr.1857.

#21: Est. of Dr.Elijah Woolfolk Cullen: decd. Intestate
(# matches Ind. to Est.#) Adm.Fletcher E.Mayfield, Sherf.
Final settlement - 4 July 1859;Inv. & App. filed 6 Oct.
1858; Let. of Adm. 6 Apr.1858; Pkt. contains a letter,
written Deer Creek, Ms. 2 Jan 1858 to Mr. Michael Jones
from Thos.Redwood, who states he is a cripple, not sure it
belongs in this Pkt. Dr.E.W.Cullen owed E.C.Westbrook, decd.
$150, asks Dr.J.P.Woolfolk to pay, since he had all of Dr.
Cullen's medical rec. No heirs named.

Est. of Fielding Davis: decd. 5 Aug,1859; Will and Est.
rec. WBk.C,p.18,19; Wit. to Will;H.J.Butterworth of Wilk.
Co.,Ms,A.Beckman of Adams Co. a merchant at Natchez,F.C.
Englessing of Claiborne - a merchant at Port Gibson. Pet.
for Adm. by Lucinda Davis of Issa. Co.
Jan.1860: Pet. of Chas.C.Balfour & Rosa Balfour who bought
land from the decd. in 1857 - part of Dunbarton Plt. - and
want land title cleared in Rosa's name. 1 July 1860; Sup.
John H.King,James A.Kelly.
5 Jan.1860: Cit. by Balfours, now names Mrs. Lucinda Davis,
exec. of Fielding Davis,decd.& Taylor Davis, a minor son
and heir of the decd.
Oct. 1860:Court appoints J.W.Prescott, Clerk, as Guard.ad
litem to Taylor Davis. Another suit, Benjamin Barbee vs
Lucinda Davis, exec. et al - Barbee also bought land from
the decd.
15 Mar 1861: Lucinda Davis declared the Est. insolvent -
tho' valued at over $76,000, indebtedness was over $114,000.
Lucinda is now of Concordia Parish, La. Included in this
Pkt. is a personal letter from S.B.Newman of New Orleans,
brother of Lucinda Davis, written Sept.1859, giving his
reasons for refusing to act as Adm.of Fieldings'Est.

Packet Gleanings: Issa. Co.
Probate Drw., Unnumbered File; A-D

#87: A.G.Deeson & M.J.Deeson: Guard. of minor ch. of
Joseph S.Clark,decd. & Matilda Jane Clark Deason. Pet.
of Guard.5 Oct. 1868 for minor ch. Eunice Mayfield Clark,
and Mary Joseph Clark under 14. A.G.Deeson is their
step-father. Land in Issa. & Penn.
Pkt. also includes Est. of J.S.Clark, decd. 25 Aug,1865,
owning land on Newsom's Bayou. 10 Apr.1868 Widow petitioned
for dower allotment; approved July Term 1868; not done unti
Jan 1869. Land desc. of 1/3 dower given in Doc. Marked #62
Jan.Term 1869.
#91: In same Pkt. as above: Est. of Mary Jane Chaney: decd.
10 Nov.1867. Pet. of Let of Adm. by Wm.J.Chaney,her husb.,
2 heirs named - Wm.B.Barnard & S.L.Barnard Hall. Filed 6
Oct.1868 (not where) (Ed.Note: Believe Wm.B.Barnard & S.L.
Barnard Hall to be sis & bro. to Mary Jane, see Census
1860, Issa. Co. Household #92)
Also incld. in this Pkt: Paper marked "Chaney". A Trustee
sale, dated 17 June 1867 - DT from Wm.J.Chaney, Thos.Y.
Chaney to Wm.T.Barnard,Wm.Myers for use of Fellows & Co.
Rec.DBk.C,p.662. Land desc.

Will of A.D.Duvall: Will rec.WBk.A,Abst. in this Vol.(1853)
No new infor. Pkt. also incld. Est. of Margaret Duvall:
Oct.4,1866: Pet.Let.Adm. by T.J.Easton, Jr.-son-in-law of
Margaret & A.D.Duvall from Parish of Terrebonne, La. He
married Gwinnet S.Duvall. Margaret decd. 2 July 1863
leaving heirs:Gwinnet S.Easton;Elizabeth P.McNairy; Caro-
line Cook;Mary C.Kelly;Claiborne Duvall;Matilda K.Baskette.
Secu.A.M.Gwinn,Jas.Mayfield. Rec.16 Nov.1866,WEk.C,p.82.
4Jan1869, A.D.McNairy appt. Adm. of Est. of M.Duvall;
Rec. Bk.of Bds. 7Jan1869, p.124.

#61: Est. of Joseph Davenport: decd 16 Mar.1877 at Glenn
Annie Pltn. left surviving him Sina,widow since decd. Ch.
are Anna Aikens,Sarah Davenport,Luke Davenport.Pet.Let.
Adm. filed 11 July1877 by C.A.Grace, member of firm of
J.C.Grace & Co. and who are creditors of Est.$1000 Bd.
secu. by E.Jeffords, Max Killian.

Probate Drw.,Unnumbered File; E-G

Est. of John H.Farr:decd. 13 June 1848, Intestate;Rec.
WBk.A.p.20:List of Minor heirs and their Guard. Elias
Pharr listed WBk.A.p.127.(1851)Additional infor: Mary
Ann Farr has married Benjamin F.Herring by 1849. Doc.
states that Elias Pharr is bro. to John H.Farr. Other
bros.& sis. are:Walter N.Pharr of N.C.; Henry N.Pharr of
N.C.;Robt.Pharr, decd.of Shelby Co.Tenn;Sarah,decd. who
marr.----Allen; James Farr of Cararrus Co.N.C.,decd;
Margaret M.Pharr who marr. ---Beavers, decd. of Meckl.
Co.NC;(The Allens were also in Shelby Co.Tenn.) The
minors listed on p.127WBk.A. are the heirs of these
bros. & sis. Further complicating the picture is the fact
that Mary Ann Farr Herring was a Farr. She defends the

Packet Gleanings: Issa.Co.
Probate Drw.,Unnumbered File: E-G

FARR,cont. holding out of slaves from the div. of the
Est. of John H.Farr, stating these slaves were hers from
her Father's Est. and also her bros. Her Father was named
Robert Farr, and her ½ bro. was named John B.Miller who
decd. 1840 Adams Co.Ms.This doc. filed 6 Apr.1850. Washington B.Farr was the Adm. of Mary Ann's Father's (Robt.
Farr) Est. in AdamsCo. **
Est. of Washington B.Farr: also in this same Pkt. Rec.
WBk.C,p.84: Will written 18 Feb.1860 "made prior to making a "trip to the Western States". Names: wife - Elizabeth
J.Farr(all slaves,7, and everything else) Wit:N.E.Robinson,
Jos.Bunn. Rec.9 Jan1867, Filed Issa.3 Oct.1866. Let. of
Adm. state that W.B.Farr decd 30 Aug.1866, widow requests
that R.M.Smith,L.T.Wade,W.L.Sibley,be appt. Apprs.
No other heirs listed. ##
Est. of John & Robt.Farr: Same Pkt.POA (Cabarrus Co.N.C.)
to Elias Pharr: states John H.Farr decd. leaving no surv.
issue.Following heirs:Walter S.Pharr,Geo.L.Morrison (wife
Margaret Maude) Guard. to Sarah Ann,Henry,Esther A.Pharr;
David D.Taylor(wife Mary C.); Cicero H.Pharr all of Cabr.
Co.N.C...Wm.Beaver, Guard.of Henry N.,John M.Wm.H.Beavers
of Mecklinburg Co.,N.C.; also Geo.L.Morrison,Jr. all give
POA to Elias Pharr, Lake Providence,La. 8 Feb.1851
An earlier POA, 13 Apr.1849 - Geo.L.Morrison to Elias.
Mar.1851: Henry N.Pharr of Iredell Co.N.C. POA to Elias
of Issa.Co...14 Apr.1851;POA by Robt.E.Pharr of Shelby
Co.Tenn. to Elias Pharr. 5 July 1851 - Saml.Allen is
Guard. to Allen ch. & Robt.'s ch. in Raliegh Springs,
Shelby Co. Tenn. The names - Margaret Bowers and Jacob
Bowers added. (Ed.Note: The spelling Pharr was consistent with the N.C.Pharrs, but John H.Always used Farr,
and Mary Ann's name was always spelled Farr.)

#89: Est. of R.F.Eastman: decd. Neshoba Co.Ms Apr.1863.
Adm. Pet. filed by decd. son Emmerson C.Eastman for Est.
of Raford F.Eastmon. Filed 6 Oct. 1868. No prop. in
Neshoba but $600 owed to him in Issa.

Est. of Horatio Eustis:WBk.C,P.13: 1859:Will written 25
July 1857, Filed 4 July 1859; names wife - Catherine C.
Eustis, ch. unnamed.Exec. wife. Pet.for Adm. Catherine
states he decd. Aug last (1858) Adm.Bd. Rich.Chotard;
Asks for Apprs. to be done by W.S.Langley,H.Hampton,
A.M.Gwin, 4 July 1859. ($96,000 est.)

Est. of Robert J.Furlow: decd. 7 May 1869, Intestate;
Pet. for Adm. filed 5 July 1869 by Amanda J.Furlow, widow
, stating the decd. left 5 ch...Paralee,Nancy,Wm.,Martha
Sue,Ruth Ann, all minors under 18. Asks that apprs. be
made by Jas.L.Boyd,H.V.Keep,Frank W.Anderson.

Marr. Rec. Adams Co.,Ms.
**John H.Farr m Mary Ann Farr: 12 - 1 - 1836 Bk.6 p.121
##Wash.B.Farr m Elvira Bedora Martin:7-7-1841 " 6 p.490

Packet Gleanings: Issa. Co.
Probate Drw., Unnumbered; E-G

Will of Mrs.Annie M.Ferriss;decd.Written 13 Sept.1878
Filed New Orleans,La. 6 Dec.1878. Mrs. Annie Maria Flood
Ferriss, widow of Dr.St.Clair Ferriss. She states she has
only 2 ch. - Leila E.Foster and Earnest Foster. Should
Leila die her ½ goes to 3 friends Rich.S.Buck,E.D.Clark,
Saml.H.Buck, who are to be Guard. & Adm. of prop.in La.,
Ms.,Tex.Wit: C.L.Walker,Leigh Watkins,Geo.W.Carey,Jas.P.
Keddell,Jos.Jones. Filed Parish of Orleans - #40691-2nd
Dw.Ct.Succession of Mrs. Anne M.Ferriss, 9 Oct.1878.
Filed Issa. 6 Dec.1878. Adm.Bd. states she decd. New
Orleans, 17 Sept 1878. (Rich.) Buck & (Ed)Clark - law firm
in Vicksburg. Will proven and accepted.

Est. of Sarah Foster: Will of Sarah Foster; filed 12 Dec.
1853 WBk.B; relict of Thos.Foster, decd. Names: Granddau.
Elizabeth Carr; dau. Nancy A.Wood; names Frederick Stanton
to get land and pay rent to son Isaac H.Foster, heir &
son of Thos.Foster,decd; dau.Caroline M.McIntosh;dau.
Sarah McMillan; dau. Mary M.Collins; dau.Frances Wells;
son Levi Foster. Asks Adm. to be Frederick Stanton,Abner
E.Green. Exec. son Isaac H.Foster. Wit: Henry D.Mandeville
Jr., Grafton Baker,Wm.Vannerson. Written 1836
Codicile: to David McIntosh & Caroline permission to have
free use of gin and mill given to Stanton for trust of
Isaac. Adams Co.Ms. Filed Issa. 3 Dec.1853.
Adams Co.Ms. 2 Mar 1838: Div. of Est. of Sarah Foster, by
Wm.Ferguson,Jos.Ferguson,Jos.H.Holt,AllenGrafton,Emanuel
Rogellio.Doc. states heirs are: Mrs. Sally McMillan, Mrs.
Mary Collins,Mrs. Frances Wells,Levi Foster,Thos.Foster,decd
Nancy A.Wood. 12 Dec.1853 - Nancy & John M.Gray pet for his
share and wife's of Est. of Sarah Frances Wells, decd.
Div. of Prop. in Issa Co. ordered 1853.
11 Jan 1854, Issa.Co. shares drawn by: E.J.& M.I.Harvey;
Catharine Carey;*WmMyer Guard. of Frances Myer son of
Henrietta F.Myers; R.R.Richardson & Mary E. his wife;
A.P. & Carsand Newport. New Adm. 14 Nov.1853, Issa.Co.
Est. of Sarah Foster,decd. (Former Adm.Saml.W.Wells has
decd) Wm.T.Baranrd, secu.Wm.Myers,E.J.Harvey,E.W.Shelby,
Pkt. includes Executrix Ann M.Foster of Est. of Jno.
Tillman Foster, decd. of Franklin Co.Va. 6 Apr.1868
Pkt. also contains: rec. of Wm.T.Barnard serving as Adm.
to Est. of John F.Chaney, filed Feb.1854; and Est. of
R.P.Shelby,decd. with Barnard as Adm. of this one, aoo.
Filed 4 Feb.1884.
(Ed.Note: Marriage Rec.Adams Co.Ms. Wm.Collins m Mary
Foster 1814)

Est.of Gideon Fitz: #16: 1st Doc: Deed of Donation, 10
June 1852, by Gideon Fitz of Sidon, Hinds Co.Ms to John
Wm.Fitz(his gr.son), son of Martha E.Fitz & Robt.J.Fitz
of Issa.Co. Gideon states: he is of advanced age, donates
537+ acrs. to JohnW.Fitz on condition of annual payment
by John W.toGideon of $200. Further states that Robert
J. is his (Gideon's) son. If John W. dies without issue
reverts to Martha, John's Mother. If Martha decd, then

*Should be Chaney

Packet Gleanings: Issa.Co.
Probate Drw., Unnumbered File; E-G

Robt.J. gets control. If for any reason the land must
be sold, then Gideon must be pd. $3,000 in lieu of any
further annuity.
#29: Same Drw. Chancery Box: May Term of Court, 1859.
Gideon Fitz vs Robt.,Martha & J.W. Fitz. Bill of Complt.
Non-payment of $200 annually, ever, and Gideon old and
infirm & dependant on others.Solic. C.L.& R.S.Buck.
May Term 1860: Gideon Fitz of Sunflower Co.Ms,decd. 1
Sept, 1859.Suit continues, saying Gideon decd. Sunf.Co.,
left a will that was prob. there in 1859.
20 Oct. 1866; Comm. sale of land to John W.Fitz to pay
complt.John W. received true title & Deed to land. (In
1860 John W.was still a minor, J.W.Prescott appt. by
court as Guard. ad Litem.)

Est. of John L.Gamble: decd. Oct. 1880 at Bear Garden PLtn.
Issa.Co.Let of Adm. 18 Mar 1881 by John G.Sessims. No
widow, one ch. unnamed, E.J.Bryan secu. on Adm.Bd.

Est. of Jacob Garrett: decd. before 2 Apr.1866; Lizzie
Garrett, widow of Jacob Pet. for Let.ofAdm. on that day.
1 ch. age 4, unnamed.Secu. on Adm.Bd.R.W.Smith,W.B.Farr;
Apprs. 2 Mar 1867 by R.W.Smith,W.L.Sibley,L.T.Wade,
1Apr.1867: it is ordered for I.Hosea Mobley to join in
the Adm of the Est. of Jacob Garrett, decd. with Lizzie
Mobley, his wife. Citation to Lawrence Co.Ms.
A/c filed 4 Jan 1868 by Elizabeth Mobley, adm. for Jacob
Garrett.

Est. of Stephen Gray: overseer on Omega Pltn. for H.R.W.
Hill. See a/c of Est. WBk.A,p.70.

Est. of George G.Gregory:decd. before 13 Mar.1854 in Issa.
Co. Let. of Adm. filed by widow Pricilla W.Gregory, with
secu. by Saml.R.Dunn, 23 May 1857.Bd. issued in Wash.Co.
Guard. of minor, Peter Gregory, son of Geo. & Pricilla
awarded to Wash.B.Farr, ad litemRec.WBk.B,p276-293.
Peter is also in Wash.Co.

Est. of Alexander M.Gwin, decd 30 Mar 1867; Adm.Jas.L.
Mayfield, Secu. WM.T.Barnard 2 July 1867. Writ of Dower
to Sarah C.Gwin Bk.C,p.119,7 Jan1867. Land in Issa. &
Warren Co...21 Feb.1872 - J.E.Mayfield declares the Est.
insolvent...26 Nov.1873 widow Sarah E.Gwinn; Thos.W;
Alexander W;Frank;& Margaret Gwin, all minor heirs of
A.M.& Sarah C.Gwin now live in Oakland, Calif.Final a/c
26 Nov.1873.(Much of Gwin's est. was in Levee Bond Script,
which had depre. to 20/25¢ on the $ from 1867 to 1873.)
Court Appts. C.S.Jeffords as Guard. of minors. Also in this
Pkt.: 2 papers concerning A.M.Gwin, Guard. of Mary H.Taylor.
J.L.Mayfield pd. $11,494 to C.I.(J?)Kiger, lawful heir
of Mary Taylor.

Census: 1850 Issa.Co.
1-1Alexander M.Gwin 33 bTenn
   Elizabeth C.   24   S.C.
   Ida H.   6   Ms.
   Robt.C.Dameron   30   "

Census 1860 Issa.
21-21 A.M.Gwin 43 bTenn
Sarah C...32 bTenn,Thos.
W...5,Alex.M...4,Mary G.
3; Jas..9/12

Packet Gleanings: Issa.Co.
Probate Drw., Unnumbered; H-L

#134: Est. of Thos.W.Hay;Decd. 1889, Intestate;owning land in Issa.Co. Pet. for Adm. by E.N.Scudder Co.Adm. Widow is Ellen E.Hays, Fitler,Ms.(Issa.CO.), son Jack P.Hays, 15 Jan.1891. Final a/c Dec.1892: Sue H.Hays of Brunswick, Warren Co.Ms & Ellen E.Hays are only surviving heirs. Relationship of Sue H.Hays unexpl.

Est. of Randall G.Higgins: (Son of Joel Higgins) decd. sometime late 1889. Joel G.Higgins Adm. of R.G.Higgins' Est. Widow Sallie Higgins, Chotard,Issa.Ms.Pltn. named "Eustasia". Will of Randall G.Higgins, dated 19 July, 1889. Widow Sallie E. inherits Life-time Est. States R.G. grew up in Lexington,Ky, had land in MS.MO.Tex. Nephew - Joel G.Higgins, eldest son of decd. bro. Richard Higgins to be exec.; Nephew Brand Higgins, son of Bro.Richard; Bro. Joel Higgins; co-exec. with Joel G.Higgins is Rosewell V.Booth of Vicksburg,Ms; to Annie Stanton, bedroom set used by her grandmother - Mrs. C.L.Maury.
Lease Doc.: Names R.G.Higgins & Sallie E.Higgins and Miss Dillie F.Maury as leasing the Pltn. "Eustacia" to W.S. Wood, Warren Co.Ms for 4 yrs. Dec. 1889. Real prop. heavily mortg. and widow and nephew at odds over person. property.

Est. of Patrick Hamel: decd. in Carolina on business date not stated; Pet.Let.Adm by widow Lavinia E.Hamel, filed 13 Oct 1869, states they have 4 ch.- James H. Hamlin(Hamel); Mary E.Jenkins, formerly Hamel; Kate A. Hamel; Wade H.Hamel, last 2 being minors. Mrs. Hamel in Orangeburg, S.C. 27 Feb.1868.
Pkt. contains Pet. of John S.Joor to dismiss his Guard. Evan Shelby since he was now 22 yrs. old.Filed 4 Dec. 1867.Rec.Bk.Inv.&a/c p.24. 25 Mar.1868; paper #33.
Pkt. also contains bills from L.Julienne..for the county for material, must have been a printer. 1860.
Pkt. also contains Est. of James R.Harris: decd. New Orleans (but res. of Issa.) 24 Mar.1860. Will written - 8 Mar.1860; presented by Bro. Wiley P.Harris 2 Apr.1860. Will names: wife Eudora - ½ of all est.; Directs exec. to sell lands and slaves. Other ½ to be div. thus; Saml.J.Moorehead in trust for James R.;L.B.;Sarah;Eliza; and Robt. Harris, ch. of bro. Wiley P.Harris; bro. Buckner Harris;bro. John H.Harris;bro. P.Harris; Wit: M. Gillespie,L.H. Aby, J.D.Mayes. Co-exec: Wiley P. and Hamilton McNeil Vance of New Orleans.

Est. of Mrs. Nancy Hardin: decd. 17 Feb.1878; Pet. for Let.of Adm. by Wirt Adams,Jr. Bd.$500 R.Cohn 21 Mar 1879. Pet. for Guard. to G.W.Pittman for minors Alma, 4 yrs. and Ida, 6 yrs. who are living with G.W.Pittman. No relationship stated. 27 Feb.1878.

PACKET GLEANINGS: Issa.Co.
Probate Drw.,Unnumbered: H-L

Est of Col.Wade Hampton, Sr.;decd. 9 Feb.1858; Pet.for
Let.of Adm. filed 24 May 1858 - Rec. 23 June 1858, p.377
(where?) by Christopher F.Hampton, son of the decd. Pet.
states that Wade Hampton,Sr. left the following ch. &
heirs: your petitioner (C.F.);Wade,Jr.; Catharine M.;
Ann M(W?); Caroline L;Frank;Mary H.Hampton-all over 21.
He decd. Intestate, leaving a widow.(unnamed)
Apr.1861: Adm. states he has sold "Walnut Ridge Pltn"
by permission of the above named heirs, + 250 negroes
for $400,000 - bought by Wade Hampton,Jr.(III) July
1858.Doc. signed by Wade Hampton,Mary F.Hampton,Frank
Hampton,Ann M.Hampton,Kate Hampton,Caroline L.Hampton
Columbia,S.C. June 18,1861 (Richland Dist.)
Final a/c by Christopher F.Hampton, Apr.1861
Ed.Note: Will of Annie F.Hampton, only dau. of Christopher
F.Hampton, Wash.Co.Ms.WBK.1,p.440 (see Vol.I this series)
Will of Wade Hampton,III; Wash.Co.WBk.1,p.415 (this Vol.)
S.C.Marr. rec: Wade Hampton,II (called Col.) marr. 1st
Ann Fitzsimmons 1817 Charleston - she decd. 1833 "at
Millwood"; marr 2nd 1838 - Margaret Preston:
"AHistory of Miss."p.349: "The Hampton Family of S.C.
had the largest absentee holdings in Ms in the mid-1840's,
in Issa.and Wash.Cos...2,700 acres in Issa. called Walnut
Ridge....Wade II owed Stephen Duncan $170,000 in 1855, and
when Wade II died 1858, Wade III assumed all debt, more
than $400,000...At the end of the War he was bankrupt -
1868. By 1875 Wade III had redeemed Walnut Ridge".
From "Marr.& Death Notices from S.C.newspapers" by Holcomb
The desc. of Gen.Wade Hampton (the 1st one) were:Caroline
Hampton,Mary Hampton,Harriet Hampton,Col.Wade Hampton,Jr.(II)

Est. of Alma & Ida Hardin: Pet. for Guard. by their Uncle
George Hardin for the minor ch. of Mrs. Nancy Hardin,decd.
and Ira Hardin decd. Feb.1878. (See Est. of Mrs. Nancy
Hardin above) No disposition noted.

Est. of John Hester: decd.---1850;Let. Ad.Coll. to Sher.
of Issa. Geo.P.Johnston - issued & Rec. 14 June 1850.

#67:Est. of Francis B.Hill, et al:Minor ch. of Isaac C.
Hill,decd.and Emily C.Hill - Francis B.-15 yrs;Eva L.-10;
(#68); Lizzie S.-8 yrs-#69; Glenora Ann-17-#92,#66; 1867
(Numbers are a/c for each minor) Pet. for Guard. by nat-
ural mother Emily C.Hill 2 Apr 1866 - minors Francis and
Glenora Ann cited to appear to choose Guard, July Term-
1866. Emily C.approved Guard. of all ch. 2 July 1866,
WBk.C,p.79 G.Bd.secu. by W.B.Farr,Jas.L.Mayfield. Inv.&
Appr. 3 Oct.1866. Glenara A.Hill pet. for release of Guard.
2 Jan 1868, "now of age 18". Pet. signed Glennie A.Hill.

Est. of Samuel Leatherman:Decd. 31 Dec.1862: (see Prob.
Pkt.#9, this Vol.) 6 ch. - Saml.E.;Robt.;Geo.W;Zachariah;
Peter R;Mrs. Martha Lindsey:2 grsons - ch. of John Leath-
erman,decd.-Frank & John W.Jr.; also survivors - Joel
Glass and Nellie Glass; Aurelia Ward wife of Carroll Ward.
Pkt. contains papers dealing with W.B.McCormick - Quit
Claim Deed on land he purchased for Levee taxes 1871

Packet Gleanings: Issa.Co.
Probate Drw.,Unnumbered: H-L

Est. of Homer V.Ledbetter; Will rec.WBk.A,Issa. p.4-5,Abst. this Vol:Pkt. contains copy of Will, rec. Issa. Co.15 Sept. 1846: Bd. for Adm. filed Sept.1846 awarded ad coll. to R.W. Pettway: Filing of final a/c by Pettway not fully accepted by Judge Bonham and said Adm owes $1667.02½ to James W. Ledbetter the present Adm. of Est. 12 Mar 1849.
19 Sept.1846: Appeal Bd. by Wm.B.Ledbetter to set aside Will. (Ed.note: can't find any action on this, but the lack of direct action may have been because 12 bros. & sisters fought over the Est. until 1860, even tho' some had sold their interest to Jas.E.Ledbetter.)
Doc. dated 1 Nov.1846, Carroll Parish,La; W.B.Ledbetter conveys his int. in Est. to J.W.Ledbetter of Madison P.La. for $250...Martha Bean sold her int.for$1020...Sarah Leighton of Jeff.Co.Ms sold her int. for $650...Martha Bean, in another sale for $500..same date...Eliza V.Deeson, Wm.M.Deeson recpt. of $1200 for their int. 13 Dec.1846.
Pet. for distribution of slaves filed 4 Oct.1859
Pet. for collection of their share,1/8th, $27,252.46 filed 2 Apr.1860 by Abner Gains,Sally Gains his wife; Jeremiah Watson as legal Guard. of Anna & Georgia Watson; Court ordered Adm.J.W.Ledbetter to pay them $3406.55 and court cost.
J.W.Ledbetter files Bill of Exception with above order 2 Apr.1860.
J.W.Prescott,Guard. of Henry L.Deeson minor distr. of Est. of Elisha Deeson,decd.heir of H.V.Ledbetter, consent to allow final settlement of J.W.Ledbetter 2 Apr.1860.
Final a/c 7 May 1860: J.W.Ledbetter gave the following run-down of the family:Jane Ledbetter - mother- decd.in La.(no date) left 12 heirs:1.Nancy Beard;2.Martha Bean; 3.Sarah Leighton;4.Eliza V.Deeson;5.Anne W.Watson(the mother of petitioners Abner Gains,Sally Gains-formerly Watson,)Jeremiah Watson,Anna Watson and Georgia Watson- the last 2 being minors;6.Jane P.Carter;7.Olivia O.Watson; 8.H.C.Ledbetter;9.James Ledbetter;10.W.B.Ledbetter;11.Homer Ledbetter;12.A.C.R.Ledbetter. Further states that when Homer V. died all bro.& sis. living and entitled to sh; James bought out all but Ann W.Watson.
(Ed.Note: No part of the Will of Homer V.Ledbetter was ever executed.)

Est. of Thos.C.Leigh; Adm.Bd. by J.M.Clark,J.J.Sullivan $1000 11Apr1853 states decd. owned land on Yazoo River. Apprs. by D.T.Williams,Thos.J.Shelby,Lewis Dameron.

Est. of John E.& Leannah T.Woolfolk, minors; (out of order) Guard. Bd. by Timothy Hughs of Woodford Co,Ky. - $1000 secu. by P.P.Woolfolk, filed 1 Jan 1866..Ch. of James B. Woolfolk of Iss. (lived on Deer Creek, Issa.Co.) Leannah under 14, John E.over 14; Rec.12Apr.1866,Bk.B of Bondsp.81.

Packet Gleanings: Issa.Co.
Probate Drw.,Unnumbered; M-O

Large Pkt. containing the following:
1. Est. of Joseph and Cynthia (Prince) McQuillan, decd. (1846)
2. Guard. of Jos.R.& Cynthia Jane McQuillan, (1851)
3. Guard. of Melissa A.McQuillan (1851)
4. Est. of Saml.W.Wells, decd. (1853)
5. Est. & Will of Sarah Foster - Div. of Prop.(1853)
6. Est. of Martha A.McQuillan (1861)
7. Est. of Jos.R.McQuillan, decd. (1862)
8. Est. of Francis C.Myers, minor

1. Est. of Jos. & Cynthia McQuillan,decd.:(abst. this Vol.) WBkA, p2,3; (1846) Guard. of minors to Wm.B.Mc Quillan...children are Jos.B.,C.J.,A.P.;Pkt. contains Guard.Bd., Inv.&Appr.(14 Oct 1851)

2. Guard. of minors stated in #1. Rec. WBkA,p.2,3; New infor. Cynthia Jane McQuillan has marr. John E.Butler, and Wm.B.McQuillen asks release from his duties as Guard. for her and Jos.R. (no mention of A.P.) 14 Nov.1853

3. Guard. of Melissa A.McQuillan (dau. of Melissa J.Mc Quillan, decd) by Wm.B.McQuillen (1851) Rec.WBkA,p.140 (abst. this Vol.)New Infor: 6 Oct. 1858 Melissa A.cites her father, Wm.B. for not attending to her business and making no Guard. reports..further states he has had rheumatism and cannot function. A Guard., ad litem,J.W. Prescott is appointed. Incl. in Pkt. is Marriage Contract between Mellissa J. & Wm.B.McQuillan - dated 23 July 1846 - listing her property - all slaves.

4. Est. of Saml.W.Wells, decd. Rec. WBkA,p.256 (abst. this Vol.)1853. New infor: by 1855, Martha A.(Chaney) Wells, widow of Saml.W. has marr. Wm.B.McQuillan who is new Adm. of Saml.W.'s est:Wm.B. & Martha A. McQuillan pet. for div. & sale of property and permission to hire out slaves..Jan Term 1855 (Saml.W.Wells left a high indebtedness)

5. The Division of the property of Est. of Sarah Foster (see WBk.B,p10-11, Abst. this Vol.) No. new Infor. (these are the issue of Saml.W.Wells and Frances Foster Wells, trying to remove their mother's Est. from that of their Father's, Saml.W.'s, since a 2nd marriage is involved.. Martha A.(Chaney) Wells m Wm.B.McQuillan)

6.Est. of Martha A.(Chaney) McQuillan, decd. 20 Oct 1861 leaving the following Will: Written 30 Sept 1861 -Rec. WBk.C, p. 49,50. Filed 6 Jan.1862.
Names: her child - James J.Wells ...14 slaves
her husb. - Wm.B.McQuillan .. 9 slaves
(little) neice - Martha A.Chaney..1 sl.
her bro. - Bailey I.Chaney..1 sl.
Exec. Husb. & E.W.Shelby with no secu.
Wit: Parminas Howard, Alonzo Givens,Mary E.Mizell allof ISSA.

Packet Gleanings: Issa. Co.
Probate Drw., Unnumbered; M-O

McQuillan Est., cont. Pkt. contains: Will;Proof of Will;
Let. Test.;Warrant of Appr. & Inv. (21 Mar.1862 - $18,000);
Pet. by E.W.Shelby - Sept.1866 asking to be dismissed as
Adm., saying he never functioned, that Wm.B.McQuillan has
handled everything and minor heir J.J.Wells agrees to
release him; An a/c by McQ. 1866.
Case #4,(Chanc) Oct. Term 1866: Pet. of James J.Wells
for settlement of his Est...he states his Guard. was
held by his mother as of Dec. 1853 (Martha A.Wells) secu.
was by E.W.Shelby,E.Jones Harvey.Then when Mother decd.
1861, his Guard. was passed on to Wm.B.McQuillen (step-
father). James J.Wells is now of age and says his mother
never made an a/c and he holds the secu. responsible for
one. Also cites Shelby, and Harvey 1867,1868,1869 (no
dispensation recorded).

7. Est. and Will of Jos.R.McQuillan (aged 24):
Will written 18 Apr.1857 - Prob.Apr.Term 1862, Rec.WBk.C
p.53-56: Names brother WmB.MCquillan to have everything
and also to serve as Exec. without secu. Wit: H.R.Hampton
(who has moved to Wilk.Co.Ms by 1862) D.D.Jackson, Issa.,
H.W.Patterson of Issa. (decd. by 1862): Pet. Let.Test.by
Wm.B.McQuillan.

8. Separate Packet, but as it involves the same family
am including it with the others.
Est. of Francis C.Myers (Meyers): MINOR HEIR OF Henrietta
F.Myers, decd. Guard. Bd. by Wm.Myers 12 Dec. 1853 -$10,000
stating that Francis is minor heir of the Est. of Mrs.
Sarah Foster, decd;S.F.Wells; decd; and Saml.W.Wells, decd.
and inf. ch. of Wm.Myers. Secu. for Guard.Bd. E.Jones
Harvey,E.W.Shelby.
Apr. 1855: Francis C.Myers, minor of Wm.Myers recd. negro
boy Eli from Est. of Sarah Frances Wells, decd.
3 Oct. 1866: An.a/c Wm.Myers, Guard. to Francis C.Myers
gives a/c of the inheritance from Saml.Wells, decd."lost
Eli due to War."

Ed.Note: Marr. Rec. from Adams Co.Ms.
Nancy Foster m 9 May 1810 Ethan A.Wood
Caroline Foster m 15 Nov.1824 David S.McIntosh
Sarah Foster m 27 June 1810 Daniel McMillan
Frances Foster m 5 Dec.1814 Saml.W.Wells
Thos.Foster, Jr. m 28 June 1820 Susanna Carson

The children of Frances Foster and Saml.W.WElls:
Martha J.Wells b 1832 m E.Jones Harvey
Catherine Wells b 1831 m John F.Chaney who decd. 1850 at
    home of Saml.W.Wells.
Henrietta F.Wells m Wm.Myers and decd before 1850
Mary E. Wells m R.R.Richardson
Carson Wells m A.R.Newport
Nancy T.Wells m John Gray

Packet Gleanings: Issa.Co.
Probate Drw.,Unnumbered: M-O

Est. of Willie Magee: decd. Pkt. contains: Pet.for L.Adm. by Fletcher E.Mayfield, Sheriff of Issa. filed 4 Oct. 1854 WBk.B,p.67: Proof of posting;Voucher;Final a/c July Term 1859.

Pkt. contains two Est. 1.**Est. of Mark H.Mayfield**; 2.**Est. of Fletcher E.Mayfield**.
1. Adm.Bd. 28 Apr.1845 by Wm.S.Mayfield, states that there are 9 heirs to divide the Est. which consists of 2 negro boys; Doc. signed by Wm.J.Mayfield;Jas.I.Mayfield;J.A.Lane, in right of wife N.P.Mayfield;Virgil H.Mayfield;F.E.Mayfield; and 1 bro. in Ga; 1 bro. in Tenn; 10 Jan 1850.
2. Est. of Fletcher E.Mayfield (born 1821), decd. 5 Mar 1868: Intestate, owning land in Issa. (most 1/3 or more "in the River") Adm. brother James L.Mayfield who listed other heirs as follows: Thomas W.Mayfield;Mary A.Lane; Heirs of Martha Freeman;Sarah Lane;Nancy Lane;Virgil H. Mayfield - all sisters and brothers of the decd. Doc. dated 5 Oct.1868. Inv. showed he also owned 1 horse and saddle.

Est. of John McLaurin,decd.28 Sept.1851: Rec.WBk.A,p.141. (Abstracted in this Vol.) No new Infor.

Est. of George William Bacon Messinger:(1863) Rec.WBk.B p.58,59 - 10 Oct 1865: Will; filed 5 Jan 1863
Wit: E.Jones Harvey,Sampson Williams
"I,George William Bacon Messinger of Issa.Co." requests that he be buried on family plot on Plantation "Baconhorn" in Warren Co.Ms. belonging to George and Sophia Messinger. Names: wife and "companion" Sybelia Antoinette Messinger; Will written: 4 June 1857: (Ed.Note: Will is rec. inWBk. C,p.53 and not in WBk.B as stated on Doc.)
Adm. is J.L.Mayfield who Pet.for sale of land, stating that only Sybelia Antoinette Foote and W.H.Foote are the only ones interested, and are living in Noxubee Co.Ms. Filed 5 Jan 1870.
Arp.Term 1870Claims are filed agst. the Est. of G.W.B. Messinger, stating he owned 880 acr. of land in Issa. and some more in Wash.Co.Ms.
2 Nov.1870 Doc.signed by H.W.Foote and S.A.Foote states the property listed in Wash.Co.Ms. was Sybelia'a as inherited from her brother Bacon Messinger.
(Ed.Note: Sybelia A.Messinger married 1863,Macon,Mis. to Judge Hezekiah William Foote as his 3rd.wife - they had 1 dau. Georgia AnnFoote b1867. See "Clements"Book by K.C. Branton,1979)

Est. of Lewis Miller: Oct. Term 1860 J.L.Mayfield, Adm. Will: written 3 Apr. at Dunbarton,1859 - Filed 3 Jan 1860 WBk.C,p.28,29:Est. consisting of money notes & book a/c owed to him he leaves to his sister Louisa Hopper of Ill. Exec:Fielding Davis; Wit:C.C.Balfour,A.Hundermark,H.Shultz. Inv.&Appr. rec. I&ABk.p.175,176 16Nov 1860.

Packet Gleanings: Issa. Co.
Probate Drw.,Unnumbered; M-O

#53: **Est of Barton W.H.Millsaps:** (on outside of cover -
"Prob. 1849") Adm.Ed. Walter C.Lofton & Jas.S.Small
$5,500 Bd.   9Nov 1852 Rec.WBk.B p.169; Bk. of Eds. A
p.116. Guard.Bd. by Walter C.Loftin & Jas.S.Small $1,600
for minors Wm.B.Loftin,Eldridge Loftin,Evan W.S.Loftin-
dated 9 Nov.1852 (Ed.note: No connection given for the
Loftins and the decd. Barton Millsaps. It's possible
that the Guard. Bd. was incld. because it was the same
date and Guard.) Inv.&Appr. of Millsaps Est. by Wm.Dodds,
I.C.Hill,E.Murphy,Louis Tillman,D.F.Castleman   2 May 1852
when Evan W.Shelby, Sherf.of Issa. was Adm.

Est. of Samuel S.(L?) Moore: (1850) decd: Pet. for L.Adm.
by Mrs. Rachael Moore, widow of decd. stating that he
died 4 July 1850, Intestate, owning negroes,stock,personal
prop., and considerable land in Hinds Co.(Ms.). She further
states that the decd. left 5 other heirs than herself:
1.Mrs. Martha Nicholson,wife of I.E.Nicholson.2.Franklin
W.Moore 3.Wm.S.Moore 4.Thos.A.Moore 5.Oliver Perry Moore
ch. of the decd. and petitioner, all being minors but
Martha.   Secu. R.Christmas,Saml.Nelson: Inv.&Appr. by
Elisha North,F.Mayfield,R.B.Cammack,R.W.Pettway,S.Leath-
erman.   Filed 15 Oct.1850/WBk.A.p.101.
Pkt. includes: #50: **Mary E.Moore Pet. for Guard.** for
minor heir of Frank W.Moore & Rachel Moore, decd.,Mary
E.Moore,Letitia M.Davis,Henry H.Davis...G.Bd. $800.
Mary E.Moore states she is the mother of minors Frank
W.& Emmet N.Moore. Doc. dated 7 Apr.1868.*
Pkt. also incld. **Sale of land** Hinds Co. 10 July 1852
Inv.& Apprs.,vouchers, **Annual a/c of S.S.Moore - Guard.**
to Martha M.Nicholson,Franklin & Wm.Moore - heirs-at-law
of **Wiley A.Walters,decd** Hds. Co.(Ms.) Jan 1850. Attest.
to this doc. Wm.H.Hampton,Hds.Co.Clerk 15 Sept.1851,at
which time Milton H.Hams was overseer on Pltn. in Issa.
          *believe this doc. belongs in next Pkt.

Est. of Rachel Moore; decd. 4th Oct.1865 Intestate:Pet.
for L.Adm. by Isaac E.Nicholson, son-in-law with secu.
by J.J.Watson,Theodore Fitler:Rec. WBk.B,p.57. Adm.Bd.
$1000, 4 Oct. 1865: Warrant of App. Filed 4 Dec.1865:
Citation to E.D.Clark Guard. ad litem to Frank Moore,
Emmet Moore - minor heirs of Frank W.Moore,decd. heir
& distributee of Est. of Rachel Moore,decd. to answ.
Pet. of Isaac E.Nicholson, Adm of Est. of Rachel Moore.
Dec. 1865: Inv.& Appr. Filed 4 Dec.1865:
23 Nov.1865:Pet by Adm.IE.Nicholson names the following
heirs: wife Martha M.Nicholson formerly Martha M.Moore;
Thos.A.Moore;Frank & Emmet Moore minor ch. of Frank.W.
Moore,decd; are only heirs and distr. of sd.Rachel Moore,
decd. who owned a pltn. in bad repair. Heirs want to
rent out the pltn. Filed 4 Dec. 1865 Bk. of I & App.p.306
1 Dec.1865 - Martha and Thos.A. sign release for sale of
pers. prop. of decd.and land rented out 1866. No final
report.

Packet Gleanings: Issa.Co.
Probate Drw.,Unnumbered M-O

Est. of G.Washington Morton: decd. 12 Dec.1859, Intestate:
Jan.Term 1860 Pet for L.Adm. by Eliza Morton & Robt.Marsh
stating the decd. left a small est. cont. land & personal
prop. @$10,000. Eliza is his widow and unable to give
required Bd. and asks that Robt.Marsh be decl. Adm...Secu.
by Isaac C.Hill; Appra & Inv. by Wm.Osborn, Benj.Osborn,
and Daniel Levy. Rec. WBk.C,p25 Jan Term 1860.
Doc. incld. in Pkt: Inv.& Appr. 15 Oct 1861; Proof of
Public posting;Pet. for sale of prop;sale of pers. est.
and hiring of slaves (3 men) 8 Apr 1862 at the "premises"
of decd. - Bunches Bend. The purchaser of the prop. was
Joseph Morton. The slaves were hired out to Jacob and
Will S.Owen (the 3 slaves were Wash,Ben,John each worth
$1000 apiece)
By 8 Oct 1861 the Adm is Jas.L.Mayfield, Sherf. de bonis
non, and there is no indication that Robt.Marsh functioned
after Jan 1860.
1st Appraisal of prop. in 1860 estimates Est. to be worth
$10,774.25, by 1861 the est. had dwindled to $4035 because
of a large stock-pile of cut wood had been allowed to
stay under water during flood. 1 voucher for cutting timber filed by D.M.Kinter, partner of J.B.McLaughlin Co...
on reverse side "money to be sent Indiana, Indiania Co.,
Pa. dated 12 Mar 1861

Est. of John H.Moseley: decd. May 1864: Filed Apr.Term 1866
#21. Pet. of L.Adm. by Alfred W.Moseley - filed 2 Apr.1866,
Rec. WBk.C, p.74,75 states: J.H.Moseley left a Will that
was never probated, he decd. owning land, around 6000acr.
+personal prop, and further states that J.H.&A.W are bros.,
and the decd. left 3 heirs: 1.Burrell Moseley 2.Eugenia
Moseley 3.Lucy Moseley ch. of sd. decd - all minors under
14. The War prevented Adm. to Est. and noth ing has been
done. Secu. by Wm.T.Barnard,Sampson Williams..Apprs. by
J.P.Woolfolk,Thos.Watson,J.Kansler.
Doc. incld. in Pkt.: Adm.Bd.;Appr.&Inv.;Pet for sale of
personal goods and household furnishings - 2 July 1866;
Answ. of heirs (minors) by Guard.E.D.Clark, Guard.Ad Litem;
Report of sale Sept.1866; 1st a/c; in Published adm.a/c
in Vicksburg Herald "Est. of John H. & Catherine Moseley"
1866. By 1869, A.W.Moseley is Guard. of minor ch.

Est of Minors, Eugenia,Lucy,Burrell Moseley: Pet. for
Guard. of minors by A.W.Moseley, stating they are the
heirs of John H.Moseley and Catherine A.Moseley both
late of said Co., decd. Alfred states he is the bro. of
John H.Moseley. From the vouchers incld. the ch. must
be living with Alfred.W. Sept. 1867 - a bill for Coffin
$12 - for Burrell Moseley, pd. by J.M.Moseley.
Last doc. 1869.

Packet Gleanings: Issa.Co.
Probate Drw.; Unnumbered - P-R.

Est. of George N.Parks and Est. of George W.Parks*(Same PKT)
Will of George N.Parks: Written 3 May 1852: Prob.20 Nov.
1854.(WBk."B",p.81)
Names: Beloved wife Susan E.Parks
      "   dau. Amanda Parks, wife of Horatio D.Coffield
      "   son George N.Parks, Jr.
      "   dau. Margaret E.Parks
All heirs to share equally, with wife to have a lifetime
interest, reverting to the children at her death. Son -
George, Jr. is a cripple and gets an extra $10,000.
Amanda and Horatio Coffield live on Pltn. called"Eldorado"
560 acrs. 40 slaves, about 8 or 10 miles South of"Ben
Lomand" the home place (1495 acrs.-130 slaves)
Exec: Son-in-law H.Coffield and brother - Thomas Parks,
     until son Geo.Jr. comes of age. They are to serve
     as Guard. to minor ch. also.
Wit: W.B.Farr,J.L.Mayfield,Robt.B.Cammack
Pkt. includes: Inv. & Appr.,Guard. Reports,Adm. reports,
Geo.N. also owned a third pltn -"Cottonwood".
Adm. seek permission to sell "Cottonwood" to pay off an
indebtedness of $149,000 owed by the Est. Jan.1855.
Expenses of Guard. for school expenses for Geo.Jr. in
Louisville,Ky...Jan.1854...Jan 1855 he's in school near
Natchez,Brighton Grammer School; Jan. 1856 he's in Port
Gibson at school. Margaret, called Maggie, was also in
school in Louisville, Ky. 1856,57,58.
Doc. Pet for sale of lands, dated Oct. Term 1856 states
that Geo.Jr. is about 19, and Maggie E. 13 yrs.
Around 1860-61, Maggie E.marr.Albert G.Ward.
Partition Pet. filed 2 July,1861..all parties in agreement.
*the 2 names are the same person.

Est. of Elias Pharr, decd. (See Est. of John H.Farr, abst.
this Vo.II - also Guard. of Minors by Elias Pharr, this
Vol.II, Est. notice WBk."A",p.127,228,233)
Additional information: Letter written by Elias Pharr in
Tallulah,Ms. Sept.4,1852 to Saml.N.Allen. P.O.A. to collect Ursilla Pharr's 1/7th share of ------ estate now in
the hands of Harper(?). He states that she does not want
to file suit. Saml.Allen and Joe Bateman to amicably arr-
ange with Baker & Bolton. "Our love to all the family and
to our sister Mary particulary. From your sincere friend
and affectionate Brother". signed by Elias Pharr. This
claim must have been settled for Ursilla requested her
$200 from that est. be separated from Elias's.
(Elias Pharr decd. sometime prior to Jan.11,1853)
Pack.contained the following doc.:
Voucher from W.C.Smedes for getting ward's,Mary E., property moved to Tenn...2 Apr.1855.
Writ of Dower for share of 568 acrs.,fully described and
map inclosed, 9 May 1853.
Public Notice of Final A/c Jan.1855 names the following
as heirs and distributees of Elias Pharr: Hampton H.Pharr,
John N.Pharr both of La.; Ursilla M.Pharr and Eunice M.Pharr
of Tenn.;Sarah E.Pharr,Albertus Pharr,and Margaret S.Smith.
(Margaret S.Smith, formerly Pharr, marr. Robt.M.Smith)

Packet Gleanings: Issa. Co.Ms.
Probate Drw: Unnumbered File, P-R.

Est. of Elizabeth Pharr,minors; Robert M.Smith Guard. to
Elizabeth A., sometimes referred to as Sarah Elizabeth;
Albertus Pharr, also signs as S.A.Pharr; who are over 14
choose R.M.Smith as their Guard. 1 Jan.1854.
Pkt. contains: Vouchers showing Albertus was in school in
North Carolina 3 yrs. and the final a/c for him was filed
1 Oct.1860 and payment recd. 28 Apr.1861 by him at Centre-
ville, La.
Another voucher dated 27 July 1854, and 8 Apr.1856 to A.T.
Travis for 5 months Board and Tuition for Henry A.Pharr.
Voucher in 1855 to Miss E.Pharr, and one to Miss Lizzie
Pharr, Cammack Landing,Ms.
Guard.Bd.1Jan 1855 by R.M.Smith for Henry A.Pharr,infant
ch. of Elias Pharr ($2,000) Also one for Sarah E.Pharr on
same date, with secu. by J.N.Porter,F.E.Mayfield.

(Ed.) Census 1850,Issa.Co.Ms.   Census 1860,Issa.
3 - 3: Elias Pharr   51 bN.C.   Robt.M.Smith   48 bKy.
       Ursilla M. " 28 Tenn.   M.S.   "   29 N.C.
       Hampton   " 16 N.C.   And living in this
       Elizabeth   " 14 Tenn.   household is S.E.Pharr,
       Albertus   " 12 "   22f..b.Tenn.

Est. of Absolem Barrow, William H.Peace adm.(See WBk."A",
pgs.5,6,7,17,19, Abst. this Vol.)
Doc. in Pkt. shows Appr. for hiring out of girl Sarah
in 1850. No new infor.

Est. of Richard W.Pettway:Pet. for Let.Adm.de bonis non
by Alex.M.Gwin,6 Jan.1862, Bd.$8,000 with secu. by Saml.
Nelson,J.L.Mayfield. Dr. Pettway decd. 13 June 1859 in
City of St.Louis, Mo. Heirs:Julia I., his wife;ch. -
Thomas R.;Ida;Sallie Gwin;Laura Danks;Richard; all under
21. Widow Julia requested that her Father Saml.Nelson
be appointed Adm.
Doc. included in Pkt: Pet. for Let.Adm.by Saml.Nelson
5 July 1859. Granted.
Pet. for sale of prop. same date.
Inv.& Appr. 7 July 1859, Recd.Oct.1859
Descript. of land and sale...2 Jan.1860
J.W.Prescott, Guard.ad litem of minor ch.
Pet. for Let.of Adm. by AlexM.Gwin 6 Jan.1862 stating that
Saml.Nelson departed this life Sept.1861.

Est. of William Rushing: decd. 10 Dec.1860. Pet. for proof
of Will and Let.of Adm. filed by Mary Rushing and E.Jones
Harvey 2 Apr.1861.
Will: (WBk."C",p.42) Written - 3 Dec.1860, Prob.19 Apr.1861.
"Everything to Mary, my wife and unborn child."
Wit:W.H.Pickens,W.D.Brown,D.W.Browder. ($40,000 Est.land
+ slaves).
Doc. incld. in Pkt.: Exec. Bd. 2 Apr.1861
Inv.&Apprs. 21 May 1861
7 July 1862 - Allowance for widow and child.
7 Oct. 1862 - E.Jones Harvey Pet. for discharge of Exec.
duties, saying Mary Rushing now marr. to R.Y.Maxwell since
July 1862.
Oct. Term 1866 - decree releasing Harvey from Exec.;

Packet Gleanings; Issa.Co.Ms.
Probate Drw.;Unnumbered P-R.

EST. OF William Rushing: cont. Vouchers and a/c show that
the unborn child was Henry, a boy, born in 1860.
In same Pkt.;Est. of Henry Rushing: in an envelope marked
1868, case #41.
Document dated Jan.Term1868 gives descript. of lands of
Wm.Rushing,decd. Rec. in WBk."C",p.112: by petitioners
Mary and R.Y.Maxwell. States that during the War they
were compelled to leave the plantation and in their absence gin house,cabins,fences and other improvements were
destroyed, slaves emancipated. Ask permission of court
to divide land between Mary and minor - Henry, saying it
is impractical to farm under the arrangements made in
Wm.Rushings's Will. Mary Maxwell - 625 acres; Henry
Maxwell - 625 acrs. Land decsriptions on N.& S. side of
Rolling Fork.
July 1868 - Frank Anderson Guard. ad litem for Henry.

#1: (Missing from Drw. 1-17) Est. of Leanah Robertson:
Non Cuperative Will dated 21 Sept.1858. "Iwill that my
son-in-law W.D.Brown be appointed Adm. My Plantation
and negroes not to be sold for debts or distr. until my
dau. Alta California becomes of age or marries".(she is 9)
W.D.Brown to have the management and control of my ch.
and their prop. until they come of age or marry. Deer
Creek, Co. of Issa.Ms. No wit. E.Jones Harvey and Verlinda Woolfolk oath to validity Jan.3,1859.
Doc. in Pkt.: Pet. for Let. of Adm. by W.D.Brown for
Leanah Robertson who decd. 21 Sept.1858. Filed 3 Jan.185
Heirs:minors Joseph W.Robertson - 11 yrs.;Alta California
9 yrs; Ella C.Robertson - 7 yrs.;Lula V.Robertson - 3 yrs
Alice V.Brown,wife of W.D.Brown; J.W.Prescott Guard. ad
litem. (Alice V.Brown is 18 yrs.)
1st a/c: vouchers.
#14:Est. of J.W.Robertson: heir of Leanah Robertson:
Pkt. contains 2 papers - Tax payments on land 1866,1867.
#96:Est. of L.Robertson: more of Leanah's Est.;1867 a/c
#98:Est. of Lula C.Robertson:minor, Vouchers, a/c by W.D.
Brown adm. to Leanah Robertson Est. 1862.- 1865.
13 Nov.1866,$55 to Miss Irene Cullen for tuition in famil
school;1866 Tuition to Lon Branch;1865 to Miss C.Boyer;
1862 to Mary Clark for instruction.
#99:Ellen C.Robertson:(Ellen on Jacket - Ella inside)
A/c by W.D.Brown 1862 - 1865. Same Tuition fees,same sch.
except for 1859 she was in sch. in Columbia,Tenn.
Some vouchers for Alta California Robertson...1866 Tuit.
to R.J.Cullen.

Census Issa.1850
				Census Issa.1860		
Joseph W.Robertson	42	bTenn.		W.D.Brown	27	bTenn.
Leanah	"	30	Ms.	A.V.	"	18f Ms.
Olive V.	"	8	"	W.	"	7/12 "
Joseph H.	"	3	"	J.H.Robertson	13m	"
Alta California	"	1	"	A.C.	"	11f "
Evan J.Harvey		23	"	E.C.	"	9f "
				L.C.	"	5f "
				N.S.Cornell	26m	N.Y.

Packet Gleanings: Issa. Co.Ms.
Probate Drw; Unnumbered S-U.

Est. of Aaron H.Sanders:decd. Oct. 1860
Will: written 13 Oct.1857 - Filed 12 Mar 1861 (not where)
Co-partnership with R.B.Cammack, details to be worked out.
Exec.:R.B.Cammack,Wm.Myers
Names: "woman Susan and her children to wit - Nancy Leaner,
Thomas,Sarah,Verlin to be free forever, unless Susan does
not conduct herself properly, in which case she must come
back to the bulk of property."
No man shall obtain any of the property by marrying any of
the ch. named above. Property must be kept together."I will
my bros. and sisters and all my relatives fifty cents apeice
and,I want my horse put in Cammack's yard."
All prop. to remain together until the ch. are 21, then
they must have equal share...A.H.(X)Sanders.
Wit:Thos.Gaddis,R.B.Cammack
Codicil: He also wanted the following 11 slaves and land
sold and the proceeds divided among the above named ch.
Proof of Will: Cit. to witnesses, reported "not found"
12 Dec.1860 Jos.L.Mayfield appointed adm.ad Col,Bd.$20,000
with Fletcher Mayfield,Alex Gwin secu. Jos.L.Mayfield
states that A.H.Sanders decd. Intestate, leaving no widow
and no children.
2 Apr. 1861 James Mayfield, Adm. sold pers. prop. at public
sale and hired out the negroes to Benj.B.Watson.
Other doc. in Pkt.:1862 list of debts owed to Est.,report
of hiring out of slaves, sale of cotton.
Case #94: Jan Term 1870: Mayfield, Adm. Pet to declare Est.
insolvent, names heirs:H.Sanders of Tippah Co.Ms;S.S.Johnson of Hinds Co.: William Graves and his wife Tabitha of
Gadsden,Ala; Stephen Sanders of Boonboro,Ark;T.B.Sanders
of Cummingsville,Tex; (Not. made public...H.Sanders not in
Tippah Co.,S.S.Johnson not in Hinds)
Nov.1871 - Est. still not settled, heirs unfound and Mayfield
avows none in this state.
In the 1866 annual a/c, Mayfield states the slaves were
carried away by U.S. troops in 1863, and the value of the
Est. reduced by $14,000.

Est. of B.M.Sellers; decd. Intestate 20 Aug.1851
Est. of Isaac Sellers; decd. Apr.1849(WBk."A"Issa.p,58)
See Est. of Thomas Sellers,decd.1843,Wash.Co.WBk.1,p.41;
Names: Sons;Silas,David,Benjamin Menus,Wrenna Breathette,
      Isaac
       Only surviving dau; Ann Hill
New Information: Ann Hill is the Adm. for the Ests. of her
brothers Issac and Benj.M.Sellers'. In Feb.1855, she states
that Silas Sellers is decd.(leaving as heirs the ch. of bro.
Wrenna's); David Sellers of La. hasn't been seen in several
years, that Isaac's children Emily C.SEllers,Thos.W.Sellers,
Edwin Ruthman Sellers under   Guard: of Isaac Hill whom
Emily has marr. Also states that the home of Isaac Sellers
was Andalusia and bro. Benj.M.Sellers lived about 3 mi.
from there. Apparently Benj.M.Sellers never marr.

PACKET GLEANINGS: Issa.Co.Ms.
Probate Drw; Unnumbered File S-U

Est. Edwin Ruthman Sellers: minor: new infor. Isaac C.
Hill Guard. has marr. E.R.Seller's sister Emily Cornelia,
and E.R. and bro. Thos.W.Sellers are still minors -Dec.1853.
when there is a sale of prop. in Holmes Co.Ms...a descript.
of the land & a/c for each minor.
Pkt. also contains a/c of other minor Seller ch...Guard. of
Henry Clinton and James F.Sellers -(sons of Isaac Sellers,
decd)10 June 1850 by Ann Hill...minors over 14.
Isaac Sellers other 5 ch.;Elbert A:Edward B:Issac F:Amelia
A;Alice G. or Susan A. are still minors under 14 - Ann
Hill is their Guard. same date as above.

Est. of Melvin H.Shellis:WBk."A",p.32 Abst. this Vol.
No new Infor.

Est. of Jacob Shoaf; WBk. "B", p.351,352,365,371.
Pet. of Henry Shoaf, resident of Davidson Co.N.C., father
of decd. states that Jacob died 23 Mar.1856 in Issa.Co.Ms.
leaving $2,200 pers. est. and asks that court appt. F.E.
Mayfield Adm. Dated 6 Apr.1857
July 1857: Pet of widow Emeline M.Smallow, late E.M.Shoaf
who has marr. Steven D.Smallow, has never recd. allowance
from Jacob's Est.
Will: written 20 Mar.1856 - Prob.Oct. Term 1856
Names: Father - Henry Shoaf)
       Mother - Elizabeth Shoaf) both of N.C.
       Friend - Burrell Bunn, Exec. with no secu.
Wit:Wm.T.Barnard, W.P.Blake
5 Jan 1857:Proof of Will by Wit. said they did not believe
Jacob was rational when he attempted to sign the will.
Other docu. in Pkt.:Apr. 1858; Inv.&Apprs., notice of sale,
vouchers,1859 - Final a/c, 1860 final a/c, 1860 James
Mayfield,Adm. allows widow $150

#43:Chanc.Dockt;Wm.T.Barnard vs E.W.Shelby,Mary B.Butts,
who was Mary B.Knox and John Butts of Wash.Co.Ms.
Nov. Term 1866: Bill of Complaint by Wm.T.Barnard,Adm.
de bonis non of R.P.Shelby with Will of attached.
Doc. states that in 1854 the Adm. of Shelby's(R.P.) Est.
was D.F.Blackburn who decd. 1861. Suit involves complaint
by Wm.T.Barnard over the selling of 1150 acrs. of land by
Blackburn. The buyers were E.W.Shelby,Mary B.Butts,who
was Mary B.Knox, now marr. to John Butts. At death of
Blackburn, Barnard took over as Adm. of R.P.Shelby's Est.
and asks for foreclosure or due payment from Shelby, and
Butts. Docu. incld.- Summons to all parties of Issa. &
Wash.Co. 1866, suit carried on into 1869.

Est. of R.P.Shelby: 2 large Pkts. Pet. by Blackburn, Adm.
for sale and division of prop. Filed Jan 1858..naming
heirs - Alberta Creath,Evan Shelby,Albert Shelby,Thos.J.
Shelby all minors..asks that W.B.Farr be appt. Guard.
1857 Guard. for Shanline, also (names sp. Shalline,Sha-
llina) 1860 - E.W.Shelby if Guard. of John Joor; W.T.
Barnard has marr. Endora Creath and is Guard. Alberta
Creath,EvanShelby,Albert Creath.

Packet Gleanings: Issa. Co.Ms.
Probate Drw; Unnumbered File S-U

R.P.Shelby, cont. Guardianship papers for John Shelby
Joor, son of George Joor, incld. here.
1866 - Evan B.Shelby is 19 yrs. ⎫
    Albert C.Shelby   17   ⎬ ch. of Thos.J.Shelby
    Thos.J.Shelby   15   ⎪
    Mollie Kate Shelby 2   ⎭
1857 - Mary B. is marr. to Geo. Waddell
Endora Creath marr.1st Thos.J.Likens, 2nd W.T.Barnard
1874: Wm.T.Barnard is Guard. of minor ch. of J.L.Barnard -
W.H. & J.L.Barnard. Mrs. J.L.Barnard,widow, is now Mrs.
Dupree.
Dec. 1888: Mollie Kate Shelby vs Wm.T.Barnard, et al:
Bill of Complaint: names: Geo.C.Waddill,Geo.Waddill,Jr.,
Nora Catchings, Ida W.Heison,Shalina C.Austin,Alberta C.
Waddell all recd. part of "Chicovea"
(In 1857, Mary B.Waddell and D.H.CReath are living Madison
Parish,La.)
All of the above are heirs of Robert Prince Shelby.

Est. of Joseph Steif: WBk."A" p.99, this Vol.
Docu. in Pkt.: Bd.of Adm.1852, Adm. notice to creditors;
Let of Adm.Nov.1850;Inv.&Apprs.;Final a/c Sept 1852.

Est. of Joseph J.Sullivan: Let. Adm. to Saml.G.Parks Filed
2 Oct.1854,Recd.WBk."B"p.68. Bd.$5,000 by Wm.Dodds,J.W.
Robertson secu.
13 Nov.1854 Warrant of Apprsl.by J.W.Robertson,James
Monroe Rushing,James B.Woolfolk.
Minor heirs: Guard. ad litem - W.B.Farr;Louisa,Ann,Martha
K. and Mary J.Sullivan.
Docu. incld. in Pkt: Annual a/c; lists of prop. sold 1855;
Pet. to court to sell 4 slaves to cover debts - 1857;
Tuition Bill for 2 ch. presented by Mrs.E.L.Williams 1854;
In report of sale of prop. buyers included H.T.Branch for
Rebecca Parks, Articles bought by C.M.Belcher for Rebecca
Parks. Final a/c 1860 by J.W.Prescott Guard. ad litem.
(Ed.note; no mention of wife Catherine who shows in 1850
Census Issa. No official Guard. appointed, just ad litem;
All the minor ch. are in Saml.and Rebecca Parks' household
in 1860 - Issa. with no vouchers showing charges against
the Est. for support for these children.
Included in this Packet: Susan Ann Sullivan, minor heir of
Saml.N.Sullivan - annual a/c by Wm.Dodds, Guard.(See WBk."A")

Est. of James Swanson: WBk."A", Abst. this Vol.
Additional infor. James Swanson decd. in Vicksburg,Ms.
28 Mar.1850. Let. of Adm.;Adm.Bd;Comm.Report on Dower;
Notice of division of slaves names the following heirs:
4 Mar.1853 - Minerva B.Smith, alias Swanson ofTenn.,
Stephen West and Mary West his wife, John P.McKay Guard.
of Monroe Swanson and Cataline Swanson, minor heirs of
James Swanson,decd. now of State of Tenn. Mary West, formerly
Mary Myrick, a dau. of James Swanson,decd.; James Swanson,Jr.

Packet Gleanings; Issa.Co.Ms.
Probate Drw.:Unnumbered File S-U

Swanson,cont. son of decd. co-Adm. of Est. stating he is
"now upward of 21".
June 1850 In pet. for Let. of Adm., James Swanson,Jr. says
Mary Myrick is his sister and the widow Minerva B.Swanson
of Williamson Co. Tenn the only heirs, but in division Pet.
dated 1854, Cataline and Monroe Swanson are named minor
heirs.
1852 - Apr.Term;Cit. to James Swanson and J.W.Miller sent
to Williamson Co.Tenn.
Writ of Dower and descript. of land - Minerva says she
marr. O.B.Smith, who is also now decd. and she can claim
her dower. Now states that Swanson left her and 4 ch.
Final a/c notice 1855 naming same heirs:
Same Pkt: Minerva B.Swanson vs James Swanson,Jr. & J.W.
Miller et al: Transcript: Filed Williamson Co.Tenn,3 Sept.
1850; James Swanson has 1200 acrs. in that county, slaves,
etc. She claims at the time of her intermarriage with Jas.
Swanson she possess. pers. prop. from Will of 1st husband
William B.Theobald (James Swanson was his Adm.) in Maury
Co.TEnn. She further claims that Swanson left no legitimite
heirs, that he had the Legislature of Tenn pass a private
act to legit. James Swanson,Jr. and Mary Myrick and that
there is a pretense set upon on behalf of Cataline Burk
and James Munroe Whitus (Wm.Johnston is Guard. of these 2)
set in motion before Swanson decd. to have courts change
their names to Swanson and legit. them and desig. them his
heirs. Minerva further states she had another inheritance
from her Mother, Mary Daniel. She filed dower in Tenn.
and asks court to have Jas.Jr. and Miller, Adm. deliver
up to her her rights and prop. in Tenn. willed to her by
her decd. husb. Wm.Theobold and her Mother, and to prove
in court the legit. heirs.
Answ. by Defendants, Swanson,Jr. and Miller: Say Minerva
and James Swanson marr. Oct. or Nov.1847 in Maury Co.Tenn.
They are co-adm. of both Tenn. and Miss. Ests. They admit
James Swanson had no ch. born in lawful wedlock, but left
surviving him ch. James Swanson,Jr. and Mary Swanson Mirick
who were made legit. by act of legis.in Will.Co.Tenn.and
they had lived with their father as family, and were recog.
as his ch. and heirs. They found the original papers in
a trunk of Decd. and a copy is filed in suit.
James Swanson,Jr. and Miller said at no time were Cataline
and Monroe made a part of the family, but a proceeding
by the Common Law and Chanc.Court of the City of Memphis
said they were his co-heirs with James and Mary.
They further claimed that Minerva's prop., willed to her
by Theobald came into Swanson's poss. by marr. and should
be considered part of the Est.
Inv.&Appr. of all Prop. and slaves,etc.
Exhibit #3: July 26 1820:Acts of Gen.Assemb.of State of
Tenn. Sec. 2 to be enacted."That the name of James Nail
and Mary Nail, the illegitimate children of James Swanson
of Williamson Co.,Tenn. be and the same are hereby changed
to that of James Swanson and Mary Swanson and they are
hereby enabled to inherit in the same manner as if they
had been born in lawful wed-lock" James Fentress,Spk. of
House of Repres.

Packet Gleanings: Issa.Co.Ms.
Probate Drw; Unnumbered File S-U.

Swanson Est.; cont. Exhibit #4: From Shelby Co.Tenn; Mar.
Term 1850 - Common-Law and Chanc.Ct. James Swanson pet.
court to change Cataline Burke of Dixon Co.Tenn. age 8,
and James Monroe Whitus - age 14 of Williamson Co.Tenn
to the name of Swanson to make them legit. and joint heirs
at law of said petitioner. (They called him Col.James
Swanson). Pet. granted.(Swanson died Mar.28,1850)
Mary Mirack (answers complaint.,Minerva). States she is
now 44 yrs. old and has lived with her father from her
earliest memories. That she never knew until the Act of
Assembly was brought to Court that she was illegit. and
had no knowledge of her father's paternity to Cataline or
Monroe. She further states that since they are legally
heirs, she"cheerfully" submits to wishes of her father for
them to inherit their share.
Monroe and Cataline answ. by Guard.Johnston.
Minerva obtained a writ to prevent sale of "her" prop.
Final paper filed Issa. June Term 1855.
(Ed.Note: We have included this Estate settlement in full
because of the many interesting aspects concerning the
heirs, unusual legalities, and the intervention of the
State Legislature.)

Probate Drw: Unnumbered File W-Z

Est. of Samuel W.Wells: (See Est. Pkt. containing McQuillan,
Wells, Foster,etc. abst. this Vol.)
Additional information:12 Dec. 1853 - Pet for sale of land
to cover $18,000 debt.of Est., signed by and for the widow
Martha A.Wells, widow; Robert R.Richardson and Mary E. his
wife of Wilkinson Co.Ms;Albert G.Newport and Sarah C. his
wife of La; John M.Gray and Nancy Viola his wife; E.Jones
Harvey and Martha J. his wife; heirs-at-law of full age,
of Saml.W.Wells. Catherine A.Chaney and her husband Bailey
Chaney also of full age. James J.Wells, a minor(Guard.
and mother - Martha A.Wells);Francis C.Myers, minor heir
of Wm.Myers, his Guard. who was the husband of Henrietta
F.Myers - a child of said S.W.Wells.
Pkt. contains: Doc.marked "non approved" Dec.Term 1853;
Cit. to all heirs 6 Jan.1855 to close out Est.;Writ of
dower to widow Martha J.Wells McQuillan Filed Jan 1855;
A map and full description of lands - 152.52 acrs. on
Deer Creek, includ. dwelling house,etc.;sale of perish.
goods - Apr.1855; Pet of widow for allowance 1857 for
herself and son J.J.Wells, stating the other heirs who
are of age are of another marriage, and the minor heir
James J. is her son by Saml.W.Wells; vouchers made out
to Col.Saml.Wells;
2nd Pkt.of Saml.Wells: Wm.T.Barnard, Adm.de bonis Non, pet.
for sale of lands to pay est. debts 2 July 1855, names
some heirs to appear in court; Another document: S.W.Wells
vs Mrs. M.A.McQuillan dated 3 May 1855 - suit for settlement
of payment of $179 recd. by Saml. 1842, due Martha A.from
Adm. of Michael Jones Est., she being an heir. Also $200
for sale of a carriage in 1844 - allowed and pd. for by
Adm.Wm.T.Barnard in 1859

Packet Gleanings: Issa.Co.Ms.
Probate Drw: Unnumbered File W-Z

Wells Est. cont: Oct. Term 1859: Final settlement by a/c of Adm.Wm.T.Barnard, cites all heirs. Nancy V.Gray is now Nancy V.Chisholm, wife of John Chisholm. All other heirs remain the same. Wm.Myers is still Guar. of Frank Myers, minor. $10,529.32 split among heirs.

Est. of Wm.E.White: decd. 1846, Mrs. Henrietta E.White Adm. Rec. in WBk."A" P.1,40,41,240,242. Abst. in this Vol. New infor; Heirs of Wm.E.White - minor ch. William,Ellen, Mary, Octavia. Court appts. W.B.Farr Guard. ad litem.

Est. of Stephen Y.Whitehead: decd. 16 Aug.1857, Rec. WBk. "B",p.354-356,380-383; No Will, Widow,or ch. or relatives known. Elisha North , a creditor, Pet.for Let.Adm. $1300 Bd. by F.E.Mayfield,James Mayfield.Oct. 1857

Supplementary material:

Marriages from Early Tenn. Newspapers - 1794-1851; by Lucas p.223: Hill, Mr. Henry R.W., married in Franklin to Miss Margaretta E. M'Alister. Nashville Banner & Nashville Whig (Sat. Aug.8.1827)

Index to Nashville Cem. :
H.R.W.Hill (white) 20 Mar.1855
Marg.Hill (age 42) 1853 (buried)

Cemetary Rec. of Williamson Co.,Tenn.: by Lynch and Hays P.12: Armstrong Cem; on Robert Adair Farm, Coleman Rd.,5th D. 5 Armstrongs and 2 "Big concrete boxes...a tree has fallen across one of them...the other one";
    James Swanson
    Born 9-28-1782
    Davidson Co.Tenn.
    Died 4-28-1850
    Vicksburg, Miss.

Mortality Schedule,1850, Miss.
James Swanson of Issa.Co.Ms, died in Vicksburg of paralysis. 28 Apr.1850.

Jefferson Co.Ms. Will Bk."A",p.26
Will of Robert Prince; dated 19 July,1817
Names: Wife - Jane
  Sons - Alexander G.
    Robert (decd.Sept.1827, Adams Co.Ms.)
    Wm.Berry (decd. Mar.1830 - married Sallie S.
      Jefferies)
    John G.T. (decd. Mar 1823 - Ouachita Parish,La.)
  Daus - Elizabeth (Married Wm.Penrice)
    Cynthia (marr. Jos.McQuillan - see Est.Issa.
      Co.Ms.WBk."A",p.2,3; decd. 1846)
    Myra Jane (Marr. Andrew Knox by 1831, lived
      Wash.Co.Ms.)
    Sally (marr. Edward Pennington of Jeff. Co.)
    Polly Berry (marr.Thomas Shelby, Wash.Co.Ms.
      Deed Bk.B,p.217)

Packet Gleanings: Issa. Co.Ms.
Drw. labeled Chancery: 1 - 32

#13:(County seat of Issa. Co. is at Tallula in 1858)
W.I.(Y?) CHANEY vs Wm.J.BRITTON & wife, Fanny I.Britton, & Helen S.Johnson, a minor under 20. Docu. dated 30 Oct. 1858.
Summons to Madison Co.Ms to Lewis W.Thompson, Guardian to Helen Johnson.
Depositions taken from Wm.Myers,B.F.Bookout, Wm.B.McQuillan, J.P.Woolfolk - Issa. Co.Ms.
Land dispute over "Old Point Comfort" Tract, south side of Rolling Fork - East of Deer Creek, sold in 1850 to S.G. Johnstone, payments made by Lewis W.Thompson, Adm. of Johnston's Est.
W.I.Chaney's brother is Thomas Y.Chaney, and his sister is Sarah E.Chaney. Thomas Y.Chaney decd. 1835 (Sr.) leaving 3 children. (His widow marr. next - Mordecai Powell).

#18: LEWIS JONES vs A.M.MULHOLLEN, et al
Suit filed Apr.27,1859 - Bk.R.,p.333-341.
Lewis Jones with wife and children, of Hinds Co.Ms. states he "bought land, 1855, from Nathaniel Mulhollen, and a series of disasters made him leave the county. In 1859 Mulhollen sells same land to John Chisholm of Issa. Co."
P.O.A., dated 27 Apr. 1854, giving Nathaniel Mulhollen power to settle matters of the Est. of Thos.J.Mulhollen, late of Union Co.Ark., and who decd. leaving the following heirs: Nathaniel Mulhollen of Ark;John M.Mulhollen - Henry C.Cage - and wife Martha W.Cage - of Lauderdale Co.Tenn. Further states that Thos.J.Mulhollen left lands in Wash., Issa.,and Sunflower Counties in Miss.
Case closed 1869.

#20: Wm.J.Chaney, Thos.Y.Chaney vs W.T.Barnard & wife,et al: Original Bill Filed 13 Dec. 1859: Wm.T.Barnard and wife Endora J., citizens of Issa.Co.; D.H.Creath, George Waddell and Mary B.Waddell his wife; Alberta Creath - minor under 21; Shalline Y.Creath - minor under 21; D.F. Blackburn, exec. of Est. of R.P.Shelby, decd. all of La.; John Joor, minor under 21; Evan Shelby, Creath Shelby, & Thos. Shelby all minors under 21 and ch. of T.J.Shelby are the defendants in a land dispute. The land is on Deer Creek with the Creek "running through the center of it."

#21: Thomas H.Christmas, et al vs Richard Christmas:
Filed Mar.1860. Family squabble over division of property. Statement of Richard Christmas says: "On 11 Feb.1840, T.H. Christmas, along with Henry Christmas and Ann D. his wife in Madison Co.Ms., gave deed to Rich.Christmas and W.B. Norfleet (Bk.G. p. 429 - 430) all rights to land in question. Richd. moved the slaves to his Pltn. in Bolivar Co.Ms. known as "Choctaw Bend". W.B.Norfleet decd. soon after this contract. T.H.Christmas acted as Richard Christmas's agent in Madison Co. 1840 - Nov.1858. Henry Christmas moved to Hinds Co.Ms 1843, and a few years later moved to Richard's in Issa. Richard Christmas had a

Packet Gleanings; Issa.Co.

wife Mary E. and a son Henry Hill Christmas. Later ,
Richard sold some of the slaves to H.B.Tibbetts and wife
Louisiana. When Thos. H.Christmas decd. he was working
for his bro. Richard and overseeing the property in
Bolivar Co.Ms.
Order, filed Mar 1860: Injunction agst. Richd.Christmas
to turn over possession of 55 slaves to Thos.H.Christmas,
minors (not named) and Wm.H.Hinton and Susan his wife.
Suit filed by James Y.Christmas, adm. of Est of Thos.H.
Christmas, decd. (Henry Christmas is also decd. by 1860)

#4: Wm.C.FORD vs ROBERT B. CAMMACK, et al
Filed 6 May 1857: Tax Assessors dispute with the Board
of Police (Supervisors). Members of the Board - Cammack,
E.J.Harvey, J.W.Robinson, E.Moore, T.B.Green.

#22: M.A.MONTGOMERY vs BURNLEY HEIRS:
Filed 29 May 1866. Mary Ann Montgomery and Hallam
Eldridge, living Issa. Co. 1859, received Mortage of
Albert T.Burnley, at that time in Ky. Recorded, Issa.
Deed Bk.C,p641,642, Feb. 16, 1859. Albert T.Burnley
decd. 1860 ,leaving the following heirs; Francis A.
Burnley, Martha A.Burnley, Lucy Victor Burnley, Robert
H.Crittenden and Harriet B. his wife.
8 Feb. 1864: POA; Mary Ann Montgomery and Hallam Eldridge
(his wife is Ann E.Eldridge) all of Binghampton, Broome
Co.N.Y. appoint Armistead Burwell, an Attorney residing
in Vicksburg to collect from Est. of Burnley, late of
Ky., decd. leaving a widow the said Frances and the
other heirs named above. Francis Burnley, widow and
Robt.H.Crittenden of Ky. are exec. of Albert Burnley's
Est....1870 - Court ordered sale of land.."foot of
Island 95, called"Burnlea", 1100 ac.

#23: T.J.Shelby, Jr. et al vs DAVID F. BLACKBURN: no
add. information.

#26: JOHN STEWART SKINNER, et al vs EASELY, et al :
Filed 1 Oct. 1860: John Stewart and Louisa Skinner by
next friend C.B.Skinner vs L.I.Easley and Edward T.
Easley, minor, et al ; John S. & Louisa are children of
Catherine B.Skinner, their Guardian. Document traces the
sale of several tracts of land from the original patent
issued to Wm.R.Norcorn, Frederick Norcorn and Robt.M.
Spicer in 1836. Robt.M.Spicer sold to Theodorick R.
Skinner ½ of these 28 Oct. 1847 Bk.C p 454-455. Complainants are heirs of Theodorich R.Skinner. Wm.R.Norcorn
sold the land to Tandy W.Easley in 1857. Tandy Easley
decd. leaving L.J.Easley, widow and exec. and a son
Edward T.Easley, minor, his mother is G.

#28: MARY I.PARKER vs GEO. HARDING, et al: Filed 14 Feb.
1861; Mrs. Mary J.Parker, widow of James P.Parker, who dec.
on 14 June, 1860 of Claiborne Co.Ms , owning land in Issa.
Co. he bought from Ben Porter,Thos.L.Lambeth,Herdaman

PACKET GLEANINGS: Issa.Co.Ms.

& Dart,W.A.Stone,T.L.Limmell. James B.Parker died leaving his widow, Mary J. and 4 children - Wm.,John M., James P., and Mary D.Parker, all over 21. The defendants George Harding, Ira Harding, ---- Whitehead, ---- Morton, and Mrs. Washington Morton have been cutting timber from her land.

#29: RICHARD CHRISTMAS VS D.W.C. BONHAM: Filed May Term 1861. Mortgage.

#34: RICHARD CHRISTMAS vs UNKNOWN OWNERS: Filed 22 Apr. 1861: tax lands.

#30: JOHN D. BEIN vs E.B.WALKER,JR.: Trans.of Bankruptcy. 1861 May Term,Original Bill; John D.Bein of New Orleans states that Edward Boylston Walker filed for bankruptcy 14 July 1842 and filed an Inventory of all holdings. He owned land on Sunflower River, 2 tracts bought at Mt.Salus - 1835. Walker was declared bankrt. Sept.1842. Lucein Herman was the assignee of Est. of E.B. Walker, and sold the land. Francis M.Fisk bought the land in Jan.1843 for $95 cash.
21 Dec.1860, John D.Bein bought the land from Fisk, and the heirs of Bein are trying to clear the title. E.B. Walker is now (1861) in Atlanta;Lucein Herman is in San Francisco; and Fisk is in New Orleans.
Nov.1866: The children of John D.Bein,decd. are: Rosina C.Bein, Lawrence G.Bein, John S.Bein,Mary S.Bein, Hugh H. Bein,Fannie M.Bein... all of New Orleans. Last document in Packet dated 1869, title still not straight.

#32: JOHN C. MAYNARD vs ALEXANDER M.GWIN:Filed 8 Apr. 1861: Document states; John C.Maynard's wife is Elizabeth S.(both of Va.) Around 1843, James Gwin, grandfather of Elizabeth Maynard, died owning 1300 ac.+slaves, and at that time Elizabeth was an infant, and now only a little over 21, and she has a sister Mary T.Bonham - wife of Dewitt W.C.Bonham, daus. of Samuel Gwinn,decd. a son of James Gwinn.
The children of James Gwinn are Alexander M.Gwin; Samuel Gwinn,decd; Wm.M.Gwinn; Catherine Danks; Margaret Duvall; Thos.Gwinn,decd - the father of Caroline E.Kiger who is the wife of G.Kiger, and Bettie Martin who is the wife of D.D.Martin. Further down in the document it states that A.J.Gwinn is the son of Thos.Gwinn, and this is struck out and"Samuel" written in above it. "Willow Grove Plantation" was the home of the Bonhams and the Gwinns until they sold it to Charles E.Balfour. At the time of the sale, Bettie Martin was Bettie Taylor.
Summons - Apr.1861:Charles C.Balfour and wife Rosa, Wm. M. Gwinn and wife Mary E.H.Gwinn, not found in Issa.Co.; the Kigers are in Warren Co.Ms. as are D.D.Martin and wife Bettie Martin.

Packet Gleanings:
Issa. Co. Probate Dr. 1 - 16

Filed in numerical sequence, many missing.
#2: John Lallien, Decd., Est. of; Pet. of Adm.Bd. of Edward D.Clark of Warren Co.,Ms. 3 Jan 1870. No relatives in State.

#3: Est. of William Chew Smith, M.D.; decd. 24 June 1870; Adm. is Addie Coffee who also is only heir "because she was faithful to my Mother and took care of me in my sickness". No will presented, owned ¼ int. in drugstore on "Esperanza Plt." called Turnbull & Smith. Will claimed and attested to by Alfred Smiley, Daniel Bruin, and J.L. Chapman, none recorded.

#6: Est. of Henry C.Barnard, decd. 26 Mar 1871, Intestate; Adm. of Est. is his bro. Wm.T.Barnard. He left Eliza Barnard, widow, and 6 ch., all minors, eldest 12 or 13 yrs.: unnamed.
Pkt. also contains documents on Est. of Joseph L. Barnard, of Adams Co.Ms., decd. father of Henry C. and Wm.T. "
Guardianship papers filed by Wm.T.Barnard, bro. of minor Henry C.Barnard 11 Dec. 1848, Adams Co.Ms., recorded 10 July 1849, Bk.A of Bonds, pgs. 66 & 67. Wm.T.Barnard moves to Issa.Co. and petitions court to move Henry C.'s slaves - 12 Dec. 1848.
2 July, 1860 - Citation to W.W.Brown and wife Rebecca F. Barnard Brown for division of Est. of Rebecca's late husband, Joseph L.Barnard, in interest of minor heirs. Wm.T.Barnard also Guardian to William H.Barnard, Joseph L. Barnard, and Mary E.Barnard, minor heirs of Joseph L. Barnard.
Will Bk.C (Issa. Co.), p. 26,27,28,;filed Dec.12, 1859, for Wm.T.Barnard, Guard. vs Brown & wife.

#9: Indexed under the name of Samuel Leatherman, but contains, also, the Est. of Saml.B.Leatherman.
Est. of Samuel Leatherman, decd. c 1865/5: Adm. of his Est. is Samuel B.Leatherman, his son. Samuel B.Leatherman died, Intestate, 20 May, 1871, and his eldest bro. Zack Leatherman takes over as the Adm. of both ests., stating that Samuel B.Leatherman died without issue, and unmarr. Final a/c of Est. of Samuel Leatherman - 12 May 1879 - names Peter R.; Robt.;(sons of Saml.) Frank and John Leatherman - sons of John Leatherman (son of Saml.); Frances Keigler, and Richard Leatherman and other heirs of Dr.G.W.Leatherman (son of Saml.) and heirs unknown, and Mary S.Leatherman - mother and G. of Richard and other unknown heirs of Dr.G.W.Leatherman, decd.; Samuel Glass and other heirs of Cornelia Glass (dau. of Saml.) and their father and G. Joshua Glass - all the heirs and divisees of said est. of Saml. Leatherman, decd.
When Zack Leatherman takes over, he states in 1877 that

Packet Gleanings: Issa. Co.

Leatherman, cont: that his bros. are Peter R.Leatherman, R.H.Leatherman. And then names all heirs and their addresses as follows; Peter R.Leatherman - Ashwood, Tensas Parish, La.; Robt.Leatherman - Frank Leatherman - Frances and Isaac Keigler - Woodville, Miss; Mary S. Leatherman, widow of G.W.Leatherman - Commerce Landing, Tunica, Co.Ms.; Glass Family - Red River Landing, La.; Court accepts final a/c 4 Oct. 1880.

#9: Also contained Petition for Dower of Sarah Neibert: Adams Co.Ms, widow of Joseph Neibert, who decd. Sept. 1837. Pet. goes to Chas.G.Dalgreen, Adm. of the est. of Joseph Neibert, dated Oct. Term 1846 - concerning 2986 acres land Issa. Co. acquired by deed from Joseph Dunbar, exec. of est. of John Foster.

#10:(cont. in File #41) Est. of James L.Boyd, decd. 7 July 1871. Adm.Bd.,Oath & Will filed 10 July 1871 by H.M.Barnes, Security - Henry Feltenberg,G.Witkowski.
Will dated 3 July,1871:(leaves no widow or issue) Charges Harry M.Barnes as Adm. until his bro. WM.B.Boyd can arrive. Will names - partner in J.L.Boyd & Co. is John L. Root; to Henrietta Rogers - house & lot in Skipwith,Ms; to Belle Millens - eldest neice - dau. of Wm. & Ann Jane Millens, gold watch and chain; to oldest son (unnamed) of Wm.B.Boyd, my sorrel mare "Queen"; to "my" bros. & sis. (unnamed) rest of property. Wit: Jas.P.McKinney, W.E.Jelley.
(Names above are spelled Miller(Millen), Baird (Beard), Braddy, (Boddy). Believe Millen, Baird, Braddy are correct.)
July 24, 1871 - W.B.Boyd arrives and pet. of Adm. Dr. Robinson submits bill of $45 for July 3,4,5, 1871. 18 Aug. 1871, WM.B.Boyd decides not to act as adm. (Interesting bill presented by Dr.R.D.Farish for $500 for prof. services rendered for injuries to the spine and ankle...and"amputation of the left thigh"..Sept.1871) 25 May 1875 Adm. is Dr.R.D.Farish.

#11: Est. of Alexander P.Boyd: decd. 14 Oct. 1867: Resid. Woodland Plt., Issa.Co. Adm.Bd. Jas.L.Boyd, brother, Sec. Edward C.Blake,D.N.Anderson...7 Jan 1868.
Appraisal of Est. by Lawrence T.Wade,W.L.Sibley,Thos. W.Sellers..14 Jan 1868.
Heirs of: Cornelius & Eliza M.Baird (Beard); Ann J. Millen (Miller); Marmaduke & Martha Boddy (Braddy); Wm.Boyd & Mary A.Boyd; Jas.L.Boyd; all residents of Marshall Co.Ms except Cornelius & Eliza Baird who reside in the State of Tenn., Tifton Co. Pet. requests that the body be sent to Collierville, Tenn. for burial(via Memphis). Ja.L.Boyd died 1871, and Wm.B.Boyd takes over Adm. Bill in pkt. shows that C.F.Hampton & dau. Miss A.F.Hampton are debtors to Est. and have not paid in 1881. R.T.& Mary A.Payne are mentioned, no relat. stated.

Packet Gleanings: Issa. Co.

#12: Est. of Benjamin B.Fore, decd. 18 July 1871, Intest.
Widow Mary Pet. for Adm. States he died in Vicksburg,
but a resident of Issa.Co... Sec. Charley Peine, Horace
Miller. Issue - 3 - William S.Fore, John T.Fore, Caroline
O.King all over 21.

#12: also in same Pkt. as above, tho' numbered #13.
Est. of John McDonald, decd. Dec. 1870; Father-in-law
of Joseph G.Davis, Adm. whose wife is sole heir (unnamed),
filed 31 July 1871.

#14: Est. of George B.Sink: Adm.W.E.Jelly (Jolly ?),Sec.
S.C.Elliott,Jas.P.McKinney - 25 Aug.1871. Bill in Pkt.
to Geo.Sink for services by Dr.D.M.Robinson dated June
1,6, 1871. Doc. 21 Aug.1871 states wife not in State at
time of death and no ch. Geo.B.Sink was maternal uncle
of W.E.Jelly(Jolly).

#15: SAMUEL Murrell, Est. of: (Index and Pkt. cover sp.
Merrill) but inside definitely Murrell) decd. 3 Sept.1871
at Homochitto Landing. Adm. Wm.Wallace, who stated the
decd. was a young man formerly residing Cave City, Ky.
unmarr. and has a sister who resides there now - Susannah
Preston. Adm.Bd. 24 Nov.1871, Sec. A.D.GRambling,John
Irwin

#16: Est. of Charles J.Fore, decd. New Orleans Jan.1866
Will recorded WBk.C, p.66,80,81. Adm. B.B.Fore, neph.
of Copiah Co.Ms. C.J.Fore decd. unmarr.
Chas.J.Fore owned ½ int. in "Onward Plt" (other ½ by
James Dick Hill). B.B.Fore decd. 1871, and G.M.Bankston
and John B.Allen pet for Adm de Bonis Non, 18 Dec.1871 -
granted 23 Jan 1872. G.M.Bankston, husband to M.J. -
neice of C.J.Fore; John B.Allen son of Sarah A.Allen,
neice of C.J.Fore.Fore owned 2144 + acr. on Porter'S
Bayou, Bolivar Co.Ms.
Apr. 1868 - Doc. #30,31 in Pkt... M.J.Roach et al vs B.B
Fore, Adm: states Peter Fore, bro. of Chas.J.Fore (both
decd) and father of B.B.Fore, Chas.J.Fore of Issa.,Sarah
Allen, Mary Bankston of Copiah Co.Ms; John Fore of Camp-
bell Co. Va; heirs-at-law of Elizabeth Harvey, address
unknown (Tenn.); and heirs of Simen Fore,decd.of Copiah
Co. leaving minors Martha, John, Wiley; Jesse Fore and
Martha Young of Mo.; Martha Roach of Ky.; Lucy Starns of
Ill. (Ind.?). Pet. for solvency Jan.1868 & sale: names
Rebecca Fore, Wm.Fore,Sarah Perkins..Tex. Martha Roach
and Lucy Starns are sisters to Chas.J.Fore. Elizabeth
Harvey is another sister, decd. Peter Fore, decd. is
bro. of C.J.Fore. John W.Fore is bro. with heirs Milton,
America, John & others unknown.
Heirs sue Adm. B.B.Fore for a/c of crops 1866/67. Inv.
& Appr. filed Bk.Of Inv. & Appr. p.556 Mar.9,1871;
Adm.Bds. rec.Bk.B. of Bds. 82,83. Apr.12,1866

Packet Gleanings: Issa. Co.Ms.
Probate Drw. #2; 17 - 37

#17: Est. of J.S.Elliott, decd. 21 Aug,1871, Intestate;
Adm.Bd. J.C.Halladen, W.H.Barnard, David Hunt, sec.$400
Feb.6,1872. Widow - Elizabeth, 3 minor ch., unnamed,...
She files exception to $100 allowance for herself and 3
ch. and asks for $300 more, May 1872. Last doc. in Pkt.

#18: Est. of Harmon Henderson, decd. 6 Apr. 1872. Pet. for
Adm. Bd. filed May 20, 1872 by father-in-law Bryant Johnson, Bd.$200 N.R.Anderson, Benj.Johnson, sec. He left
a widow - Hester, 4 minor ch., unnamed.
Apr.21,1873 suit brought by Geo.C.Harris vs Hester Britton
& Henderson over poss. of 1 horse & colt.

#19: Est. of Henry T.Branch, decd.27 Oct 1870:Widow - Martha
Pet. for Adm. 11 June 1871; states she has 2 ch. Wm.Henry
Branch - 8 yrs., Thomas Anne Branch (female) 4 yrs. Gard.
Bd. $1500 signed by Hester J.Branch, Thos. G.Parks - 11
June 1872. (Clerical error on no. of ch. & sex. in a/c
treating Thomas as 1 ch. & Anne as another.)

#20: Est. of Henry (Harry ?)Christmas: d Nov.1870, stating he was over 21. (Rec.WEk.C,p.128, Issa.) Will: dated
21 Feb.1868; "I Harry Christmas of Co.Of Jefferson, State
of Ky...property goes to step-mother Mary E.Christmas,
wife of my father Richard Christmas." Adm. father, Rich.
Christmas 17 June 1872, to adm. without bond. Wit: H.
Smith,Thos.Hays,J.J.Watson.
Harry H.Christmas, late of Issa.Co.Ms, died poss. of a
lg. Plt. on Miss. River in Issa.

#22: Guard. of Thos.A.Heath, age 13 & James A.Heath, age
11; 24 Dec. 1872. John Heath is father (inheiritance of
of Real Prop. $2000) David Mayer, sec.

#23: Guard. of John W.Heath, who is over 14 (19 yrs.) Pet.
Court to appoint father John Heath Guard. 24 Dec.1872.
$1000 sec. by David Mayer.

#24: Guard. of Parks minors: King.P.Parks, 13 Yrs.; Geo.
C. Parks, 11 yrs.; James M.Parks, 18 yrs; George N.Parks
Guard. and Albert G.Warde sec. $3,000...21 Jan.1873.

#25: Est. of Georgie P.Parks: decd. Jan. 1873 at Ben Lomand Pltn. Husband - George N.Parks Pet for Let. Of Adm.
21 Jan.1873. Ch. King P.(R?), Geo.C.,James M.Parks Pet.
granted same day.

#26: Est. of Jesse Moore: decd. 4 Mar 1873 at Rolling
Fork Landing. Adm.Bd. to Saml.Fischel of Warren Co.Ms.
with David Mayer sec. 24 Mar. 1873. No widow,no ch.,
relatives unknown. Jesse Moore partner in firm of Jeans
& Moore. Appr. 24 Sept. 1873 by Wm.Chaney, E.C.Clements,
D.Clark, W.D.Brown, agent. Inv. mentions C.F.Ring,J.
Coker, J.O.Stevens,N.B.Parker.

Packet Gleanings: Issa. Co.Ms.
Probate Drw. #2 17 - 37

#27: Guard. of Robert Lee Hallberg & Ida Hallberg: 14 Apr. 1873, minor ch. of Charles J.Hallberg, late of Issa. Co. Guard.Bd. to John B.Dirker, Secu. Thos.W.Hays,A.D.Sloan. No est. real or personal; Nearest of kin - John B.Dirker, cousin. No natural guardian.

#28: Est. of Martha Binney: Inside cover - Est. of Matthew Birney; decd. Feb. 1873 Issa. Co.Jams.L.Mayfield (large creditor) pet. for let. of adm. 13 May 1873. Bd. $750 L.C.Watson, D.H.Alexander, secu. No heirs. No per. prop.

#30: Est. of Smith Williams: decd. Sept 1868 at "Danover" Issa.Co..Pet. of Noah B.Parker 16 Sept.1873 states "Bounty claim agst. the U.S." $195. Widow - Sylvia Williams, dau. Melissa Williams about 18, Noah B.Parker - distant rela. of decd. Adm.Bd. $400, secu. A.W.Brooks, Nash Hamilton, Henry Turner, 16 Sept. 1873.

#31: Est. of Wm.B.Paddleford: decd. 26 July 1873, surv. partner of firm Davis & Paddleford, Lewis R.Davis already decd. 2 mo. previous. Pet. of Adm. C.Edward Paddleford of Edwards, Hinds Co.Ms.,30 Sept. 1873 States Wm.B.Paddleford in partnership with Davis farmed on Deer Creek a plt. "Council Bend" Widow - Louella, no ch. In answer to citation for a/c/ 1882, C.E.Paddleford states "his home burned & all records are gone...but all debts are pd.

#32: Est. of John Wheeler: decd. 9 Oct. 1873 at"Burnlea Plt. Intestate. Julia Wheeler, widow of John, pet. for Let. of Adm. 22 Oct. 1873. No ch.

#33: Est. of George B.Wedley, M.D.: (could be Nedley) decd. 13 Sept. 1873; Widow - Mary Wedley, 4 ch. unnamed. Est. consisted of medical bills, uncollectable.

#34: Guard. of Aurora and Winfield Lax (Lacks): Pet. for Guard. by Soloman Blackwell, who states Annie Blackwell of Issa.Co. decd. and left 2 ch. - Aurora Lax - 10 yrs.; Winfield Lacks - 15 yrs. Solomon Blackwell is their stepfather. Secu. Harrison Bradshaw, Anthony Croxton, Wm. Bradshaw, Isaac Brooks. 27 Sept 1873. Owned a lot on Locust St., Greenville (in the river, now) and a lot on Bachelor's Bend addition. Final a/c - dated 30 May 1882 by Guard. states Winfield now over 21 and Aurora (Rosa) married.

#35: Guard. of Paul and Viney Grooms: Pet. of Millie Walls, sister of Louisa Grooms - decd. Nov. 1872, for Guard. of Paul - 13 yrs., and Viney - 11 yrs, minor ch. of Louisa Grooms and Jake Grooms, decd. The ch. have lived with Millie Walls since death of her sister ; Millie Walls husband is Jacob Walls; Jake Grooms decd. in service of U.S.Gov. Adm. and secu.iss. Nov 5, 1873, $500, to Millie Walls, Jacob Walls, John French, Peter Holmes.

Packet Gleanings: Issa.Co.
Probate Drw. 2; 17 - 37

#36: Est. of D.H.Alexander: decd. 4 Nov. 1873; Will filed 13 Nov. 1873 (not where). Will dated 1 Feb. 1873: "All my Est. to be divided between my 3 beloved ch. (unnamed) and exec. to see that they are educated, especially my dau." Exec. is A.G.Ward who lived on Ben Lomand Plt., witnessed by D.H.McCue. Exec.Bd. $2500, A.G.Ward, Leon Fischel, Wm.J.Toy, sec. 13 Nov.1873.Home of Daniel H. Alexander was "Bavarian Plt." The following vouchers were included in Pkt. gives clues to idenity of 3 ch.: voucher #43, dated Feb.1876 - for clothing for James W.Alexander; Voucher #4 dated 13 Jan 1874 - $15 to J.W.Alexander travel exp. to Fort Adams, Ms. Voucher unnumb. - 13 Nov 1873 to 13 Nov.1874 from Mrs. E.A.Bell of Fort Adams, Ms. received $300 for board of Mollie and Daniel Alexander. V #34, June 1876 - letter from Fort Adams, Ms from Mrs. E.T.Bell, about Mollie and Daniel.

#37: Est. & Guard. of James W., Daniel, and Mary Alexander: ch. of D.W.Alexander, decd. Guard.Bd. filed 13 Nov.1873 to A.G.Ward, Leon Fischel,WM.J.Toy sec. $1000. A/c - filed 16 Apr. 1877 said Est. consisted of "Bavarian Plt.", 140 acr. of cleared land, 20 acr. of woods, all formerly of "Ben Lomand Plt." By 1877 all but 80 acr. had caved in the River, being outside new levee.

Probate Drw. #3: 38 - 55

#38: Est. of M.S. Wakefield; decd. 1 Nov..1873; near Skipwith; Adm. wife Melissa, filed 13 Nov. 1873. No ch. J.C.Grace, S.M.Spencer sec. of Adm.Bd.

#39: (In pkg. #40) Est. of Mrs. Elizabeth Green:decd. July 1871. Adm.Bd. filed 18 Nov. 1873 by Walter V.Crouch, stating that Mrs. Green's husband, T.B.Green has decd. since the death of his wife. Names the following heirs: Daus. Mary Case, wife of James Case of New Orleans, La.;
" Melissa Jones, wife of James Jones of N.O., La.
" Annie E.Crouch, wife of Walter V.Crouch " " "
Sons - Oscar P.Green, decd. of Issa. Co., Ely Green, Issa. Co., Thomas Green, Jr., _____ W.Green, since decd. all over 21.
Dr. H.D.Coffield presented a bill to "ElDorada Plt." 1869 Zach Leatherman, John C.Calhoun sec. Atty. T.Marshall Miller.Last docu. dated 11 May 1905, a citation to Crouch for a/c - W.W.Catchings, Sher. says "not in my county".

#40: Guard. Bd. for Lelia A.Foster & Earnest Foster : minor ch. of Annie M.Ferriss. filed 19 Jan. 1874 by Annie B.Ferriss, stating these are the ch. of John L. Foster, decd. with $12,000 Est in Botetourt Co.Va. The widow is now married to T.ST.Clair Ferriss. Last cit. is to Adams Co.Ms 11 May 1905

Packet Gleanings: Issa.Co.
Probate Drw. #3, 38 - 55

#41: Est. of James L.Boyd: continuation of #10. Pet. of R.D.Farrish to replace H.M.Barnes as Adm. Filed 23 Nov 1873. May 29, 1873 court appt. Farrish Adm. Final A/c 25 Apr. 1879.

#42: Andrew Jackson, Est.: decd. 4 Mar 1873 at home of his mother, Rachel Johnson on part of "Muscadine Plt.", having been there 10 days before death. Will - verbal - wit. by Ned Spurlock, Ann Spurlock, Rose Gary,Rachel Johnson, and others. Named - widow, Sally Jackson; bros. Daniel and Henry Johnson; sis. Mary Ann Gary wife of Adolphus Gary; sis. Nancy Thompson wife of Peter Thompson; Attested will filed 5 Mar 1873, wit. by W.L.Sibley, R.W.Smith, Jr. Pet. for proof of will & Let. of Testa. filed 19 May 1874. He left "Muscadine" to his mother, bros. & sisters; Wife Sally got stock and personal prop. May 25,1874 - Sallie filed suit challenging validity of Will. On 26 Nov.1875, court took the matter under advisement until next term of court. Case now called Jackson vs Sallie Ann Ingram. Disposition of case missing.

#43: Guard. Bd. for Jimmie Simmons, minor son of Phillip Simmons, decd. Bd. by David Early, nearest kin.Filed 9 July 1874. Sec. Anderson Hardy, James White,

#44: Est. of LouisCWatson; decd. 11 Sept. 1874. Adm. Let. filed & granted 30 Oct. 1874 - L.W.Watson,Capt. Wm.W. Moore. Est. in Issa. Co. and Jefferson Co. (Ms.)worth $6000.Wife of Louis C.Watson has decd. Louis W.Watson is his son; Ernestine Moore - wife of Wm.W.Moore his dau.; L.C.Watson,Jr. and B.E.Watson are minor sons of L.W.Watson and his wife Olivia Watson. (Olivia decd. by 1880)Most of the papers issued by Wm.W.Moore are from Port Gibson, Ms. Louis W.Watson is in Issa.Co. and then Sharkey (county split) Final a/c 3 Apr.1880. L.W.Watson states he managed the "Mills and Cammack Plts." on Deer Creek for 8 yrs. 67-1874, claims back salary of $12,000. Included in Pkt. is a personal letter from Wm.Moore to Judge Jeffords, 9 Sept.1876, Mayersville, Ms. complaining about the mess his taxes were in because of the split in the counties.By 1905 Capt. Moore lives in Sharkey Co.

#45: Est. of Leon Fischel: of Ben Lomand Plt., decd. 17 Nov. 1874. Adm.Bd. filed 24 Nov.1874 by wife Babette Fische sec. by David Mayer, Maurice Van Os $15,000. Owned storehouse and stock at Ben Lomand Landing, Issa. Co. Had 3 ch.- Albert Fischel, age 4; Leopold age 2½; Maurice 1yr. Named Saml.Fischel (no relationsip given). Citation to Mrs. Babette Sartuius (sp.Sartimus,Sartirnus) Mar. 14, 1881 for a/c. Apr. 1879 Babette is in Warren Co.

#46: Guard. Bd. for Albert,Leopold,Maurice Fischel: filed 24 Nov 1874 by Babette Fischel, widow of Leon Fischel, for their 3 minor sons.

Packet Gleanings: Issa. Co.
Probate Drw. #3, 38-55

#47: Est. of J.E.Barrett, decd. 24 Sept 1874. Intestate, owning ½ int. in Plt. called"Burnlea", leaving 5 minor ch.- Stella age 11, oldest; Ernest; Lucian;Percy;Claudia. Adm.Bd. & Pet. filed 10 Dec. 1874 by Sallie R.Barrett, his widow. Adm.Pet. filed 13 Nov 1874 by David C.Perkins brother of Sallie E.Barrettt. Bd. issued to David C. Perkins, John Heath, A.C.Gilliam, 11 Nov. 1874. (One paper calls him CharlesE.Barrett) Sallie Barett signs Adm.order 22 Feb.1875, with POA to J.M.Miller. 1877 Sheriff states she is now in Wash.Co.Ms. (See Pkt.#51)

#48: Est. of John Hennessy: decd. at Tenn. Landing, Ms. 30 Jan.1875, leaving a widow - Margaret Adelaide Hennessy, ch. James,Mary,Dennis Mc, Margaret Hennessy. Pet. for let. of Adm.25 Feb.1875, Frederick Hall,E.P.Toy sec. Body taken to Vicksburg 2 Feb.1875. Last doc. dated 1905 a citation deliverd to M.A.Hennessy by Sherf. in Issa.Co. (Will of Margaret Adelaide Hennessy, WBk.C,p.248,Issa.)

#49: Est. of William Alonzo Collins, decd 25 Aug 1874; Adm.Bd.Saml.B.Harwood, sec.G.W.Cooley,Agnes Eugenia Harwood (his mother) 20 Mar 1875. States W.A.Collins' wife Emma D.Collins decd. 9June 1873. A.E.Harwood request that her nephew Saml.B.Harwood to be Adm.of her sons' est., since she is an invalid.By 7 Apr. 1877, S.B.Harwood is adm. of est. of A.E.Collins.(See Pkt.56)

#50: Est. of Mrs. Rebecca (sp.Rebela) B.Holmes, decd. 31 May 1875. Adm.Bd. J.P.Strong, her brother; sec. Jas.M.Moore, Melbourne Bean. Will(not listed in WBk. Index)dated 24 May 1875, admitted to Probate 25 June 1875. Residence Chotard Landing; left house and land called "Right Side Plt", 790 acr. to Jas.M.Moore, + store,a/c notes,etc.;Mrs. Elizabeth Strong, wife of J.P.Strong- $1000; H.J.Holmes $500 yrly.for life;Miss Ellen Gardner 1/4th int. in store house. Writing very faint.

#51: Guard. of Barrett minors, Pet. of Sallie R.Barrett 27 Aug 1875 for Guard. of Stella E.-13;Earnest A.-9; Lucien J.7;Percy N. 5; Claudia P. 3., minor ch. of Jos. E.Barrett and Sallie R. (See Pkt.#47)

#52: Margaret S.Smith vs Robt.M.Smith: (should have been filed under Chancery Docket) filed 27 Apr. 1868. Marg. charges her husb. Robt.M. $1400+int. in money due her from the Est of her father, Elias Pharr, whose Adm. since 1855 was Robt.M.. Court finds in her behalf and orders Robt. M.to pay $2,627 +6% int.. 3Aug 1872 order to Sherf in Issa. to seize Robt.M.Smith's goods, chattels,land for sale to settle dispute. No rec. of dispos.

#52(2):(in folder marked Smith vs Smith) Thomas J. Shelby, Jr.et al by next friend T.J.Shelby, Sr. vs D.F.Blackburn. Jos.W.Prescott appt. by Court to ascertain amt. of money due complainant heirs of R.P.Shelby, from his Adm. - D.F.Blackburn & to suggest a Guard. for receiving such amts. Chas.L.Buck named Solicitor for complts. May term

Packet Gleanings: Issa. Co.
Probate Drw. #3, 38-55

#52:(cont.) of Court 1860. Court also ordered Blackburn to pay each legatee $500 for yr. Feb.20, 1860 to Feb.20 1861. Paper filed 26 Apr.1861, William T.Barnard now Adm. de bonis non of R.P.Shelby Est., David Blackburn,decd. (Both cases in this folder should have been in Chanc.files)

#52: **Est. of Susan Wilson** (this 2nd folder numb.52), decd. at Tallula, Issa. Co. Ms.9 Oct 1874. Pet.for Adm. filed 3 May 1875 by Stephen Wilson, son of Susan Wilson, Names other ch. Jack;Gilmore;Ann;Rachel Hamilton. Est. $250 in litigation in Circuit Ct. agst. H.P.Scott for the recovery of personal property. Adm.Bd.Sec. James L.Mayfield, Peter Brown. Mar.1877 citation returned - Stephen Wilson not found in Iss.Co. Same for 1905.

#53: **Est. of J.A.McDonald**, decd. 5 Aug 1875, at Holland Landing, Issa.Co. leaving no widow or ch. or relatives in U.S.Adm.Pet by Jole O.Stevens, sec.E.P.Toy,E.Jeffords, 10 Aug 1875. 2 bills in Pkt. filed 10 Sept.1875,17 Feb. 1876 are to the Est. of A.McDonald of Mackville, Ms.

#54: **Est. of Charles A.Hester**: decd. 11 Aug.1875 in Vicksburg, Ms., resident of Issa. Co. Widow - H.O.G.Hester, encinte at time of his death. Other issue - Annie Loyle, Marshall J., David. Pet for Adm. 6 Jan 1876 - C.T.Brown, L.W.Watson, sec.Bd.J.W.Ellis, Gen.Grant.

#55: **Guar.of George May Knight**: Guard.Bd.by Elizabeth A.M. Strong and Isaac P.Strong, her husband. Sureties A.W. Acker,Gabe Brown - 12 Feb.1876. George May Knight, minor dau. of George M.Knight, decd. and Elizabeth A.M.Strong. Also heir of John Knight with $162.50 annuity.

Last Pkt. in Drw.38-55 is unnumbered and contains Pet.& Bds. for apprentice indentures of freedmen or women, Minors, indigents, freed negro, mulatto...all filed during the year 1867 under"Apprentice Act approved by Ms. Legislature 22 Nov 1865."(A small Index was found for this listing , and is included in this Vol.II)

Probate Drw. 56-80

#56: **Est. of Agnes E.Harwood**: Will rec. WBk.C, p.130-132 Filed 3 July 1876. Names: Robt.Hughes,Archie Hughes,Mary Agnes Hughes - ch. of decd. sister Lucia L.Hughes & James Hughes, Harris Co.Texas. Will written 4 Dec.1874 at Ingamar, Issa.Co. Wit: C.I.Kiger,S.B.Harwood,G.W.Cooley. Codicil written the same day, same wit.: Robt. and Archie Hughes to have 1/4 each and Mary Agnes Hughes ½ of est.+ jewelry; Mrs. ____ N.Beveridge (?) of Richmond, Va.hair jewerly except gentl. hair chain to Robt.D.McRaven;Mrs. Eliza Burton of Richmond,Va. - gold locket;Anna H.Boswell of Shelbyville,Ky. -bracelet;Anna E.Harwood, dau of Mary E.Harwood o Vicksburg - gold thimble; Wm.Alonzo Morrison

Packet Gleanings: Issa. Co.
Probate Drw. 56-80

#56: (cont) of Richmond,Va., son of Mary Collins Morrison,
$300; Wm.Boswell, son of Anna E.Boswell of Shelbyville,Ky.
$300; Anna E.Harwood, dau. of Mary E.Harwood of Vicksburg,
$350; Lowry E.Harwood, son of Mary E.Harwood, Vicksburg
$150. In case of death of Robt.,Archie,Mary Hughes, prop.
to be sold and an Orphans Home called "Lowry Orphan Assylum" be establ. in V'Burg. Mr. Richmond Peeler of Warren
Co.Ms signed Bd. 16 June 1876.
Codicil #2: Mrs. MaryE.Moore,Miss Josie McWhirter, Miss
Lizzie Herbert - ea.$100. Desire remains of son - Wm.A.
Collins removed to V'burg and buried beside his wife.
Desire remains of Lizzie Gwin,Ida Gwin,Sue Lowry and my
dau. Mary Collins removed from Brunswick next yr. and
interred in the Old Gwin Burial ground in V'burg.with
my bro. Wm.T.Lowry. Mrs. B.G.Kiger to attend to same.
Doc. states: Agnes E.Harwood dept. life V'burg 4 May 1876.
Ingomar Plt., 590 acr. in lower end of Iss.Co., I.,a/c.
P.O.A.to Charles E.Smith of Harrisburg, Harris Co.Texas,
signed by Mary.Agnes Hughes , now Mrs. Charles Emile
Smith and Archie Hughes (Robt. Hughes is decd.) to collect
from the Est. of A.E.Harwood. 21 Sept.1880.

#57: Est. of Ira Hardin: of Bunches Bend, Ms.(sometimes
called Bunches cutoff), decd. 10 Oct.1875 leaving widow -
Nancy Hardin - 2 ch. unnamed. Nancy declines to act as
Adm. and asks court to app. James Andrews. (ch. are 3 yrs.
and 6 - 8 mos.) Adm.Bd. 16 Nov. 1875.

#58: Est. S.S.Nelson: (2 #58's, 1 in red ink,1-blue)of Issa.
Co., decd. 11 Mar 1876 in New Orleans, La.; Pet. for Let
of Adm. filed 23 Mar 1876 by widow Margaret D.Nelson,
saying there were no ch., further states that Saml.Nelson
had been cultivating Valewood Plt. as tenant for yrs.
Final a/c filed 3 Mar 1880. Pkt. cont. I.& Appr.
Red Ink Pkt. contains debts owed & collected, and a letter
from Atty. Chapman, on same Est.

#59: Guard. of James Johnson, Lunatic. 24 Mar.1876. G.
is W.L.Sibley.

#60: Apprentice of Alex Anderson: Bd. filed 26 Apr.1877;
minor negro appr. to Mrs. Malvina F.Peyton.

#62: (2 #62) Est. of R.M.Smith: decd. 5 July 1877.Pet. for
Let.of Adm. filed 20 July 1877 by M.S.Smith, widow and
Robt.M.Smith, Jr. eldest son of decd.Bd.$7000, sec. Will
E.Collins, Morris VanOs, J.Irving. Lists heirs Margaret
S.Smith, widow; ch. Robt.Jr., Walter J.,Mrs. Tina (M.C.)
Hill, Mrs. Mary E.Collins, Preston H.Smith, Lee A.Smith,
Lawrence W.Smith,Lovena Smith.Guard. Pet. by Mrs. Margaret
S.Smith and Robt.M.Smith,Jr. mother and eldest bro. of
Preston H.-16 yrs.old, and Lee A.Smith - 14 yrs. Filed 20
July, 1877.(Pkt. #52 contains suit Margaret S.Smith vs
Robt. M.Smith over money owed Marg. from her father's
est. Some duplicate doc. incl. here. No add. infor.)
Guard.Pet. filed by Marg.S.Smith and Robt.M.Smith,Jr.
filed same day as above Guard. for Lawrence W.Smith 10

Packet Gleanings: Issa.Co,
Probate Drw. 56-80

#62: (cont.)yrs. Lovena Smith - 8 yrs. Final a/c dated
29 Jan 1906 states that Robt.Jr. had taken charge of
Robt.Smith,Sr.'s Plt, Clover Hill, which was mort. for
$18,000 at time of his father's death, and Robt.Jr. had'
worked it out of debt. in 10 yrs...unencumbent lands
div. to heirs - 1/7 to eac.By this time Preston had marr.
now decd; Lee marr. now decd; Lawrence - unmarr, decd.
before majority; sister Lou marr. J.P.Heath.Partition
Deed, S 519.

#63 & #64: Robt.M.Smith,Est. empty.

#66: Est. of James M.McQuaid: decd 1865. Adm.Bd. issued
to Nelson Fulton, I.(orJ.)G.Cortright. 5 Apr.1878. Appraisal - 21 Aug.1878. Doc. states that McQuaid was a
school teacher in Issa. (now Sharkey) Co.. Never marr.,
father decd. mother- Mrs. Sarah Davis decd. 1866, 2 sis.
Mary C.McQuaide, now Mrs. Allison Fulton (bro. of Nelson
Fulton) of Well Co.Ind. and Dorcas McQuaide, now Mrs.
James L.Lemmon, Westmoreland Co.Penn.

#67: Est. of Elias Bernstein: decd. 25 Oct.1878: Resident
of Shiloh Landing. Let. of Adm. granted Julius Fox - 13
Mar 1879Bd. signed 20 May 1879, sec. Max Pribatsch, Lincoln Co. Ms., Saml.Fox, Amite Co.Ms. States he left no
widow, but did leave 4 infants "of tender age" no relatives in State. JOS. Hirsh is Guard. of minor ch. (unnamed), and states that Bernstein died of yellowfever.
John L.Chapman was Atty. for the Est. but decd. July 1884.

#68: Est. of Amanda E.Coffield: decd. in her home 16 Feb
1879; Will rec. WBk.C,p.132; Husband H.D.Coffield, son
Robert Nelson Coffield - share everything. Husband -G
of son and exec. Will written 1 Nov 1855, no wit. 14 Apr.
1879, A.G.Ward,J.J.Watson attested to handwriting & signature.

#69: Est. of Abraham Heyman:(sp.Heiman) decd. at Tallula
30 Sept.1878.Pet. for Adm. by widow Amelia Heyman 22 Oct
1878; ch. Hannah,Samuel,Henrietta - all minors. Adm.Bd.
sec. Chas.C.Reynolds, T.J.Brennan, Bros. of Warren Co.
30 Dec.1878, denied, than accepted 29 Apr.1879. Doc.
include Inven. and Appraisles.

#70: Est. of Selden Spencer: decd. 3 June 1878 at Skipwith Landing. Will dated 29 Aug 1870, filed Dec.2,1878,
Rec. WBk.C,p.296 24 May 1918. Left everything to bro.
James G.Spencer of Claiborne Co.Ms..Otterburn Plt.was
Seldon Spencer's address. Adm.Bd. 2 Dec.1878 by S.M.
Spencer,Bd.Max Killiam,John L.Chapman, W.S.Farrish.

Packet Gleanings: Issa. Co.
Probate Drw. 56-80

#71: Est. of Franklin Dunn: decd. 21 Sept.1879. Wright Stanley Collector., Est. consists of Burleigh (Burnlea?) Plt.crop of cotton, etc..No wife or ch. Mrs. Catherine M.Stanley (Wright's wife) is sister of Dunn, Thomas J. Dunn is Bro..Dr. John A.Dunn - son of bro. Dr. Jno.A. Dunn. Pet for Adm. ad collengendum, by Wright Stanley 11 Oct. 1879.sureties - John M.Parker, Robt.Mollison of Issa.Co. Same day all heirs sign agreement to allow Stanley to remove dwelling house,store-house, and any other buildings in danger of caving into the River on Burleigh Plt.

#72: Est. of Mrs.Ada L.Gilkey: decd. 28 May 1879 at Duncansby, Ms. Will prob. WBk.C, p.133, Issa.Co., Andrew J.Gilkey, husband of decd. presents will and asks for probate. 1,000 acr. land in Issa, and land in N.C. Will dated 10 Mar 1879: Ada states she is 40 yrs. old, leaves land to husband A.J.Gilkey until his death, and then for the land to be divided between her ch. Rolf.W., LLoyd L., Mary Eva,Laura H.,Ida C.,Anna G., Ada L. and their heirs. A.J.Gilkey to be exec. Wit: Francis B.Hill, Wm.Anderson, S.W.Lachs, J.P. Filed 20 Oct.1879. Mar.1882 Pet for Guard. for 6 of the 7 ch."because they are entit- led to the sum of $300 now in the hands of M.(W?) Justice of Rutherford, S.C" Rolf. W.Gilkey is only ch. not a minor. Guard. granted 1 May 1882. A.J.Gilkey is called Colonel. (Ada Logan Gilkey is buried "Greenfield Cemetary", Wash. Co.Ms. her dates 11 Jan1838 - 29 May 1879)

#73: Est. of Franklin Dunn: continuation of #71.Pet. of Let. of Adm. dated 19 Dec.1879, challenges court app. of Wright Stanley adm. of Dunn's est. Same heirs named as in #71 with the addition of Mrs.Mary E.Wilkerson, sister. Stanley's Adm. revoked and Milton Royster, acting for J.L. Harris & Co.of New Orleans - a large creditor- declared new Adm. Inv. & Appr. - sale of personal prop.19 Apr.1880

#74: Est. of H.D.Coffield, decd. 25 Oct. 1879; Pet.for Let. of Adm. by J.J.Watson - 5 Nov.1879. Bd. by Saml. Nelson, Julius Fox granted 12 Jan.1880. Names heirs - 2 ch., minors (ed. note: only 1 ch. listed in wife's will.. Robert Nelson Coffield #68) Appras. 12 Jan 1880 T.W.Hays, N.L.Norwood,Wm.S.Gwin. Amts. pd. for Misses Dora and Lee Coffield...sundries,tuition,servants. Exceptions of Mrs. Eldora Burditt to J.J.Watson Adm. to a/c, filed 8 Apr. 1884. No disp. in this pkt.

#75: Guard. of Frank Barlow,Jr.: G.Bd. to Frank Barlow 12 Jan 1880. Frank,Jr. is son of Indiana C.Barlow, decd.& Frank Barlow. Sec.E.Jeffords,D.Strachan (sp.)

#76: Est. of Jacob Price; decd. 27 Jan.1880 at Farland Plt. Adm. Wm.F.Keene - 9 Feb.1880. States he has 3 ch. James - 15, Anna - 12, Jacob 9. Wm.Keene was chosen by next of kin Alfred Murray, Wm.Henderson as Adm. Sec. Cornelius Diggs,John Diggs, Demus Coursey. Alfred Murray alias Price, adult son of Jacob Price,Wm.Henserson is his

PACKET GLEANINGS: Issa. Co.Ms.
Probate Drawer. 56-80

#76: (cont); (Jacob Price's) brother-in-law.

#77: **GURADIANSHIP OF GEORGE ROBERTSON**: G.Bd. to Frank Barlow - step-father. George Robertson's mother was Mrs. Indiana C.Barlow,decd.,of Bolivar Co.Ms. Bond issued 9 Feb.1880, Issa Co...for $1500. Sec.J.L.Chapman,C.S. Jeffords,S.L.Hussey. George - between 14/18 yrs.,by law chose his Guard.

#78: **EST. OF OLIVER BLANTON**:et al minors; Pet. for Guard. Bd.by O.R.Daugherty for 5 minor ch. of Mary Fitzpatrick Daughtery; Irmgarde & Oliver Blanton, Lucia, Belle, & Nora Daugherty, last named since decd. 13 Mar.1880. Sec. for Bd($2,200) P.Scott,J.L.Chapman. No other papers.

#79: **EST. OF ALEXANDER CHASE**: decd.25 June 1880,Intestate at residence "Oakley Plt.",Issa.Co. Adm.Pet. by Andrew Chase,son,only heir of Est. 30 June 1880 - Sec.($300)by J.L.Chapman,W.S.Ingram.

#80: **EST. OF JOSEPH C. GRACE**:decd. 26 June 1880 at Duncanby,Ms.Intestate;Let. of Adm. filed jointly by A.J.Gilkey,Wm. F.Wescott - 10 July 1880. Widow Harriet B.Grace declined to Adm.Est. Adm.Bd.$16,000,signed by C.A.Grace,Harriet B.Grace,W.H.Clark,E.Jeffords,F.W.Anderson,F.B.Hill,J.L. Root,R.Cohn,H.Sommers.
Inv. & Apprs. - 10 July 1880 - by Sam C.Elliott,J.P.Kershaw, T.W.Lachs. The decd. owned a store called "Red Store", and a saloon called "White Store" (co-owned with C.A.Grace) in the town of Duncansby,Ms. The widow and ch.,including 3 minors, were allowed an allowance of $1200 for the 1st yr., later reduced to $1,000. Also a list of household and personal prop. in Rising Sun, Ohio Co.,Indiana---later claimed by widow Harriet B.Grace as "in her own right". July 1880, P.O.A.to Wm.H.Clark of Rising Sunn,Ind.,signed by Harriet B.Grace, also in Rising Sun...
1881: 6 heirs to undivided Est. of J.C.Grace; Mrs. Harriet B.Grace,T.E.Grace,Mrs.C.E.Wescott,George C.Grace,Harry Louis Grace, Eva Grace.
1882:T.E.Grace sold his 1/6th to Mrs. C.E.Wescott & Harriet.
1887:Mrs. H.B.Grace,decd; her 1/4 int. in Est. went equally to her 5 children - named above.
1892: Geo.C.Grace,decd.of Diptheria, his int. went to 4 remaining heirs.
1897:Louis Grace sold his int. to Mrs.Carrie E.Wescott. T.C.Grace was appt.Guard. to Eva Grace and Louis Grace after the death of their mother.(Bond not in Packet)
Final Report filed 27 Feb.1897 (Ed.Note:The Nov.28,1881 list of open a/c and notes due Est.,6 pages, reads like a telephone directory of present time of this area)
#98: Included in Pkt.#80,above;**EST. OF GEORGE C.GRACE**: decd. of Diptheria,10 Feb.1892; Sister- Carrie Westcott Adm.12 Mar.1892;Adm.Bd.$300,sec. by Virginia C.Grace (Mrs. T.C.)and M.S.Hicks.No widow,no ch. - bro.and sis. are heirs; T.C.Grace waived right as brother to serve as Adm.
#99: **The GUARD. OF MINOR CH. OF JOSEPH C.GRACE**:filed 12 May 1884 by Harriet B.Grace;States - Geo.C.Grace is 20 yrs.,

Packet Gleanings: Issa.Co.
Probate Drw: 56-80

#80: cont.(There were four large envelopes under the #80,
containing the Est. of Joseph C.Grace,The Est. of Geo.C.
Grace, Guard. of Minor Heirs of Jos.C.Grace.)
Harry Louis Grace is 9 , Eva.E. is 6, all live Rising Sun.
17, Sept.1891: T.C.Grace, Guard. of Louis and Eva Grace
signs a new G.Bd. required because of the sale of the prop.
in Rising Sun, Ind.

Drw.2, Prob.Issa. Overlooked, so is out of sequence
#18: Pkt. marked Est. of Burwell Bunn,decd.Rec.WBk.C,p.31;
Pet. for Adm. 2 Apr.1860 by bro.W.H.Bunn, states the decd.
had no wife,no ch.,5 brothers,2 sisters heirs. Inv.1861
by W.B.Farr,Isaac Hill,A.Turnbull,Jr.Rec.Bk. of Inv.&Appr.
p.193-196,25 Jan 1861, $19,150 in slaves,$700 pers. prop.
Apr.1861: Cit. to J.Z.Bunn,Mary J.Dollar and her husband
Jas.C.Dollar by Adm. of Est. Wm.Bunn. Date same, summons
to heirs of Burwell Bunn - Jos.Bunn; Alex.Bunn;Rich.G.Bunn;
Catherine Ann Mosley and her husb.John H.Moseley
Apr.1866: Cit. to A.W.Mosley - Guard. of Burwell,Eugenia,
and Lucy Moseley and Alezander Bunn,Rich.G.Bunn,Jos.Bunn
to speak up if final a/c unacceptablr.
In same Pkt. Est. of Jas.M.Briscoe: decd. (See WBk.A, abst.
in this Vol) Only addit.infor.: Wm.P.Briscoe, Adm. of Est.
of James M.Briscoe, decd. 20 June 1853. Private letter from
R.Duncan,Jeff.Co.,to W.B.Farr dated 5 May1857. Wm.B.Farr
Guard. ad Litem to minors after Wm.P.Briscoe's death, doc.
dated 2 Oct.1855.
In same Pkt. Est. J.L.Barnard: decd. Testate
Pkt. contains Will of J.L.Barnard, rec. WBk.B,p.5,6 Dec.
16,1853. Names wife Rebecca F.;2 ch. - Henry & Joseph;
appoints bro. Wm.T.BArnard exec; Wit; Saml. Wells,E.Jones
Harvey,D.D.Jackson.
In 2 doc. dated 1857 cit. to minor heirs on final settle.
heirs listed as R.F.Barnard,widow;Wm.H.;Joseph L;and Mary
E.Barnard with W.B.Farr Guard.Ad Litem. 1860 Census Rebecca
has married W.W.Brown and her ch. (Barnards) W.H.11yrs;
J.L.8 yrs; Mary L.6yrs. (Was Rebecca carrying a child when
J.L.Barnard died?)
Final a/c 1 Oct. 1860

PROBATE DRW: 80 - 97:

4 Packets of #80, J.C.Grace, included#98,99 - already Abst.
above.

#81: Est. of Marshall Turner: In the matter of the lunacy
of Marshall Turner, 20 Nov.1880.
Docu. incld. in Pkt.: Summons for Jury to decide matter -
6 men; Verdict of Jury - 5 yes - 1 no. He was sent to
State Hospital; Suggestion to court by Father - John Turner
that Jury investigate his son's lunacy; Supoena to John
Turner,Clara Turner,Lizzie Williams to testify.

#82: Est. of Henry Fox: decd. 14 Oct. 1880 at Rosalie Pltn.
Mrs. Rosalie Fox, Adm. Pet. Let. Adm. to J.I.Chapman, Atty.
Est. worth about $2,100. 4 Dec.1880 Rosalie Fox, widow;
Julius Fox;Theodore R.Fox;Mrs. Charlotte G.Levy; Miss
Augusta C.Fox ch. of decd.

Packet Gleanings: Issa.Co.Ms.
Probate Drw: 80 - 97

Fox Est. cont.: Kaufman Levy and Julius Fox secu. on Adm.
Bd.; Inv. & Apprs. by T.L.Neal, Chas.A.Fitler,Jno.R.Linville - Dec.18,1880. List of merchandise suggests he owned a store. Allowance for 1 ch. of $500 suggest one was a minor - a years provision for herself and ch. $1,000, part of personal prop. set aside as widow's portion.

#83: Est. of Moses Johnson: decd. 20 Dec. 1880: at "Cottonwood Pltn." Intestate. Pet. Let.Adm. by D.A.Dreyfus - 10 Mar.1881. States Johnson had no heirs or relatives. Small est.

#85: Guard. of Agnes,Lucy, and Jinny Tedo, minors: John Napper Guard. with A.W.Farish, Atty. Filed 11Apr.1881 Pet. for Guard. by John Napper states: William Tedo decd. and left surviving him 3 ch.,all minors, Agnes-12 yrs; Lucy - 6; Jinny- 8, all being the ch. of a former marriage. He states they are entitled to an $800 share apiece of the Est. of Wm.Tedo. Napper further states that he is the Uncle of the Tedo Minors. Guard.Bd.Secu. by Thos.Skipwith, Andrew W.Farish - $1,000.

#89:ANNA & JOHN PRICE (James inside): Three folders:
In the matter of James Price,Jacob Price,Anna Price:
1st folder: Pet. from James A.Price, minor heir of Jacob Price,decd. 27 Jan.1880, over 14 yrs. and asks Wm.F.Keene be appt. Guard. Pet. further states that Jacob left 3 ch. James,Anna and Jacob: Guard.Bd. $284 with secu. by Cornelius Diggs,Chas.Coursey,Demus Coursey, & John Diggs - 1 Aug.1881 6 Apr.1892, Keene seeks disch. from Guard. duties "as James Price has reached his majority".
20 Oct. 1890 Report of J.A.Price,by Keene, signed by J.A. and Anna Jackson, written from Hays Landing.
6 June 1881 - Pet. for Guard. for Jimmie Price - age 16.
Folder #2. In the matter of Jacob Price:Guard.Pet. by Wm. Keene 6 June 1881 states that Anna - 13;Jacob - 9;James A. 16 had been in his care since the death of their father Jacob Price. States further that he,Wm.Keene is a friend of the family, and Adm. of Jacob's Est. States his affection for the ch. and love and friendship for their father and at request of close relatives asks for Guard. of Jacob, minor.
Folder #3: Anna Price - Guard. Bd. by same ones, same dates as above for James and Jacob.

#89(2nd) Marked Price Minors: Duplicated infor. in #89(1st)

#91: Est. A.M.Tillman: decd. wife of Lewis Tillman,decd.
Adm.Pet. by John D.Lee - states that A.M.Tillman was Adm. of her husband's Est. and their children are Mattie M. Tillman now wife of John D.Lee; petitioner; Junius P.Tillman and Sallie A.Tillman - dated 6 May 1891.
Doc. incld.: Pet. for Let.of Adm by Ann Maria Tillman,Adm. to Lewis Tillman Est. dated Mar.1864, and she asks for her portion in 1866 of 240 acrs. of "Bear Lake" Filed 8 Oct.1867 Guard. Pet. for minor heirs of Lewis Tillman rec. WBk."C" p.33 asks appt. of Ann Maria Tillman as Guard. of Laura A. aged 15;Junius P. aged 12;Sallie A. 10; Mattie M. 5. 2 Apr. 1866.
Pet. of Junius P.Tillman for Adm. to Est. of mother Ann M.

Packet Gleanings: Issa Co.Ms
Probate Drw: 80 - 97

Tillman Est. cont. Tillman who decd. 18 Oct. 1880. Filed
31 Sept.1881. Names heirs Junius P.Tillman;Mrs. Sallie A.
Moseley;Mrs. Mattie M.Coner; her children and Eddie Hauff -
a grandch.,minor.
Sequence of Doc. confusing:Papers of Adm. of Ann M.Tillman
who decd. 1880 - 1st Adm. was son Junius, then in 1891
the Adm. was John D.Lee who had marr. Mattie Tillman Coner
Lee.
An earlier doc. in Pkt. was the Guard. Pet. by Lewis Tillman for 5 yr.old son Junius dated July Term 1860 - for the
purpose of selling 140 acrs. of land Lewis had bought in
his young son's name, stating the taxes had been raised
and the land pract. worthless. Pet. to sellgranted.

Loose paper in this drw:J.M.Butts, Guard. of Mary T.Butts
(in pencil - "these are all the papers found in this case"
Feb.7,1897) Lett. of Guard. to John M.Butts; Bd. $4,000.
Jan.1,1855 to Mary,Bettie,Eva,Edward Butts of Green Co.
Ala. children of John Butts. Rec. WBk."B" p.94.
Inv. of prop. and slaves.

#92: Est. of Antram Weleig:(Sp. Welling in Index to Est.)
Let. of Adm. 3 Oct.1881 by F.W.Anderson; Final a/c 2 Apr.
1892 statesAfter Let. of Adm. granted, an Inv. &Apprs. made
pers. prop.sold and all reports made to court in Fall 1883.
All of which papers have disappeared, lost from the files
of this court. Has reconstructed the a/c as best he can
and had some duplicate vouchers, States he hired W.S.Farish
to defend suits agst. Est. by Laura Walker, and D.Mayer,
which he won & the Est. owes Farish $50 fee.
By request of heirs (only one named,here) L.A.Evans of St.
Cloud, Minn. Anderson pd. taxes for 1881,82 and has not
been repaid. Anderson swears that Henry Welling is the
only heir of Antram Welling, to his knowledge. Henry
Welling is now in New Munich, Minn. (1892)

#93: Est. of Dr.R.J.Turnbull:(2 Pkts.) decd. 13 Feb.1882,
of Duncansby Pltn.,Issa.Co.Ms. (Ed.Note: Dr. R.J.Turnbull
was the Adm. for the family Ests. for a period of years,
and also the only one of this large group of land-owners
(absentee) who made a permanent home in the Delta.Therefore this Pkt. is a hodge-podge of Family documents)
Will and Est. of R.J.Turnbull: (Abst. in Vol.I, this series)
Filed for rec. 3 Jan 1855, Issa Co.Ms. Gouverneur M.Wilkins
brother-in-law of R.J.Turnbull stated - 24 June 1854, Westchester, N.Y. that R.J.decd. Cincinatti in 1854, but that
R.J. lived in Westchester, N.Y. and decd. leaving the following heirs: Widow - Cornelia Turnbull;Robt;Lewis;Sinclair;
Ann;Matthena;Catherine Turnbull - all minors living Westchester except Robert and Lewis who are absent at school.
The decd.'s brother - Andrew Turnbull and Wilkins are the
minors' Testamentary Guard.
28 June 1854 - John P.Jenkins of White Plains,N.Y. is appt.
Special Guard. of 6 ch. of R.J.Turnbull.
R.J.Turnbull's Will was written 17 Nov.1847,Westchester,N.Y.
carefully protective of each ch. and giving his widow -
Cornelia a $10,000 allowance + other things.

Packet Gleanings: Issa. Co.Ms
Probate Drw: 80 - 97

Turnbull, cont: The remaining documents in this folder deal with the Est. of Dr.R.J.Turnbull who decd. 13 Feb.1882. Adm.Bd. filed 3 Apr.1882 by Robt.J.Turnbull, Secu. J.L. Chapman,F.W.Anderson, H.V.Keep:
Insurance policy , fire, for "his one story frame shingle roof building and kitchen adjacent, occupied as a dwelling, and situated on Duncansby Pltn.Issa.Co.Ms, with special permission to use Coal Oil for lights. $300 prem.,$4.50 per yr with W.N.O.Insurance Ass. 15 Feb.1885
Release of Mahala P.H.Roach to Robert J.Turnbull, Exec. of Dr.R.J.Turnbull's Est. stating she had received $770 in 1883 - 1885 and expects no more. (Mahala P.H.Roach was the mother of the decd. wife of Dr. R.J. - Heonaro Elizabeth Roach)
Annual a/c Filed 18 Apr.1887
Final A/c Apr. 1891
Other docu. incld. Vouchers for rent,druggist bills,ect.

#93(2nd) Apr. Term 1880: Guard. of Lewis A.K.Turnbull and Mary Reubine Turnbull: Pet. of Rosa K.Walker, Guard. and formerly Rosa K.Turnbull, mother and Guard. of the above minors who are now about 17 and 13 yrs. old. She states that she qualified as Guard. for her 2 ch. 20 June 1871 (Her husband Charles Frederick Turnbull decd.27 July 1870.) She further states that Andrew Turnbull "the Senior" decd. in Issa. 30 Mar.1870 Intestate owning "Esperanza Pltn." and leaving the following heirs: Robert J.Turnbull, M.D. a son;Andrew Turnbull, a son; E.H.Bay Turnbull, a son; Charles Frederick Turnbull, a son; Claudia B.Turnbull, a dau; Elizabeth C.Walker, a dau. And that Chas.F.Trunbull decd. Intestate leaving her, the widow, and his 2 ch. named above. She states that Andrew's Est. is encumbered by debt - mortaged 27 Sept. to A.W.Campbell of S.C. under marriage settlement between T.O.Elliott and his wife. By 1847"Esperanza" was mortd. , other creditors were Jas.O'Neal, R.A. Furlow,Robt.L.Maitland of N.Y., dated 1867. A Bill of foreclosure was filed on Mort. held by Campbell on 16 July 1870 by one Hannah Eusten, exectx. of Wm.Eusten,decd. The court decreed the sale of "Esperanza" and it was bought 5 Jan.1874 by Edmund Richardson who occupied it several years and made valuable improvements, then sold it to Tarleton B. Cowan who is now in Possession, and who has also made valuable improvements. On 5 Aug. 1878, Hannah Eusten filed suit vs the heirs of Andrew Turnbull.#71 on Chanc. Dockt. She further states that the Uncle of said minors, Dr.R.J. Turnbull, pet. for relief of said minors - Lewis and Mary R. (End of Guard. Pet. by Rosa K.Turnbull Walker)
31 Mar. 1879 - An action of Ejectment was begun in Circuit Court of Issa.Co.Ms.by all heirs of Andrew Turnbull, but E.. H.Bay Turnbull who had quit-claimed all his rights to Edm. Richardson. The heirs claim that land not included as part of "Esperanza" had erroneoulsy been included in the sale. Edm.Richardson offered a settlement of $5,000 - $2,000 to go to the said minors, and $3,000 to be split between 4 adult heirs, and the heirs agreed. Rosa Kershaw Turnbull Walker's attys. were Owen McGarr, Esq. and Hon.T.C.Catchings Atty.Gen. of State of Ms. who recommends she settle.

Packet Gleanings: Issa.Co.Ms.
Probate Drw. 80-97

Turnbull; cont. Rosa K.T.Walker signed the docu. in St. Louis,Mo. Mar 1880, stating that Dr.R.J.Turnbull was the only Uncle in Issa. and no Aunts were here.
"Office of Sec. of State", Jackson,Ms. Henry C.Myers, Sec. of State gives permission to act for minors 8 Mar. 1880 (took an act of the Legislature!)
6 Apr.1880 - Guard.Bd. Rosa K.Walker as principal and Robt. Cohn and J.P.Kershaw, sureties.
14 June 1871: **Est. of Chas.F.Turnbull,**decd. Guard. and Adm. Bd. Rosa K.Turnbull as principal, O.R.Daughtery and Mrs. Ann Matthews, in Wash.Co.Ms., secu. Bd. $2,500.
Nov. 1877 - Sherf. states Rosa not to be found in Issa. Co. for annual a/c. (same in 1874) By Apr. 1880 - Rosa is marr. to -----Walker.
Docu. filed 28 May 1871 shows minors, Lewis and Mary R. as 8 and 5 yrs. and both living in Issa. Co.Ms.
Docu. states that Chas.F.Turnbull owned no Est. in Issa. Co., but had large holdings in Mexico, (Republic of)
Adm.Pet. by Dr.R.J.Turnbull, Adm. of Andrew Turnbull, who decd. 20 Mar.1870 - Issa.Co. gives the location of Andrew's heirs as follows: Andrew,Jr. is in Ala; Chas.F. now decd; leaving 2 ch; E.H.Bay now decd.;and without any ch.; Claudia lives in Maryland; Elizabeth, who marr. Jno.Walker and the said John Walker is decd. leaving Dr.R.J.Turnbull as nearest kin of Andrew's in Issa. Ms. Filed 17 Nov.1879.
(Ed.Note: There were 3 R.J.Turnbulls in the above a/c, with others in S.C., and one other in early Wash.Co.)

#95: Est. of Walter Elliott: Minor son of Emma Elliott,decd. and S.C.Elliott. S.C.Elliott Pet. for Guard. of 2 minor ch. Walter W. - 7; Charles S.Elloitt - 4. 3 July 1882.
Minors own land in Wash.Co.Ms. Guard. S.C.Elliott pd. taxes on it 1894 - Walter's half is $100 per yr. and Chas. the same.A/c 1882,1883.
Inv. and Apprs. of prop. owned by Emma Elliott - 1 1/3 int. in tract of land in Wash.Co.,value $1,000 - rent per yr. $250. 1 1/3 int. in house and lot in Mayersville (Ms.)

#96: Est. of Mrs. Emma Elliott: Guard. Pet by Father S.C. Elliott for minor son Charles S.Elliott 2 July 1882 , same as above.
Additional Information: Sometime between 1894 - 1896 S.C. Elliott died and Walter W. petitioned Court for Guard. of younger brother Charles. Bd. $2,000.R.M.Smith, W.Kaufman secu. 23 Sept.1896, stating Charles is now 18 and by Nov. 1896 **Charles**filed and Application for Emancipation from infancy to act on his own and to manage his own business affairs. Next friend is his grandmother - Mrs. Ann Walker. Bro. Walter testifies in Cha rles' behalf. Pet. granted.

#97:Est. of Augusta G.Luhm; decd. 13 Oct. 1882,Pet.Let Adm. Max Summers,R.Cohn secu. 17 Dec. 1882. Mary Frederick Luhm,widow and 3 minor ch.(unnmd) Apr. Term1883, Chas.Wilham, trustee, pet. for Adm. of Est. states Max Sommers intends to go "beyond limits of U.S. and wants relief". Pet. granted.

Issa.Co.
Index to Apprentice Records: Bk.A
Apr.30,1866 - July 5,1869: 85 pgs.

Last Packet in Drw. 38-55 is unnumbered and contains Petitions and Bonds for Apprentice indentures for freedmen or women, minors, indigents, freed negro, mulatto... all filed during the year 1867 under "Apprentice Act" approved by the Mississippi Legislature 22 Nov. 1865. A small Index was found for this listing, which is reproduced here. The actual documents tell age, condition under which supervision was needed, sometimes location of missing kin. It was difficult to tell the correct name for the Apprentices so have copied exactly as they appeared in the Index.

APPRENTICE NAMES:	Page	MASTER or MISTRESS
Benjamin	34	Thomas J.Shelby
Chaney John	12	Bailey I.Chaney
Dixie	34	Thomas J.Shelby
Dangerfield Thomas	59	Joel Ossterns (?)
Eugenia (col minor)	3	Henrietta N.Creath
Edward " "	17	J.J.Watson
Esquire Harvey	29	E.Jones Harvey
Florence (col minor)	3	Mordicai Powell
Grant Martha	57	Joel Ossierens (?)
Grant Bettie	51	" "
Hal (col minor)	--	A.W.Mosley
Henry Hamilton Jackson	54	Emily C.Hill
Letitia Walker	50	Emily C.Hill
Milly	40	Saml.G.Parks
Phillis (col minor)	3	Mordicai Powell
Roseanna Johnson	48	Emily C.Hill
Sarena Johnson	46	" " "
Scott Mary	71	D.H.Alexander
Talfour Johnson	52	Emily C.Hill
Tyler Nancy	73	Charles Courser
Woodward Thomton	65	D.H.Alexander
Woodward Alfred	69	" "

The Master/Mistress who accepted an Apprentice, guaranteed them care, protection, and had to post a bond ($300). The Apprentice was then under the protection of the Court.

' A History of Miss." by McLemore:Table 7: List: showing Planters owning 300 or more slaves in 1860..the ones shown from Issa. were Wade HamptonIII - 249 slaves - Overseer was P.Hamel: Stephen Duncan - 706 sl.-Ovsr. O.H.T.Rich,J.Garrett,S.C.Heard,Wm.J.Rowe,S.T.LeMay: J.D.Hill - 502 sl.- Ovsr. W.P.Branch,B.B.Mills,N.Rutland, S.J.Eakin;R.J.Turnbull, est. -401 sl.-Ovsr. Jos.Bunn, T.F.Alford,Alex.Bunn,G.Jamison.

Ibid: p.550: The Apprentice Act was part of Civil Rights Legislature, later known as the "Black Code", and all phases of the Black Code were repealed "except a vagrancy measure"...in 1867.

BOOK OF ORIGINAL PATENTS:*1827 - 1840
Washington Co.,Ms.

ABERCROMBIE,Chas.S.	1835	CAIN,Jas.	1829
AINSWORTH,L.	1834	CALDANIS,Peter R.	1837
ALEXANDER,Amos	1830	CALDWELL,Isaac	1831
ALLEN,Chas.W.	1835	" ,I.	1833
ALSOBROOKS,Willis	1834	CAMPBELL,Beasley	1834
ANDERSON,Hiram	183-	" ,Chas.R.	1835
" ,Horace	----	" ,John C.	1834
ATCHINSON,Elijah F.	1830	" ,Josepha	----
		" ,Wm.R.	1829
BACON,Larkin	1831	" , "	1834
" ,Wm.	"	CARNES,G.	1831
BALL,Geo.W.	1836	" ,Welles	----
BANKS,Margaret	1834	CARPENTER,Horace	1833
BARLOW,Geo.W.	"	" ,John M.	----
" ,Lydia	"	CARSON,A.	1835
" ,Noah	1835	CHAMBLISS,Peter C.	1834
BARNARD,Thos.	1833	CHANEY,Jas.I.	1830
BASS,Council R.	1832	CHANDLEY,D.H.	18--
" ,Edmund P.	"	CHANEY,Bailey D.	1830
" ,Jordan R.	1834	CHAPLAIN,Wm.R.T.	1835
BEAL,Geo.	1831	CHEWNING,Jas.J.	1831
" ,Marshall R.	----	CHILTON,John M.	1835
BENNETT,Elijah	1834	CHRISTMAS,Rich.	1836
BERRY,John G.	1836	CLARY,Thos.	1831
BIBB,Geo.B.	1835	CLOY,Michael	1834
BIRMINGHAM,Ben	1836	COCKS,Susan A.	1829
BLACK,Andrew J.	1834	COMPTON,Wm.H.	1835
" ,Ezekiel,Sr.	1831	CONNELLI,D.W.	18--
" , " ,Jr.	"	CONNELLY,D.W.	1834
" ,John	1836	COOK,Wm.B.	1829
" ,R.	1833	COOPER,Jas.	1834
BLANTON,Wm.W.	1831	COURTER,Jos.	1831
BODLEY,Wm.S.	1834	COWDRAY,Wm.C.	1831
BOOKER,Rich.L.	1835	COX,Alfred	1830
BOOKOUT,Ben	"	" ,John G.	1829
BRABSTON,Thos.	1831	" ,John S.	1835
BREELAND,Malvina	1834	" , Phillip A.	1831
BRISCOE,E.C.	1835	" , " "	1835
BRISCONET,S.	"	CRAFT,John	1831
BROWN,Rich.	1832	" ,Major	----
BROWNING,Joshua	1831	CREATH,Albert G.	183-
" ,Wm.	----	CROCKETT,Leonard	1834
BRYANT, Wm.P.	1835	" ,Martha	----
BUCKNER,Robt.H.	1834	CROW,Henry	1834
BUTTLER,Joshua	"	CRUTCHER,Geo.B.	----
" ,Noble	----	CUNNINGHAM,Belinda	1834
BYRD,Geo.	1834		
" ,John	----	DARDEN,David M.	1835
BYRNE,J.B.	1836	" ,J.	1834

---

*Taken from "THE STOCKWELL PAPERS",Wm.A.Percy Memorial Library, Greenville,Miss.

BOOK OF ORIGINAL PATENTS:* 1827 - 1840
Washington Co., Ms.

Name	Year	Name	Year
DART, C.	1835	EVERETT, R.H.P.	----
DASHEAR, Geo.	"	" , Thos.T.	----
DAVENPORT, Rich.G.	1834		
DAVIDSON, Christopher	1834	FAKE, Henry	1829
" , Wm.L.	----	FAULKNER, John W.	1834
DAVIS, Daniel	1835	" , Saml.C.	----
" , Stephen	----	" " "	1832
" , Jos.E.	1835	FELTS, D.W.	1834
" , J.	1834	FERGUSON, James	1833
" , Laban	----	FIRRANO, Manuel	1831
DAWSON, Henry S.	1835	FISK, Alvarez	1831
DAY, W.T.	"	FITZ, Gideon	1833
DEARING, Thos.	"	FLOURNOY, Matthew	1829
" , Wm.	----	FORD, James C.	1835
DEARMAN, Soloman, Sr.	1834	" , Wm.G.	"
" , " , Jr.	----	FOSTER, John	1832
DECOIN, Robt.L.	1836	FRAZER, Wm.	1830
DEHART, John	1832	FREELAND, Thos.	1835
DENHAM, Simpson	1834	FULTON, Zenos X.	----
DENTON, Gabriel W.	1835		
DESAULLIS, Louis	1835	GARLAND, Burr	1834
DICKENS, David	1834	GATES, John & John B.	----
" , Jas.C.	1833	GIBSON, Claudius	1831
DICKENSON, John	1834	" , Wm.	1834
DICKSON, Jas.C.	1833	GRUBBS, Francis	----
DOSWELL, Jas.	1831	GILBERT, Webster	1834
DOWNING, Alex	1833	" , Wm.	----
DOWNS, Alfred C.	1835	GLOYD, Spencer	1835
" , Thos.D.	1831	GOOCH, John S.	1830
DOZIER, John D.	1834	GORDON, Nancy	1834
DROMGOOLE, Wm.A.	1829	GORMAN, Starling	1830
DUKE, Simeon	1834	GOWAN, Wm.	1834
DUNBAR, Albert N.	1834	GREEN, David	1834
DUNBAR, Jos.	1832	" , Leonard	----
DUNN, Bartholomew	1831	GRIFFIN, Francis	1831
" , Wm.	----	" , Dennis	"
DUNLAP, Hugh W.	1835	" , Elizabeth	1834
		GRIMES, Thos.	"
EDRINGTON, Burwell T.	1835	GWIN, Wm.M.	1835
EDWARDS, Daniel	1834		
" , John	----	HALL, John B.	1835
" , B.W.	1834	HAMBERLIN, Mary	1834
EGG, Chas.	1831	HANNUM, Fisher A.	1835
" , Jos.	----	HARPER, James T.	----
" , " .	1829	" , Jesse	----
ELLIOTT, Theodore D.	1832	HARRELSON, A.W.	1834
ERSKINE, Alex	1835	HARRIS, Ezekiel	1835
ESTES, Arch.H.	1830	HARRISON, Abner G.	1837
" , Jos.E.	1831	" , Gilson P.	1835
EVANS, McLin	1835	HARVEY, John	1834

*Taken from "THE STOCKWELL PAPERS", Wm.A.Percy Memorial Library, Greenville, Miss.

BOOK OF ORIGINAL PATENTS:* 1827 - 1840
Washington Co.,Ms.

HARVEY,Mary	1834	KELLUM,Nathl.K.	1836
HATCH,Benj.	"	KENNY,Archibald S.	1833
HERALD,Jas.J.	"	KILPATRICK,Ebenezer	1832
HERRING,Redding B.	1835	" ,Elihu	1830
HESTER,E.	1831	KINCAID,John	1835
HIGGINS,Joel	1829	KNIGHT,Wm.	1834
HILL,Parley	1831	KNOX,Andrew	1832
" ,Caleb	----		
" ,Orren	1831	LABUZAN,Chas.A.	----
HINDS,Howell	1831	LACY,F.	1831
HOFF,Moses	1835	" ,Thos.	1830
HOFFMAN,Daniel	1831	LAIRD,Archibald	1835
" ,Delilah	----	" ,Geo.W.	----
HOLLIDAY,Thos.	1834	LASHLEY,Alexander	1834
HOOPER,P.	1834	" ,H.	----
HOUGH,Jos.	1829	" ,John	----
HOWARD,Arthur	1834	LATHAN,Lorenzo	1835
HUGHES,B.	1833	LAWSTE,Chas.A.	"
HUNT,David	1834	LEE,Jas.D.	1834
" ,Wm.	1831	LILES,Chas.	1831
HUSTON,F.	1832	LINDER,Daniel	1834
" ,Wm.	1834	LINSEY,Ephraim	1831
HYDE,Ezekiel	1831	LLOYD,Spencer	----
" , " ,Jr.	"	(see GLOYD)	
		LOFTON,Walter C.	1830
INGRAM,James	1833	LONGELY,A.	1836
" ,Wm.	----	LUDLOW,Ben A.	1835
IRISH,Geo.	1831	LUM,Erastus & Wm.	1835
" ,Henry T.	1833	LUNEY,Ephraim	----
IRVIN,Archibald	1835	(see LUISEY)	
JACKSON,Ben	1831	MANNIFEE,Robt.C.	1833
JOHNSON,Wm.	----	MARLOW,Jos.	1834
JAFFREY,Robt.	1837	MARSHALL,Geo.,Sr.	1831
JAMES,Gabriel	1834	" , "	"
" ,Thos.I.	"	MARTIN,John	1835
" ,Theodoric J.	----	MAY,John	1831
JEFFRIES,Wm.F.	1835	MAYFIELD,Saunders	1837
JENKINS,Baley	1834	" ,Mary	----
" ,Crittenden	----	MAXWELL,Laurence P.	1835
" ,John	1834	McALLISTER,Archibald	1831
JELKS,Dixon	1831	" ,John	----
" ,Geo.W.	----	" ,Augustus W.	1831
JOHNSON,Henry	1833	" ,David	1835
" ,Launcelot	1834	McALPIN,Duncan	1831
JONES,Saml.	"	McCAMERON,Sarah M.	"
" ,Susannah	----	McCaughan,John J.	1835
" ,Thos.	1835	McCRASKEN,Arthur	"
" ,Zachariah	1831	McDANIEL,Jos.	1831

* Ibid

BOOK OF ORIGINAL PATENTS:* 1827 - 1840
Washington Co., Ms.

McDANIEL, Wm.	----		PARKER, Benj.	----	
McDUFFIE, Angus	1834		" , Rich.	1831	
" , Murdock	----		" , Wm. L.V.	1834	
McFADDEN, John	1829		PAXTON, John G.	1838	
McGHEE,	----		" , Wm.	1835	
(see MeGHEE)			PEACOCK, Wm.	1834	
McINTYRE, Hugh	1834		PECK, A.H.	"	
" , John	----		" , G.H.	----	
McKAY, Robt.	1833		PENRICE, Francis	1835	
McLARAN, Jas.	1831		" , Wm.	1832	
McMURRAY, John T.	1835		PERCY, Thos. G.	1834	
McNUTT, Alexander	1834		PESCOD, Wm.	----	
McRAE, C.	1834		PETTIT, Absolom	1835	
MEAD, Cowles	1833		PIERSON, Jos. O.	1836	
MEGHEE, Evan	1834		PINTARD, John M.	183-	
" , Holden	----		POINDEXTER, Geo.	1835	
METCALFE, Albert G.	1829		POOL, Wm.	183-	
MIDDLETON, John	1834		POWELL, E.&.R.	1831	
MIERS, Jesse E.	"		PRINCE, Catherine	1829	
MILLER, Harvey	1833		PRINCE, Sarah S.	"	
" , Henry	"		PUCKETT, Henry L.	1835	
" , Anderson	1835		" , Walter A.	1836	
" , Hiram D.	1831		PURVIS, James	1831	
" , John C.	1829		" , John	"	
" , Joslin	1831		" , Jos.	"	
" , Wm.	----				
MILLS, Wm.	1835		RAGLAND, Arthur S.	1831	
MOFFETT, John	1836		" , John	----	
" , Ulysses W.	1835		" , "	1834	
MONTGOMERY, Alex. B.	1831		READING, Abraham B.	1836	
" , Davis	1834		" , Absolom B.	1835	
" , John	1835		" , Sidney	1831	
" , Wm. P.	1831		REILY, James	1835	
MOORE, Edmund	1835		RHYMES, Alex	1831	
MOORE, Lewis	----		" , Allen	----	
MORRIS, Wm.	1835		RIFE, Wm.	1831	
MORTON, Francis	"		RIMES, Zena	1834	
			" , Peggy	----	
NEIBERT, Jos.	1834		ROACH, Benj.	1831	
NEWMAN, Jos. H.	1832		ROBERTSON, Jos. W.	1831	
NEWTON, W.E.	1834		" , Wm. T.	----	
NICHOLSON, Isaac R.	1833		ROBINSON, Henry W.	1834	
NUTT, Rittenhouse	"		ROSE, Elizabeth	1831	
			" , Rebecca	----	
OATS, Jacob	1831		" , Enoch	1831	
OFFUTT, Zach. E.	1835		ROSS, D.	"	
			" , Hugh	"	
PARHAM, John G.	1835		" , Thos.	"	
PRYOR, Wm. B.	----		" , John	"	
PARKER, Anderson	1831		" , Mary	1830	

* Ibid;

BOOK OF ORIGINAL PATENTS:* 1827 - 1840
Washington Co.,Ms.

RUNNELS,Hiram G.	1830	THERELKERD,David H.	1832
RUSSELL,Wm.	1831	TIDWELL,Rich.	1831
		" ,Wm.	----
SAVAGE,Dolly	1831	TILLMAN,Hardin	1834
" ,Rowland	1834	" ,Malachi	----
SCHMIDT,Frederick W.	----	TONEY,Jas.C.	1834
SCOTT,Abraham M.	1831	TRAYTON,M.	----
" ,John A.	1835	TOOLEY,Mary	1834
" ,John F.	"	TOUCHSTONE,Dempsey	"
" ,Perry	1834	" ,Wm.H.	----
SELSER,Elisha	1830	TUCKER,John	1831
SHANKS,Geo.	1830	TUNSTALL,John	1834
SHARKEY,Wm.L.	1833	" ,Lynch	"
SHARP,Absolom	1830	" ,Thos.	1830
SHARPLIN,Wm.	1834	TURNBULL,Andrew	1834
SHELBY,Bayliss P.	----	" ,Frederick	1829
" ,Mary	1830		
" ,Thos.(heirs of)	--	VANCLIVE,Thos.	1834
" ,Robt.P.	1829	VINING,Jeptha	1835
SHERIDAN,Thos.	1834	VINSON,Stokey	"
" ,Victoria	----		
SIMMONS,Geo.W.	1835	WALKER,Robt.J.	1834
" ,Saml.	"	WALLACE,Jos.	1832
SIMPSON,Sarah	1831	WALWORTH,Horace F.	1833
SIMS,Wm.H.	"	WARD,Jeremiah S.	1831
SKINE,Ben	1835	" ,Robt.J.	1833
" ,Vergil	----	WARE,Nathl.A.	1834
SMITH,Benj.	1829	WARFIELD,Thos.B.	1835
" ,Francis P.	1832	WATSON,John	1834
" ,Jos.	1834	WEBB,John & Mary	1835
" ,Jas.M.	1835	WEESE,Henry	"
SMYLIE,Mat	1834	WELCH,Chas.	1831
SPELL,Jos.G.	"	WHEELER,Mark	1834
STAMPS,John	1834	WILKERSON,	----
" ,Volney	"	(see WILKINSON)	
STARKE,Theodore O.	1836	WILKINSON,Isaac S.	1831
STEPHENSON,John	1831	" ,Jane	----
" ,Mary	----	" ,Jefferson	----
STILE,John	1835	" ,Peter	1831
STRINGER,Drusilla	1830	WILLIAMS,Benj.	1835
" ,Jos.	"	" ,Peter W.	1830
" ,Leonard	1831	" ,Putnam	1834
SUMRALL,Drury	1834	WILLIAMSON,Mary N.	"
" ,Thos.L.	1835	WINCHESTER,Geo.	1833
SURGET,Jas.	1834	WINN,Allen	1834
SWAN,John C.	1835	WINTOR,Thacker W.	1836
		WITMIRE,John	----
TANNER,Saml.	1838	WOMACK,Abner	1834
TATUM,John	1834	" ,Martha	----
" ,Wm.C.	"	WOODSON,Frederick	1836
TAYLOR,Harrison	"	WORTHINGTON,Isaac	1829
		" ,Saml.	"

* Ibid:

BOOK OF ORIGINAL PATENTS:* 1827 - 1840
Washington Co., Ms.

"The following names were in the early part of the listing but the dates were too faint to read on the original."

ARTHUR, J.W.
BRYAN, Wm.H
BODLEY, Wm.L.
CHEWNING, J.J.
CASTLEMAN, S.
COX, W.L.
CRAWFORD, John
DANIEL, Smith C.
DAVENPORT, Jas.
ELLIS, Wm.S.
FORSYTHE, Wm.
FOLKES, Miles C.
   " , Saml.
FUSELL, Wm.
   " , Sherwood
FISHER, Alex.
GRAVES, Nancy
HUNTINGTON, Geo.W.
HUDDLESTON, John
HENRY, Saml.G.
HENDERSON, John
JARRETT, Thos.R.
JOHNSON, Edw.P.
KEEN, M.
KIRBY, Soloman
LYONS, Rich.J.
McGinty, Delia
MARSHALL, Reuben
   " , L.R.
MILLSAPS, Wm.
MAYFIELD, E.
MORRISS, Henry T.
   " , Jane
MAHOFFEY, J.T.
MILLER, Polly Ann
MOORE, Michael
MERRICK, P.F.
NEWMAN, Ben.F.
NEELY, Mary
OLIVER, Saml.C.

OUSLEY, Thos.
OFTEEN, M.
OSTEEN, Simon
REGIONS, Jos.
REYNOLDS, G.W.
ROBERTS, John C.
SPIKES, Wm.
STEPHENSON, Wm.
SCOTT, Alfred V.
SIMS, John
   " , Rich.S.
SMITH, Geo.N.
STRANGE, Joshiah
STEADMAN, B.M.
SHIRLEY, Adam
STEWART, J.S.
TAYLOR, Wm.
   " , Ben
THOMPSON, Wm.
TUTTLE, Abraham
THOMAS, M.
TOMLINSON, W.E.
TAYLOR, Alvin
UNDERWOOD, R.
VICK, Henry W.
WILKINSON, D.M.
WELLS, Wm.C.
WILSON, A.L.
WARTHUR, Isaac
WARD, Thos.
   " , G.W.
WHITFIELD, Ben
WRIGHT, Abraham
WHITE, John
WINGATE, E.F.
PUCKETT, Walter
PHILLIPS, B.E.
PRYOR, Wm.B.
PRESCOTT, Wm.
PIERCE, Granville S.

Washington Co.Ms.
#Marriage Records,Bk."A":(Marked colored, but is not)

P.1.John Buckner to Parolee M.Copeland: Bds.E.S.Wallis.
License issued 11 Jan.1858 - marr.14Jan1858

2.Cyrus Johnson to Mary M.Worthington:Bds.Jefferson
Compton:L.I. 8 Jan 1858 - Marr. 14 Jan 1858:Groom from
Chicot Co.Ark: consent by Bride's Mother, Ann Worthington in handwritten note: License spells name M.Marie.

3.R.A.Young to Victoria O.Sullivan: Bds.Thos.Hinds,Robt.
Davenport:Ceremony perf.by Wm.B.Hines,Min.:L.I.30 Jan
1857 - ret. 2 Feb 1858.

4.Edward O.Lampkins to Frances Ann Grissom:Bds.Joseph
J.Cooper,James D.Blincoe:Perf. by Wm.B.Hines,M.G.;L.I.
21 June 1858 - perf.21 June 1858.

5.John J.Ross to Mary L.Carson: Bds. WM.A.Haycraft: Perf.
by T.D.Lea:L.I. 7 July 1858 - pfd.8 July 1858.

6.G.H.Buford to Sallie Fulton: Bds.Andrew Crow;L.I. 3
Aug 1858 - perf. 14 Aug 1858.

7.David Friley to Catherine J.Hatcher:Bds.E.J.Pace:Ceremony perf. by E.J.Mullins,M.G.:L.I. 14 Aug 1857 - marr.
26 Aug 1858.

8.Isaac Bankston to Martha E.White:Bds.Wm.Browning:Perf.
by James Abell,M.B.P.:L.I. 16 Aug 1858 - Marr.26 Aug 1858

9.Wm.H.Browning to Maggie M.Moore: Bds.Isaac Bankston:
Perf. by James Abell,M.B.P.:L.I. 20 Aug 1858 - marr. 26
Aug.1858.

10.John G.Walton of Madison Co.La. to Gracia M.Turnbull
of Wash.Co.Ms:Bds.Wm.Turnbull:Wit,Geo.T.Blackburn:Perf.
by Benj.M.Miller - Rector of Christ Church,Church Hill,
Ms.;L.I.27 Nov.1858 - Marr. 30 Nov 1858.

11.Robert H.Hord to Mrs. Mary I.Jackson: Bds.Robt.W.
Durfey: Perf. by WM.B.Hines,M.G.:L.I. 30 Nov.1858 -
Marr. 2 Dec.1858.

12.W.T.Ashford to Mrs.Mary J.Haney:Bds.W.S.Nugent: Perf.
by E.F.Mullins,M.E.C.S.:18 Jan 1859 - marr. 19 Jan 1859.

13.Thomas M.Worthington to Louisa Montgomery: Bds.Russell
Montgomery: Perf. by Wm.B.Hines: L.I.7 Feb 1859 - marr.8 Feb.

14.George T.Blackburn to M.Belle Johnson:Bds.Matt F.Johnson:Perf.by Whitefield Harrington,M.G.:22 Mar 1859 - L.I.
Marr.12 Apr. 1859.

15.Richard Brown to Miss Margaret Orr:Bds.Geo.T.Blackburn:Perf.by Wm.B.Hines: L.I.22 Mar 1859 - Marr.30 Mar 1859.

#Marriage Bk."A" is in the Wash.Co.Circuit Clerk's Office.

Washington Co.Ms.
Marriage Records,Bk."A"

P. 16.Handwritten notes attached:Ulysses Merchant gives consent for dau.Roxana Merchant to marry William Richard Nash:note dated 28 Mar.1858 & wit.by Robert Vance: Wm.R.Nash to Roxanna Merchant.Bds.Robt.Vance:L.I.26 Mar. 1859 - marr,28 Mar.1859;Perf. by E.F.Mullins,M.G.

17.Edward P.Johnson,Jr. to Isabella Griffin: Bds.John R. Woodburn:Perf. by W.W.Lord,Minister of P.E.Church,Vicksburg,(Ms.) L.I.16 Apr.1859 - marr. 19 Apr.1859.

18.Blank

19.George P.Powell to Nancy J.James:both of Wash.Co.; Bds.Ira M.Powell: Perf. by Wm.F.Camp: L.I.2 May 1859- Marr. 4 May 1859.

22.(page numbers skip 20,21) Harris H.Johnston to Miss Anna Brooks: Bds.Thos.W.Wilson:Perf. by Whitfield Harrington: L.I.6 June 1859 - marr.8 June 1859.

23.Ira M.Powell to Amanda Susan Vanmeter:Bds.E.A.Wallis: Perf. by Wm.F.Camp:L.I. 23 June 1859 - marr. 26 June 1859.

24.James O.Wilcox to Sarah Jane Scott:Bds.A.F.Smith: Perf. by Whitfield Harrington: L.I.29 Sept 1859 - marr. 29 Oct.1859.

25.John Norwood to Jane Smith:Bds. (blank): L.I. 10 Nov. 1859 - marriage license not returned.

26.Paper attached:Judge of Probate R.L.Dixon authorizes marr. between Grant A.Bowen & Amanda V.Yerger: paper dated 4 Jan.1855:L.I. 12 Feb.1855 - marr.20 Feb.1855 by Wm. Parker Scott,Rector of Trinity Church,Yazoo City, Ms.

27.Wm.L.Nugent to Eleanor F.Smith: Bds.D.C.Montgomery: Perf. by Wm.P.Barton,M.G.:L.I.5 Nov.1860 -Marr.6 Nov.1859.

28.John S.Nelson to Belinda J.James:Bds. John H.Nelson: Perf. by G.C.Fore:L.I.19 Dec.1860 - marr.20 Dec.1860.

29.Franklin Valliant to Marian Rucks: Bds.Leroy B.Valliant: Perf. by Wm.C.Crane,Rector of St.Andrew Church,Jackson, Ms.:L.I. 14 Jan.1861 - marr. 17 Jan.1861.

30.Loose paper:State of Ms.,Wash.Co.,Mr. Dudley and Mrs. M.A.Dudley consent to marriage between "our" dau.Miss Lillie J.Erwin and Oliver T.Morgan,Esq. Note dated 29 Jan.1861 and wit. by Geo.T.Blackburn:On p. 30 - Oliver T.Morgan to Miss Lillie Erwin: Bds.Wm.L.Nugent:Perf. by C.G.Andrews,Minister: L.I.24 Jan.1861 - marr.7 Feb.1861.

31.Blank: Reverse side - Petition of Charles G.Andrews, Minister, to be allowed to perform marriages in Ms. dated 28 Jan.1861 - M.E.C.S.(Methodist Episcopal Church South)

32.George P.Worthington to Josie M.Bott: Bds.John M.Bott: Perf. by Wm.P.Barton,M.G.;L.I.29 Jan.1861 - marr. same.

33.Blank: Reverse side - Handwritten petition of Stevenson Archer,Minister, for license to perform marriages in Ms; Dated 27 May 1861 - Presbytery of Ms.

Washington Co.Ms.
Marriage Records Bk."A".

P. 34.Wm.H.Douglas to Miss Kate Sutton: Bds.W.T.Penny;L.I.
27 May 1860 - marr. 29 May 1860 by Stevenson Archer,M.
35.Wyndon R.Trigg to Nannie S.Hurst:Bds.John L.Finlay:
L.I. 31 May 1861 - marr. same:Perf.by Wm.P.Barton,M.G.
36.Wm.B.Dunn to Miss Bettie M.Dunn:Bds.Wm.L.Nugent; L.I.
31 May 1861 - marr. same:Perf.by Wm.P.Barton,M.G.
37.Loose paper:Issa.Co.(Ms.) 15 June 1861 - "Give approval for the marriage of Charles F.Turnbull to Miss Rosa Sarah Kershaw" - Andrew Turnbull signs for Charles and Thomas Kershaw signs for the bride. Wit. by Andrew Turnbull,Jr. and R.J.Turnbull,MD. L.I.17 June 1861 - marr. 20 June 1861 by W.W.Lord.L.I. to Charles Frederick Turnbull and Miss Rosa Sarah Kershaw.
38.John W.Crisler to Miss Josephine E.Foster:Bds.Thos.H. Hill: L.I.12 July 1861 - marr. 16 July by C.G.Andrews.
39.F.H.Boyer to Virginia L.Brooks:Bds.W.P.Montgomery:L.I. 2 Nov.1861 - marr. 4 Nov. by Wm.P.Barton,M.G.
40.J.W.Green to Miss Virginia Skipworth: Bds.Percy Roberts; L.I.19 Feb.1862 - marr. 20 Feb by Jno.W.Beckwith.
41.Blank: Reverse side:Petition of John W.Beckwith for license to perform marriages as a Priest in Protestant Episcopal Church by Bishop of Diocese of N.C. - 24 Feb. 1862.
42.Leroy B.Valliant to Theodosia Worthington: Bds.Andrew B.Carson:L.I. 17 Oct.1862 - marr.21 Oct.by Wm.P.Barton,M.G.
43.Samuel W.Ferguson to Catherine S.Lee:Bds.N.W.Lee:L.I. 24 Aug.1862 - marr.25 Aug. by Jno.W.Beckwith.
44. Repeats p.43.
45.J.L.Phillips to Elizabeth Brown:Bds.Andrew Carson:L.I. 9 Dec.1862 - marr.11 Dec. by Stevenson Archer.

---------2 year gap---------
46.Bascom T.Pearson to Fannie A.Maloy:Bds.J.W.Murphy: L.I. 8 Dec.1864 - no return.
On reverse - Petition of Wm.H.Phillips of Protestant Episcopal Church for license to perform marriages,28Jan.1863
47.N.Cummings to Matilda E.Perry:no bds.;L.I.28 July 1864 marr. 1 Aug by Stevenson Archer.
48.Henry Kober to Pricilla Tamplin:Bds.Zachariah Tamplin: L.I. 29 Dec. 1864 - marr. 3 Jan 1865 by Stevenson Archer.
49.James Pritchard to Gertrude Laws: Bds. N.C.Skinner:L.I. 1 Mar.1865 - marr 2 Mar. by Stevenson Archer.
50.Christopher Gillespie to Maggie King:Bds.Jno.T.Courtney and J.M.Heathman:L.I.14 Mar 1865 - marr.22 Mar.by J.L.Shaw.

Washington Co.Ms.
Marr. Records, Bk.A;cont.

p. 51: A.J.Lawson to Mary R.Dunn: Bds. F.F.Voohies & Jno.T. Courtney: L.I. 15 Mar 1865 - Marr. 16 Mar by J.L.Shaw

52: B.F.Penny to Amelia A.Charnley: Bds. F.H.Boyce: L.I. 17 Apr 1865 - Marr 20 Apr. by Stevenson Archer.

53: H.P.Eckford to Ella Bland: Bds. Jno.T.Courtney: L.I. 12 July 1865 - no return.

54: Jno.T.Switzer to Nannette Abell: Bds. N.J.Nelson: L.I. 18 Dec 1865 - Marr. 20 Mar 1866 by Stevenson Archer.

55: Chas. W.Johnston to Annie F.Dunn: Bds. Andrew Carson: L.I. 21 Dec 1865 - Marr. 22 Dec. by Stevenson Archer.

56: Lyman G.Aldrich to Bettie A.Wilson: Bds. Davis M. Buckner: L.I. 6 Feb 1866 - Marr.8 Feb. by Stevenson Archer.

57: Albert Gammeter to Julia Stiess: Bds. F.A.Metcalf: L.I. 13 Mar 1866 - Marr. 15 Mar. by Lytton L.Taylor

58: Jno.T.F.Waters to Nancy C.Mooran: Bds. J.T.Smith:L.I. 27 Mar.1866 - Marr. 28 Mar. by Geo. T. Blackburn, member of Board of Police, Wash.Co.Ms.(Ed.Note:Later called the Board of Supervisors)

59: _____Blank

60: Thomas W.Powell to Lizzie D.Marsh: Bds. N.J.Nelson: L.I. 27 Mar 1866 - Marr. 28 Mar by Stevenson Archer.

61: Frank Williams to Sarah Jane Drummond: Bds Stuart White: L.I. 14 Apr 1866 - Marr. 15 Apr: Reverse side; David (X) Spells swears he is Step-father of Sarah Jane and she is over 18.

62: Louis de N.Evans to Emma E.Buckner: Bds. J.M.Davis: L.I. 4 Dec 1866 - Marr. 5 Dec by Stevenson Archer.

63: Davis M.Buckner to Amanda Worthington: Bds.James Stone: L.I. 4 Dec 1866 - Marr. 5 Dec. by Stevenson Archer.

64: _____
65: _____Reverse: Petition of William Winans Drake, Minis. of the Gospel Methodist Episcopla Church South (MECS), by Rev.Robt.Paine, Bishop, to perform marriages in Ms. 27 June 1866.

66: E.S.Crandle to Helen Glemser: Bds. A.C.Caperton: L.I. 12 Julu 1866 - Marr. 13 July by A.C.Carpenter, M.G.

67: A.J.Petty to Laura James: Bds. Jno.S.Nelson: L.I.26 Sept 1866 Marr.27 Sept.by Stevenson Archer.

L.I: License Issued, next date the date the Marriage was performed.

Washington Co.Ms.
Marriage Records Bk."A".

68. John H.Maclin to Sallie E.Hill:Bds.Saml.T.Taylor:L.I. 8 Oct.1866 - marr. same day by S.Archer.

69. Zachariah Tamplin to Margaret V.Hamberlin:Bds.J.Kirkland:L.I.13 Oct.1866 - marr. 18 Oct. by W.W.Drake.

70. Harry Yerger to Miss Sallie Miller:Bds.Wm.G.Yerger: L.I.18 Oct.1866 - marr.23 Oct.by S.Archer.

71. James M.Smith to Anna L.Wilmot:Bds. W.G.Yerger and John L.Wilmot:L.I.22 Oct.1866 - marr.25 Oct. by S.Archer.

72. Oliver T.Morgan to Emma Erwin:Bds.Chas.B.Talbutt:L.I. 3 Nov,1866 - marr. not returned.

73. Wm.G.Yerger to Jennie Hunter:Bds.W.R.Trigg:L.I.4 Dec. 1866 - marr.6 Dec.by Stevenson Archer.

74. James Stone to Mary B.Worthington:Bds.Davis M.Buckner: L.I.4 Dec.1866 - marr.5 Dec. by S.Archer.

75. J.W.Winpigler to Mollie J.Bar(e)field: E.Collum,Bds.: L.I.4 Dec.1866 - marr.5 Dec.by Augustine Chew,J.P.

Loose paper (out of chronological order):Petition of Charles G.Andrews, M.E.C.S.to perform marriages,28 Jan.1861.

Reverse side of p.75: J.H.Barfield, brother of Mollie J. Barfield says she is over 18. See above.

76. G.W.Sanders to Harriet Leppard:Bds.Isom Sanders;L.I. 7 Jan 1867 - no return.

77. M.F.Spells to Mary Ann Drummond:Bds.David (X) Spells: L.I.18 Jan.1867 - marr.20 Jan. by Wm.T.Ashford,M.G.: Reverse side:David (X)Spells says he is the Guardian of Mary Ann who was born Jan 1848 and is of age.

77. (Duplicate numbers):H.Rogers McIlwain to Mattie G. Campbell:Bds. W.R.Campbell:L.I.22 Jan.1867 - marr.23 Jan. by Stevenson Archer.

78. James W.Oswald to Julia Ann Shell:Bds.Andrew Carson: L.I.14 Feb.1867 - Not returned, but James W.Oswald swore that he was the guardian of Julia Ann and she "is over 18".

79. James M.Miller to Jennie G.Raffington:Bds.O.M.Blanton: L.I.9 Apr.1867 - marr.same day by W.W.Drake.

80. Wm.T.Cole to Kate A.Russell:Bds.Wm.A.Haycraft: L.I. 11 Apr.1867 - marr. 13 Apr.by S.Archer.

81. Thos.J.Sutton to Sarah Jane Melchoir: Bds.W.R.Trigg: L.I.4 May 1867 - Marr. 7 May by S.Archer.

82. Page attached to front of p. 82: Calvin W.Baldridge to Mrs.Sarah Ray: Bds.J.M.Collins: L.I.10 June 1867 - marr.by Sam.T.Taylor.

Information above repeated on p.82.

Washington Co. Ms.
Marriage Records, Bk. A; cont.

p.83: Wm.L.Nugent to Mary C.Montgomery: Bds. W.R.Trigg: L.I. 20 June 1867 - Marr. same day by Stevenson Archer.

84: H.L.Baker to Annie C.James: Bds. W.R.Trigg: L.I. 28 Sept. 1867 - not returned.

85: C.W.Dudley to Lois Elley: Bds. Benjamin Johnson: L.I. 12 Oct 1867 - not returned.

86: Michael M.Deterly to Mrs. Mary E.Elmore: Bds.J.D.Harper: L.I. 22 Oct 1867 - not returned.

Loose Paper:Dated 7 June 1870: H.R.Williams and Eli Butler give permission for H.R.Williams to marry Miss Emma Newton.

87: J.D.Hopper to Annie K.F.Satterwhite: Bds. M.M.Deterly: L.I. 22 Oct. 1867 - Not returned.

88: Wm.T. Norment to Julia Montgomery: Bds. J.M.Montgomery: L.I. 24 Dec.1867 - Marr. 25 Dec 1867 by Stevenson Archer.

89: Jno. Kanatzer to Mrs. Nellie Davis: Bds. Henry Miller: L.I. 30 Dec. 1867 - not returned.

90: E.J.Comstock to Evie H.Smith: Bds. Jas.Stone Wilson: L.I. 1 Jan 1868 - Marr same day by W.W.Drake.

91: Jos. McGraw to Martha A.Williams: Bds.J.F.Waters: L.I. 22 Jan 1867 - not returned.

92: Hugh G.Gwyn to Jennie Buckner: Bds. T.R.Wallis: L.I. 3 Feb 1868 - Marr. 6 Feb. by Stevenson Archer, Minister.

93: D.A.Love to Katrude Douglass: Bds. A.B.Carson: L.I. 3 Feb. 1867 - Marr 4 Feb 1868 by Stevenson Archer.

94: E.J. Bryant to Mary Macklin Evans: Bds. C.Heard: L.I. 10 Mar 1867 - Not returned.

95: L.A. Melchoir to Sarah V.Copeland: Bds. D.M.Shanahan: L.I. 27 Apr.1868 - Marr same day by Stevenson Archer.

96: John Heath to Mollie L.Taylor: Bds. J.L.Lengsfield: L.I. 14 June 1868 - Marr. 3 July 1868 by Ben Johnson,J.P.

97: Attached paper: Sunflower, June 26, 1868...Seek permission to marry:John C.MCGregor to Permely Lee: Bds. Jos. Keys:

On p. 97: John C.McGregor (by Jno. Collier) to Permelia Lee: Bds. J.C.Collier: L.I. 30 June 1868 - Marr 2 July by W.A. Hopkins, M.G.

98: R.Gillespie to Rebecca Watts: Bds. W.W.Drake: L.I. 24 July 1868 - Marr same day by W.W.Drake.

99: L.M.Brown to Rebecca Roberts: Bds. H.B.Putnam: L.I. 16 Oct 1868 - No return.

100: Harry Percy Lee to Sallie E.Scott: Bds. Geo.Y.Scott: L.I. 23 Nov. 1868 - no return.

101: Willy Bailey Barnard to Lizzie Mauray West: Bds. W.E. West: L.I. 12 Dec. 1868 - Marr. 17 Dec. by Augustine Chew, J.P.

Washington Co.Ms.
Marriage Records, Bk. A; cont.

p.102: D.L.Stone to Katie B.Hunt: Bds. J.S.Wilson: L.I.
15 Dec. 1868 - Marr 16 Dec by Stevenson Archer.

103: Charles W.Standard to Mollie E.Reddin: Bds. Jn.W.
Wingpegler: L.I. 20 May 1868 - Marr 17 Dec 1868
by Augustine Chew, J.P.

104: Archie Baugh to Harriet McAllister: Bds. Columbus
Heard: L.I. 24 Dec.1868 - Marr. same day by Stevenson Archer.

105: Benjamin T.Worthington to Mary D. Elly: Bds. Jo.H.
Robb: L.I. 2 Jan 1869 - Marr 5 Jan by Stevenson Archer.

106: Edward Enos to Mary Farmer: Bds. John Weiss: L.I.
19 Jan 1869 - Marr 20 Jan by Henry C.Liponsky.

107: Wm.Wells to Mary E.Abell: Bds. Wm.Allison: L.I.
24 Jan 1869 - Marr 28 Jan by Stevenson Archer.

108: J.H.Barefield to Jane P.Morgan: Bds. Geo.F.Farmer:
L.I. 1 Feb 1869 - Marr 4 Feb. by Jas. Macleman,M.G.

109: L.B. Weems to Mary B.Rives: Bds. N.T. Nelson: L.I.
1 Mar 1869 - Marr. 18 Mar. by Stevenson Archer, M.G.

110: H.K. McEvers to Rachel Kelly: Jn.T.Nelson Bds.:L.I.
12 Mar 1869 - Marr. same day by S.C.Elliott, J.P.

111: Henry T.Irish to Bettie Taylor: Bds. K.R.Wilson:
L.I. 15 May 1869 - Marr same day by Stevenson Archer.

112: Wm.F.Randolph to Ann B.Carter: Bds. R.M.Carter: L.I.
1 June 1869 - Marr. 6 June by Stevenson Archer.

113: F.M.Hoppin to Mattie O.Pierce: Bds. J.O.Pierce: L.I.
30 July 1869 - Marr. 5 Aug by Stevenson Archer.

114: Henry H.Melchoir to Frances Ann Elizabeth Gibbons:
Bds. Raphl. L.Marshall: L.I.11Aug 1869 - Marr. same
day by Wm. T.Ashford, M.G.

115: Jas.S.Dunn to Miss Martha Carter: Bds. G.L.Dunn:L.I.
11 Aug 1869 - Marr 12 Aug by W.W.Drake.

116:Joseph McDonald to Sarah Ann Murphy: BDS. P.W.Carroll:
L.I. 25 Sept 1869 - Marr. same day by W.W.Drake.

117: A.C.West to Mrs. C.A.Vaughn: Bds. A.D.Aldridge: L.I.
2 Oct 1869 - Marr. 6 Oct. by W.W.Drake.

118: Jesse J.Duncan to Josephine Moore: Bds. B.J.Foley:
L.I. 13 Oct. 1869 - Marr. 21 Oct.

119: James H. Brown to Martha Eleanor Watson: Bds. Willis
Watson: L.I. 1 Nov. 1869 - Marr. 10 Nov. by Stevenson
Archer, M.G.

120: P.B.Holly to Miss M.J.Simpson: Bds. W.B.Wheatly: L.I.
17 Nov. 1869 - Marr. 18 Nov. by J.M.Collier, J.P.

121: E.Collum to Mrs. K.F.Barefield: Bds. J.F.Wilkerson:
L.I.6 Dec 1869 - Marr. 7 Dec. by Jas. M.Coburn, J.P.

Washington Co.Ms.
Marriage Records Bk."A".

P. 122.F.A.Poggel to Julia R.Putnam:Bds.C.F.Putnam:L.I.
11 Dec.1869 - marr.12 Dec.by Stevenson Archer.

123.O.D.Thomas to Miss May Yerger:Bds.Alex.Yerger:L.I.
16 Dec.1869 - marr.23 Dec. by Wallace Carnahan,P.E.C.

124.Angelo Gargaro to MrsH.C.LeRiemondie: Bds.Julius J.
Lengsfield:L.I. 28 Jan 1870 - marr.28 Jan by Wm.A.Alford.

125.Geo.Roden to Elizabeth Jane Lacey: Bds.Andrew Pogle:
L.I.5 Feb.1870 - marr.14 Feb.by Robt.A.Davis,M.G.

126.J.Dudley Murff to Miss Mattie A.Rives:Bds.W.W.Drake:
L.I.22 Feb.1870 - marr.24 Feb.by W.W.Drake.

127. J.B.Strothers to Josephine Jennings:Bds.W.R.Saunders:
L.I.27 Feb.1870 - marr.3 Mar.by Albert M.Mott,J.P.

128.W.B.Hunter to Miss Belle Bott: Bds.Wm.G.Yerger:L.I.
2 Mar.1870 - marr.3 Mar.by Wallace Carnahan,P.E.C.

129.Charles Scott and Miss Malvina Yerger:Bds.Alex Yerger:
L.I.7 Mar.1870 - marr.10 Mar by Wallace Carnahan,P.E.C.

130.Charles Elliott to Loujenia Jennings: Bds.J.A.Newman:
L.I.8 Mar.1870 - marr.10 Mar by A.B.Mott,J.P.

131.John J.Cox to Miss Alice Nelson: Bds.T.A.Wallis:L.I.
31 Mar.1870 - marr.same day by W.W.Drake.

132.W.P.Hawkins to Miss Nancy Georgia Moore:Bds.R.M.
Carter:L.I.8 Apr.1870 - marr. 10 Apr. By S.Archer.

133.Frank E.Smith to Miss Lena Frances Woods:BdsR.A.Wilshire: L.I.2 May 1870 - marr.same by Wm.T.Ashford,M.G.

134.Jacob Heidingsfelder to Miss Rowina Goldman:Bds.J.A.
Goldman:L.I.23 May 1870 - marr.30 May by S.Archer.

135.Ed.H.Hodge to Miss Mary Merchant:Bds.Jas.Wilson:L.I.
23 May 1870 - marr.30 May by S.Archer.

136.H.R.Williams to Miss Emma Newton:Bds.Eli Butler;L.I.
4 June 1870 - marr.7 June by W.W.Drake.

137.W.T.Embry to M.C.McCallam (sp.):Bds.D.J.Cochran:L.I.
9 Aug.1870 -marr. 10 Aug. by S.Archer: Permission granted
by her mother, J.L.McCallum.

138.Henry Herman to Johanna Leveret:Bds.John Habicht:L.I.
3 Sept.1870 - marr.13 Sept.by Wallace Carnahan.

139.John Cox to Ella Tillman: Bds.Geo.R.Farmer and F.M.
Tillman:L.I.5 Sept.1870 - marr.same by G.R.Farmer,J.P.

140.D.B.Obanion to Mary P.Heard:Bds.N.A.Herd: L.I.3 Oct.
1870 - marr.13 Oct. by Stevenson Archer.

141.Samuel Oram Elwell to Ida Geary:Bds.Lomax Anderson:
L.I.12 Dec.1870 - marr.14 Dec.by S.Archer.

142.James C.Estill to R.C.Ryals:Bds.Geo.R.Farmer:L.I.14
Dec.1870 - marr same by Geo.R.Farmer,J.P.

Washington Co.Ms.
Marriage Records, Bk.A; cont.

p. 143: James Thompson to Mary Meade: Bds. Jas. D.Shanks:
L.I.1 Jan 1871 - Marr. same by Geo.Waldo Stickney,
Rector St.James (Prot. Epis.) Ch., Greenville.

144: James (X) Williams to Mollie Judon: Bds. J.B.Benson:
L.I. 7 Jan 1871 - Marr. 8 Jan by Geo.R.Farmer, J.P.

145: W.S.Winter to Mary Clark: Bds. J.P.Finlay: L.I.
14 Jan. 1871 - Marr. 19 Jan. by F.A.S.Adams.

146: Joseph H.Robb to Mattie Buckner: Bds. J.H.Buckner:
L.I. 16 Jan 1871 - Marr. 19 Jan ;by S.Archer.

147: Robert R.(X)Wright to Frances Hicks: Bds. Jno.
Sinsabaugh: L.I. 19 Jan 1871 - Marr. same by Geo.
R.Farmer, J.P.

Page between 147 - 148 is unnumbered:the following
Marriage is noted: Madison M.Arnold to Mrs. Sarah
McDonald: Bds. John Sinsabaugh: L.I. 19 Jan 1871 -
Marr. same by Geo.F.Farmer,J.P.

148: Wm. (X) Stinson to Mrs. Jane Barefield: Bds. J.H.
(X)Morgan: L.I. 31 Jan 1871 - Marr. same by J.Duche;
Murff.

149: Francis C.Carter to Annie A.McCallum: Bds. John L.
McCallum: L.I. 20 Feb.1871 - Marr. 21 Feb. by S.
Archer,M.G.

150: T.J.Rushing (X) to Ida R.Roghers: Bds. Jno.H.Welser:
L.I. 7 Mar 1871 - Marr. 12 Mar by ____ Murff, M.G.

150: John H. Cook to Mary Dridy: Bds. J.Hirsch: L.I.
18 Mar. 1871 - Marr. 19 Mar by John L.Griffin, J.P.

Attached to reverse of 2nd 150; Wesley O. Wetherbee
to Miss Belle V.Elliott: L.I. 3 Apr.1871 - Marr.
same by A.D.Brooks, Minister.

151: Wm.Jackson to Eliza Sigler: Bds. Geo.R.Farmer: L.I.
15 May 1871 - Form returned but not dated or signed
by the minister.

152: J.H.Steadman to E.D Jones: Jno.H.Penrice, Bds: L.I.
27 May 1871 - no returns

153: Ceasar McMillan to Caroline Jones: Bds. J.M.McFarland:
L.I. 26 Aug. 1871 - no return.

154: Monroe (X) Bannister to Ellen Kinney: Bds. Albert (X)
Johnson: L.I. 26 Aug. 1871 - no return.

155: Wesley O.Wetherbee to Belle V.Elliott: Bds. M.R.
Sanders: L.I. 3 Apr. 1871 - no return

Microfilmed - Unindexed

L.I.: License Issued
M.G.: Minister of the Gospel
MECS: Methodist Episcopal Church South
PEC : Protestant Episcopal Church
J.P.: Justice of the Peace

MARRIAGE RECORDS FROM THE GREENVILLE "TIMES"*

Mr. Benjamin F. Therrel, formerly of G'ville, to Miss Mary E. Grier, of Ga., in Lake Providence, La. 9/19/1874

Mr. H.E. Wetherbee, of G'ville to Miss Dora McCoy, of Golconda, in Golconda, Ill. 11/7/1874

Mr. Hinds Holmes and Miss Annie Shelby, both of G'ville, in St. James Church bu Rev. Duncan Green. 11/17/1874

Mr. M.I. Morzinski and Miss Pauline Hassberg, of G'ville, at the residence of Mr. Wm. Marshall, by the Rev. Dr. Gotthelf, of Vicksburg. 12/27/1874

Mr. H.J. Hollingsworth and Miss Martina Wright, both of this county, at the residence of the bride's father by Rev. Jos. S. Oakley. 2/6/1875

Mr. David Friley and Mrs. Mary L. White, both of Wash. Co. in the Methodist Church by the Rev. Jos. S. Oakley. 1/31/75

Mr. R. Lee Sims, of Brandon, Miss., and Miss Mary Nelson Finlay, of G'ville, by the Rev. Stevenson Archer.

Mr. Wm. H. Lyons and Miss Cecelia C. Dash, in St. James Church by Rev. Duncan Green.

Rev. Duncan Green, Rector of St. James Church, and Mrs. Belle Hunter, both of G'ville, by Bishop Green. 6/10/1875

Mr. Benjamin F. Lengsfield and Miss Fannie Hassberg, both of G'ville, at the residence of Mr. Wm. Marshall, by Rev. Dr. Gotthelf, of Vicksburg. 6/13/1875

Dr. C.W. Lewis and Miss Maggie Campbell, both of Wash. Co. at the residence of the bride's mother in G'ville, by Rev. Father Miale.

Mr. Louis Vaughn and Miss Alice Robards, both of G'ville, at the residence of the bride's Uncle, Mr. Pat Campion, in Louisville, Ky. 9/12/1875

Mr. Wm. C. Maddox, of Water Proof, La. and Miss Sallie R. Dunn, at the residence of Dr. S.R. Dunn, by Rev. Stevenson Archer. 11/20/1875

Dr. R.D. Farish, of Issaquena Co. and Miss Callie H. Power, elder dau. of Mr. Stephen H. Power, in Trinity Church in Natchez, by Rev. Alexander Marks. 11/11/1875

----

*Copied from the "Stockwell Papers", available in the Greenville, Miss. Public Library, and the Archives in Jackson, Miss. Taken from original newspapers, some of which are no longer in existence. K.B.

MARRIAGE RECORDS FROM THE GREENVILLE "TIMES"

Mr. Chas.Sheffner and Miss Helen B.Small, at the home of the bride's mother in G'ville, by Chancellor Stafford. 12/25/1875

Mr. Robert Smith and Miss Amelia McClenan, at the Panola Plantation of Rev.Stevenson Archer. 1/8/1876

Mr. John H.Moore and Miss Eliza B.Finlay, at the residence of the bride's mother in G'ville, by Rev.Stevenson Archer. 1/27/1876

Mr. Samuel D.Finlay and Miss Georgie Blanton at the residence of Dr.O.M.Blanton, by Rev.S.Archer. 4/18/1876

Mr. Walter Quick and Miss Alice Van Allen, both of G'ville, at the residence of the British Consul, Thomas P.Perry,Esq. in G'ville, by Rev.T.Page.

Mr. Nathan Goldstein and Miss Emeline Weiss, of G'ville, at Alexander's Hall, by Rev. Chas. Rawitzer. Mr.andMrs. Morris Weiss, parents of the bride, celebrated the 25th anniversary of their marriage at the same time and place. 6/8/1876

Mr.James McConnell and Miss Sallie R.Burrett, at the residence of the bride's father in G'ville, by the Rev.T. Page. 7/1/1876

Mr.J.M.Montgomery and Miss Carrie Mosly,* at Loughborough, by Rev. Stevenson Archer. 11/2/1876

Mr.G.C.Vaught and Miss Mary Perrotte, at St.James Ch. by Rev.D.C. Green. 12/12/1876

Mr.Jas.E.Negus,Jr. and Miss Louisa M.McAllister, in G'ville by the Rev.S.Archer. 12/28/1876

Mr.W.P.Kretschmar and Miss Kate Cox, in G'ville, by the Rev.T.Page. 12/20/1876

Mr. JohnNeff and Miss Louisa Williams at the parsonage by Rev.T.Page. 1/1/1877

Mr. Edward Kennedy and Miss Maggie Biggins, at the Catholic Church in G'ville, by Rev.Father Queler. 1/8/77

Mr. Francis G.Toomer and Miss Lillian H.Stickney, at Zion's Church, Wadmalaw Island, by Rev.G.W.Stickney. 1/27/1877

Mr.R.C.Ryals and Miss Frances E.Dixon, at the residence of Saml.Barefield on Deer Creek, by J.N.Collier,J.P. 1/31/77

----

*Ed. Mosley should be spelled Mosby.

MARRIAGE RECORDS FROM THE GREENVILLE "TIMES"

Mr. Green F. Slater and Miss Mary E. Barwick, at the residence of the bride's father on Deer Creek, by J.N. Collier, J.P. 2/1/1877

Mr. Jos. Strum and Miss Sarah Ann Small, at the residence of the bride's mother in G'ville, by Rev. T. Page. 3/4/1877

Mr. Kendrick R. Wilson, of G'ville, and Miss Mary R. Anthony, of Elizabeth, N.J. at home in Elizabeth, N.J. 4/4/1877

Mr. Jos. A. Schall and Miss Euella McCall, both of G'ville, in St. James Church by Rev. D. Green. 4/26/1877

Mr. James Hair and Miss Fannie M. Newton, at the residence of J.G. Beck, by Rev. T. Page. 6/10/1877

Mr. Chas. S. Farrar, of New Orleans, and Miss Hattie Leonard, of G'ville, at the residence of the bride's father, Mr. A.R. Leonard, by Rev. S. Archer. 6/24/1877

Mr. H.M. Snowberger and Miss Minnie Wolfenstein, at the residence of Mr. Sol Morris, by Rev. Chas. Rawitzer. 7/8/77

Mr. John Hanway and Miss Annie Shanahan, in St. Joseph Catholic Church, by Rev. Father Quelar. 7/18/1877

Mr. Lee Hartman and Miss Marcella Marshall, at the residence of Wm. Marshall, bt Rev. C. Rawitzer. 8/12/1877

Dr. A.S. Gerdine and Miss Sallie B. West, at the residence of Dr. Morson, by Rev. T. Page. 8/19/1877

Mr. S.A. Thompson, of Bolivar Co. and Miss Anna C. Pilchers, of New Orleans, at the residence of Col. W.G. Myers, Belmont Lake, Bolivar, by Rev. J.T. Oakley. 8/26/1877

Dr. W.G. Allen, of Wash. Co. and Miss Sue Banks, at the residence of the bride's father, Mr. JohnO. Banks, Clinton, Miss. by the Rev. Chas. B. Galloway, of Jackson.

Mr. Tristrim L. Skinner, late of G'ville, and Mamie Uznay, of San Francisco, at the Church of Notre Dame des Victoiries, in San Francisco. 12/20/1877

Mr. Jacob Y. Johnson, of G'ville, and Mrs. Mary M. Butterfield, of Hot Springs, Ark., in the Episcopal Church at Little Rock, Ark. 12/23/1877

Mr. Geo. Johnson and Miss Julia Morgan, at the residence of Col. Matt F. Johnson on Lake Wash., by Rev. S. Archer. 1/1/1878

Mr. JohnD. Taylor, of Bolivar Co. and Mrs. G.A. Young, at her residence, with REv. D. Green officiating. 1/3/1878

MARRIAGE RECORDS FROM THE GREENVILLE "TIMES"

Mr. J.C.Greenley and Miss Julia McGrath, at St.James Episcopal Church, by Rev.D.C.Green. 1/19/1878

Mr.S.O.Shorey and Miss Laura L.Church, at the residence of H.B.Putnam. 2/5/1878

Mr. John Church and Miss Fannie A.Putnam, at the same time and place. 2/5/1878

Mr.John C.Head, of Griffin, Ga. and Miss Mamie A.Buckner, of Bolivar Co., at the residence of the bride's mother, by Rev.Mr.Fleming. 3/21/1878

Mr. A.P.Wingfield and Miss Mattie D.Buckner, at the residence of A.J.Paxton, by Rev.S.Archer. 4/13/1878

Dr.J.S.Walker and Miss Orville Blanton, of G'ville, at St.James Episcopal Church. by Rev.D.C.Green. 4/23/1878

Mr. Mark Eckstone and Miss Bertha Solomon, both of G'ville, at the Grand Central Hotel, by Rev.Chas.Rawitzer. 5/1/1878

Mr. Arthur A.Morson and Miss Bessie Dameron, at the residence of John T.Casey, Warsaw Place, Deer Creek, by Rev.Mr.Lee. The bride is from Hinds Co. and at the late tournament at Rolling Fork was chosen "Queen of Beauty". 5/1/1878

Dr.R.R.Stockard of Wash.Co. and Miss Ella Hyde Fowlkes, of Va., at the residence of the bride's father in Burkville, Va. by Rev. Mr. Newhill. 5/11/1878

Mr.S.A.Jones, son of A.L.Jones, of Alliance, Ohio. and Miss Isadore French, of Damascoville, Mahoning Co., at the residence of the bride's father, Honorable O.C.French, formerly of Miss., by Rev. Anderson. 6/15/1878

Mr. R.W.C.Mitchell, of Wash.City, and Miss Anna G.Elloitt, of G'ville, at the residence of Mr.G.W.Elliott, by the Rev. S.Archer. Mr.Mitchell is the private secretary of Carl Schurz. 7/13/1878

Mr.P.T.Dwyer and Mrs. C.K.Teats, both of G'ville, in St. Joseph's Catholic Ch., by Rev.Mr.Bomar. 7/25/1878

Mr. Joseph Hobson and Miss Mattie Lee, by Capt.W.E.West., member of the Board of Supervisors. 8/10/1878

Mr.A.Downs Pace and Fanny Percy, both of this county, at the residence of the bride's father, Hon.W.A.Percy, by Rev.S.Archer. 12/26/1878.

Mr.Augustine Benoit and Miss Ida Blanton, at the Presbyterian Church by Rev.S.Archer. 1/29/1879

MARRIAGE RECORDS FROM THE GREENVILLE "TIMES"

Mr. John M. Lee, of Wash. Co. and Miss A.P. Farrar, of New Orleans, at the residence of the bride's mother in New Orleans by Father Lamie. 2/20/1879

Mr. Charles H. Smith and Miss M. Georgie Miller, both of Wash. Co., at the residence of Mrs. Urquhart by Rev. S. Archer. 4/23/1879

Mr. A.M. St. Clair and Miss Charlotte Feltus, at the residence of Mr. J.A.V. Feltus by Right Rev. Bishop Adams. 6/10/1879

Mr. W.T. Carpenter and Miss Sallie Montgomery, at the residence of Mr. J.M. Montgomery, by Rev. S. Archer. 6/11/79

Mr. Andrew Aldridge**and Miss Lucy Paxton, at the residence of Col. A.J. Paxton, on Deer Creek by Rev. S. Archer. 7/1/1879

Mr. John Dabney and Miss Lola Blanton, at the residence of Dr. O.M. Blanton, by Rev. Dr. Juny. 7/24/1879

Maj. Wade Hampton, of G'ville, and Miss Kate O. Phelan, of Memphis, dau. of the late Senator Phelan of Miss., in Louisville. 8/23/1879

Mr. Isadore Hexter, of G'ville and Miss Yetta Scherer, of Cleveland, Ohio, in Cleveland. 9/10/1879

Mr. Joshua Skinner, of G'ville, and Miss Bettie Mardens, of Fairfax Co., Va., at Pohick Church, Fairfax Co. Va. by Rev. Walker Nelson. 9/23/1879

Mr. Ed. Whiteway, of the wharf-boat, and Miss Nellie Perry, by Rev. Dr. Juny. 11/19/1879

Mr. Alex Anderson and Miss Nellie Burke, both of G'ville, in St. Joseph's Ch. by Rev. Father Bohmert. 12/8/1879

Mr. E.A. Dennett and Miss Fannie Bell, at the residence of Dr. Montgomery, by Rev. S. Archer. 12/10/1879

Mr. L.P. Yerger and Miss Susie Southworth, at the Episcopal Church in Vaiden, by Rev. Mr. Halstead. 12/10/1879

Mr. James Bruckway and Mrs. Annie De Montaigue, nee Miss Henshaw, dau. of Co. Henshaw, one of Wash. Cos. earliest and most worthy citizens, at Leadville, Colo. 2/17/1880

Mr. Lee Simmons, of Stoneville, and Miss Nancy Hasberg, of G'ville, by Rev. Mr. Subler of Vicksburg. 3/11/1880

Mr. Chas. P. Manfield and Miss Fredreka Leake, at the Methodist Parsonage in G'ville, by Rev. J.L. Futrell. 4/8/1880

**Ed. Lucy Paxton married Frank Saunders Aldridge, not Andrew, as this account states.

MARRIAGE RECORDS FROM THE GREENVILLE "TIMES"

Mr. Samuel Davis and Miss C.M.Jobe at the residence of
Mr.J.P.Jeneen, in G'Ville, by Rev.S.Archer. 4/7/1880

Mr.A.M.Kirk and Mrs. Georgia Blanton, of this county,
at Belle Air Place, by Rev.S.Archer. 4/13/1880

Mr. Edward K.Stafford, of G'ville, and Miss Ida B.Kelly,
of Wisconsin, at the Methodist Church in G'ville, by
Rev. J.L.Futrell. 5/6/1880

Mr.C.M.Johnson and Miss Alice Hunt, belonging to two
of the worthiest and largest families in Wash.Co., at
the residence of Capt.W.E.Hunt, by Rev.S.Archer. 6/7/80

Mr.W.L.Canfield and Miss Mary Rucks, both of Friar's
Point, at the Methodist Church in Friar's Point, by
Right Rev.BishopPearce, of Ark. assisted by Right Rev.
Mr. Bruce, of Helena (Ark.) both of the Episcopal
Church. 6/29/1880

Mr. Edward Storm, of Storm's Landing, Bolivar Co.(Ms.)
and Miss Julia Kuhn, of this county, at the residence
of Mr. J.Alexander, by his Honor, Mayor Valliant and
Mr. Steinberg. His Honor and Col.Storm were comrades
in war, as they are friends in peace; both belonged to
Co.D, 28th Miss. Calv., and the Mayor read the marriage
service with the force and vim of a battle order. The
Col. stood to his colors like a man, serene, but a little
shaky, as the solemn sentences were fired at him like a
shower of grape from a smoking battery. After the
ceremony by the Mayor, Mr. Steinberg administered the
Jewish Marriage rite. 8/29/1880

Mr.A.J.Paxton,Jr. and Miss Lena Wilmot, at the residence
of Dr. James Smith, near Egg's Point, by Rev.S.Archer.
10/7/1880

Mr. James C.Estill, of Wash.Co. and Miss Mattie A.Eckford
of Aberdeen, at the residence of the bride's mother in
Aberdeen, by Rev.Richard Hines, of Meridian. 9/25/1880

Mr. John Sager and Miss Agnes Caffall, both of G'ville,
at the residence of the bride's father, by Rev.Dr.Juny.
10/14/1880

Mr.J.Hamner and Miss Mattie Powell, both of G'ville,
at the residence of the bride's Uncle,Thos.Powell,
by Rev.S.Archer. 10/24/1880

Mr. Geo.Wade, of Bolivar City, and Miss Kate Curell,
of G'ville, at the Catholic Church, by Rev.Father
Bohmert. 11/10/1880

Mr. Thomas Powell and Miss Fannie Abell, at the residence
of the bride's mother, Mrs. Switzer, on Lake Lee, by
Rev.S.Archer. 11/17/1880

MARRIAGE RECORDS FROM THE GREENVILLE "TIMES"

Mr.C.S.White and Miss Manny Gray, at the Episcopal Church by Rev.Dr.Juny. 12/15/1880

Mr. Isidore Wise, of St.Joseph, La. and Miss Sarah Alder, of Barnes Landing, Miss., at the residence of the bride's parents, by D.B.O'Bannon, Esq. 1/21/1881

Mr. John Bowen and Miss Wilsey Sutton, at the Presbyterian Ch. by Rev.S.Archer. 1/27/1881

Mr. James Edwards and Miss Fannie Willis, both of G'ville at the residence of the bride's mother at Stoneville, by Rev. S.Archer. 1/31/1881

Mr.G.B.Lancaster and Miss Nannie Bedon, at the residence of Calhoun Haile, in Bolivar Co., by Rev.S.Archer. 3/22/81

Mr. Benjamin James and Miss Nannette Able, at the residence of the bride's mother, by Rev.S.Archer. 5/21/1881

Dr. Henry Robinson and Miss Mary Childs, at St.James Episcopal Church, by Rev.Dr.Juny. 5/22/1881

Mr.J.S.McNeily, and Miss M.M.Berkeley, at the residence of her father, Col.E.Berkeley, Prince Wm.Co.,Va. by Rev. Arthur Gray. 6/21/1881

Mr. Robert Ingram and Miss Virginia Watson, at the residence of the bride's father in Sunflower Co., by Rev.S.Archer. 7/26/1881

Mr.T.B.Shaw and Mrs.Belle V.Wetherbee, at the residence of the bride, in G'ville, by Rev.Mr.Gates. 9/26/1881

Mr. Walter Helm and Miss Mannie Bowen, at the St.James Episcopal Ch. by Rev.Dr.Juny. 10/25/1881

Mr.A.F.Dunbar and Miss Sallie Rucks, at St.James Episcopal Ch., by Rev.Dr.Juny. 10/26/1881

Mr. Albert Olin and Miss Bettie Shelby, at the Methodist Church by Rev. Mr.Moon. 10/27/1881

Dr. Owen Stone, of G'ville, and Miss Mary Holt, dau. of the late Dr.A.C.Holt, of New Orleans, at Summit,Miss. 11/17/1881

Dr.Wm.M.Eggleston, of Wash.Co., and Miss Sallie S.Starke of Vicksburg, at the church of the Holy Trinity,Vicksburg by the Rev.Bishop Adams. 12/6/1881

Mr.Geo.Pearce and Miss Nana Bourges, at the residence of the bride's father,Capt.E.Bourges, by Rev.Father Bohmert. They will live in Kansas City. 12/28/1881

MARRIAGE RECORDS FROM THE GREENVILLE "TIMES"

Dr. Henry B.Blackburn, of Laconda,Ark. and Miss Lucy Johnson, of Nelson Co.,Ky. at the residence of Mr.A.W. Wickliffe, by Rev.S.Archer. 12/26/1881

Mr.Geo.B.Alexander, of G'ville, and Miss Eliza Overton Green of Frankfort, Ky. in Frankfort, by Rev.E.A.Penick.12/28/

Mr.S.Brill and Miss Sarah Goldstein, at the Synagogue by Dr.Bogan, Rabbi. 1/15/1882

Mr. Peyton S.Kincaid, of Versailles,Ky. and Miss Sallie Johnson, at Aldama, the residence of the bride's father, Capt. Henry Johnson, by the Rev. S.Archer. 2/9/1882

Mr.W.K.Gildart and Miss Della Montgomery, at the residence of Mrs.E.J.D.Gray, by Rev.S.Archer. 3/8/1882

Mr. John G.Archer and Miss Pricilla W.Finlay, at the residence of the bride's mother, by Rev.S.Archer.3/12/1882

Mr. Abraham Kirshner, of G'ville, and Miss Katie Levy, of Summit, at Summit, by Rev.Dr.Bien, of Vicksburg. 3/22/1882

Mr. John J.Pettit and Miss Julia H.Peters, at the residence of the bride's mother, by Rev.S.Archer. 4/13/1882

Mr. Benjamin F.Hughes and Miss Lelia Manifold, both of G'ville, at the Methodist Ch.by Rev.E.H.Moon. 4/19/1882
          Attendants
R.W.Tilford   Claudia Walton
H.P.Raworth   M.B.Worthington
Henry Crittenden   Julia Blackburn
H.P.Hawkins   Nellie Nugent
LeRoy Percy   Carrie Bell
T.P.Finlay   Bettie McGrath

Mr. Saml.R.Dunn and Miss May Seay, at the residence of Dr.Seay, on Lake Lee, by Rev.F.A.Juny. 5/27/1882

Mr.Edward W.Scott, formerly of Warren Co.Ms. and Miss Lutie C.Mosely, of Cape Girardeau, Mo. at the residence of Dr.W.E.Satterfield, in Wash.Co.Ms, by Rev.L.Ball. 11/19/1882

Mr.R.W.Tilford and Miss Claudia Walton, both of G;ville, in the Episcopal Ch. by Rev.D.B.Ramsey. 12/20/1882
          Attendants
Mr.John Griffin   Miss Carrie Worthington
Mr. Henry Crittenden Miss Lucy Robinson
Mr. Thomas P.Finlay Miss Laura Nelson
Mr.Sam Worthington   Miss Sadie Urquhart
Mr.H.P.Hawkins   Miss Estelle Pintard

Mr.A.G.Paxton, of Wash.Co. and Miss Mary H.Noland, of Warren Co. at the residence of Mr.Hal Noland, in Warren Co.,by Rev.Mr.Cross, of the Episc.Ch. 12/12/1882

MARRIAGE RECORDS FROM THE GREENVILLE "TIMES"

Mr.C.Steffgen and Miss Minnie Polle, of Port Gibson,(MS.) in G'ville, by Rev.S.Archer. 12/17/1882

Mr.J.W.Scott and Miss Fannie A.Powell, at the residence of Mrs. T.W.Powell, in Wash.Co. by Rev.S.Archer. 12/7/1882

Mr.Arthur Whitehead and Miss Mollie James, at the same time and place, by the same. (double wedding).12/7/1882

Mr.Wm.Beach and Miss Eugenia Tamplin, at the residnece of Mr.E.B.McDaniel, by Rev.S.Archer. 12/19/1882

Mr.J.L.Lee and Miss Jenny Flowers, both of G'ville, at the residence of Mrs.E.J.D.Gray, by Rev.S.Archer. 1/16/83

Mr.E.G.Marshall and Miss Bertha Waldauer, at the Synagogue by Rev.Dr.Bogen. 1/21/1883

Mr.Max Lemler and Miss Bertha Landau, at the Synagogue by Rev.Dr.Bogen. 1/23/1883

Attendents

C.E.Levingston   Malinda Weiss
L.E.Goldsmith   Rachel Alexander
Jacob Scott   Mollie Lewy
L.Fiest   Sarah Eckstone
H.Levy   Mamie Scott
J.Sherman   Lena Wineberg

Mr.Morris Rachelman, of Burn City, and Miss Mamie Scott of G'Ville, at the Synagogue by Rev.Jos.Bogen. 2/11/1883

Mr.C.H.Cofer and Miss Fannie Burdett, both of Wash.Co. at the residence of Miss Annie Lampkin, aunt of the bride, by Rev.S.Archer. 3/11/1883

Mr. Emile Aydam and Miss Lula Caffal, at the Episc. Parsonage, by Rev.D.B.Ramsey. 5/9/1883

Mr. Henry Levy and Miss Bertha Goldman, at the Synag. by Rev.Dr.Bogen. 5/24/1883

Mr.JohnHolmes and Miss Emma Sessford, at the residence of Mr.F.J.Craig, the bride's uncle, by the Rev.S.Archer 5/16/1883

Mr.Leopold Schlesinger and Miss Aline Koufman, both formerly of G'ville, at the residence of Mr.Sam Hirsch, in Memphis, by Rev. Dr.Samfield. 5/27/1883

Mr.Doswell Walker and Miss Laura Nelson, at the Presb. Ch. by Rev.S.Archer. The bride is a native of this community, and Mr.Walker is the popular conductor for the Ga.& Pacific R.R. 6/19/1883

MARRIAGE RECORDS FROM THE GREENVILLE "TIMES"

Mr.H.S.Magruder and Miss Bettie Lewis McGrath, at St.
James Church, by Rev.D.B.Ramsey. 6/25/1883
    Attendants
    Mr.R.W.Magruder   Miss Mamie McGrath
    Mr. J.H.Moore   Miss Lena McCall
    Mr. Hy. Crittenden   Miss Carrie Worthington
    Mr.LeRoy Percy   Miss Tenie Bell
The bride has been a resident of G'ville since her childhood, and Mr.Magruder is a native of Port Gibson.

Dr.D.C.Montgomery and Mrs.Mamie Simś, at the residence of Mrs.A.B.Finlay, by Rev.S.Archer. 7/26/1883

Mr.Thomas P.Finlay and Miss Julia Blackburn, at the residence of Mr.A.B.Carson, by Rev.S.Archer. 9/4/1883

Mr.R.Lee Clack and Miss Bettie M.Edgar, in Vicksburg, by Rev.Dr.Sansom. 9/4/1883

Mr.Thomas Worthington, of G'ville, and Miss Rosine Adams, of New Orleans, at the residence of the bride's parents in New Orleans, by Rev.J.Subileau, of St. Augustine's Church. 10/25/1883.

Mr.E.B.McDaniel,Jr. and Miss Josephine Axman, at the residence of the bride's mother, by Rev.S.Archer.11/22/83

Mr. John A.Rowells, of Memphis and Miss Emma Laws Raily, at the residence of Dr.N.C.Skinner, by Rev.D.B.Ramsey. They will live in Ocalla, Fla. 2/10/1884

Mr.D.B.Bell and Mrs. Lawson, at the Kossuth House, by Rev.F.C.Bohmert. 2/10/1884

Dr.Dedrick Hood and Mrs. Mary L.Page on Silver Lake, by Rev. J.W.Price. 5/15/1884

Mr. Jacob Scott and Miss Mollie Lewy, at the residence of Mr.S.Pepperman, by Rev.Dr.Bogen. 6/11/1884

Mr. Robert Watts and Miss Henrietta Woods, at the residence of Mr. Thomas McRaven, on Indian Bayou,Sunf.Co., by Rev. S.Archer. 7/11/1884

Mr.Robert Lacey and Miss Cora Kanatzer, at the residence of H.F.Kriger, by Rev.S.Archer. 7/13/1884

Mr.J.A.Cannon and Miss Margaret T.Shanahan, in St.Joseph's Catholic Church by Rev.Father Bohmert. 7/23/1884

Mr.A.B.Nance, of Wash.Co. and Miss M.W.Berkeley, of Prince Wm.Co.,Va.at the residence of the bride's father, Col. Edmund Berkeley, in Prince Wm.Co.Va.by Rev.A.Gray. 9/6/84

MARRIAGE RECORDS FROM THE GREENVILLE "TIMES"

Dr.J.L.Young, of G'ville, and Miss Mary Killian, of Mayersville, Miss. at the residence of the bride's father, Mr.Mark Killian, one of Mayersville's most thriving merchants, besides being a large planter in Issa.Co. by Rev. S.Archer. 10/28/1884

Mr.Jacob Sherman and Mrs. Eva Silverberg, at the residence of Mr.I.Isenberg, by Rabbi Bogen. 11/20/1884

Mr. Lep Lewy and Miss Sarah Eckstone, at the Synagogue by Rabbi Bogen. 11/25/1884

Mr. James W.Goodwin and Miss Ida A.Beck, both of this county, at the residence of Mrs.E.N.Wheatly, in Arcola, by Rev.Mr.Scrugg. 12/6/1884

Mr. JohnJ.Harty, of G'ville, and Miss Katie Ryan, of Port Gibson, at the Catholic Church in Port Gibson, by Father Lennan. 11/25/1884

Mr.John Avery and Miss Sarah Aulder, at the residence of Mr.Avery, by Rev.S.Archer. 12/24/1884

Mr.Thomas Sutton and Miss Fleta Avery, at the residence of Mr.Avery, by Rev.S.Archer. 12/24/1884

Mr.A.D.Pace and Miss Carrie Bell, BOTH OF G'ville, at the residence of Dr.D.C.Montgomery, by Rev.R.M.Standifer. 1/14/1885

Mr.G.S.Davison and Miss Belle Roy, at the residence of the bride's father in G'ville, by Rev.S.Archer. 1/21/1885

Mr.T.E.LaFoe and Miss Nettie Swain, at the residence of the bride's father, on Deer Creek, by Rev.S.Archer. 1/23/1885

Mr. James Ward, of Wash.Co., son of Mr.G.V.Ward, and Miss Nutt, of Natchez, at St.Mary's Cathedral, Natchez. 1/24/85

Mr.B.N.Rucks and Miss Lee B.Hunter, at the Presbyterian Church in G'ville, by Rev.S.Archer. 1/20/1885

Mr.Herman G.Franklin and Miss Rachel Levey, at the synagogue, by Rev.Dr.Bogen. 1/25/1885

Mr.W.N.Moore and Miss Keith, both of Wash.Co., at the residence of the bride's father,Mr.S.N.Keith, by W.D. Ferriss, Esq. 2/1/1885

Mr.A.J.Aldridge and Miss Hannah Paxton, at the residence of the bride's father, Mr.A.J.Paxton,By Rev.Archer.2/10/85

MARRIAGE RECORDS FROM THE GREENVILLE "TIMES"

Mr. Oscar Ignace and Miss Belle Lemle, at the Synagogue, by Rabbi Bogen. 2/14/1885

Mr.A.Fares and Miss Eudora Moseby, both of this county, at the residence of Mr. Overby, at Overby Station, by Rev.Joseph D.Newsom. 1/13/1885

Dr.W.C.Miller and Miss Jennie Gravitt, both of this county at the residence of the bride's father, by Rev.J.D.Newsom. 2/12/1885

Mr. Henry Crittenden and Miss Loula Blackburn, at the residence of Mr.A.B.Carson, by Rev.S.Archer. 2/16/1885

Dr.W.M.Bagley and Mrs.Jennie Joyes at the residence of Mr.J.D.Smith, by Rev.S.Archer. 2/22/1885

Mr.E.W.Baker and Miss Cora Lee Vaughn, at Wayside, by Rev.S.Archer. 3/3/1885

Mr.Albert Vormus and Miss Pauline E.Levy, dau. of Mr.E. Levy, of Summit, at the Synagogue in Summit, by Rev. Dr.BOGEN. 2/18/1885

Mr. Horace C.Brashear and Miss Mary Love, at the residence of the bride's father on William's Bayou, By Rev.S.ARcher. 3/11/1885

Mr.Berry Batz and Miss Addie Weilenman, at the bride's residence near Stoneville, by Rev.R.M.Standifer. 5/29/1885

Mr. Jonte Ecuin, of New Orleans, and Miss Willie E.Sykes, at the residence of the bride's parents in Columbus. Mr. Equin is well known in G'ville where he lived for a number of yrs. 4/28/1885

Mr.Ferdinand Strauss and Miss Lulu Woolf, at the Synagogue by Rabbi Bogen. 8/12/1885

Mr.Robert Somerville, of G'ville, and Miss Nellie Nugent, eldest dau.of Col.W.L.Nugent of Jackson, at the residence of the bride's father in Jackson, by Dr.C.G.Andrews.

Mr.Sam T.Rucks and Miss Alice Gray, in St.James Epis.Ch. by Rev. Wm.Cross. 10/14/1885
               Attendants

W.A.Percy,Jr.	Miss Nellie Gray
O.B.Crittenden	Miss Lillie Gray
Joe G. Webb	Miss Carrie Worthington
Tom F. Davis	Miss Lady Percy
Hal Rucks	Miss Lommie Webb
William Hood	Miss Fanny Valliant.

Mr. J.C.Brumley and Mrs. Mattie A.Craig, at the residence of the bride, by Rev.S.Archer. 10/13/1885

MARRIAGE RECORDS FROM THE GREENVILLE "TIMES"

Mr. Archer Harmon, Louisville, Ky. and Miss Mary Livingston Lee, of G'ville, at St.James Ch. in G'ville, by Rev.Wm.Cross. Gen.Ferguson, her brother-in-law and Guardian, gave the bride away. 11/4/1885

Mr. JohnM.Moore, of G'ville, and Miss Lucy D.McRaven, of Jackson, at St.Andrews Episcopal Church,Jackson,by Rev. Dr.Short. 11/10/1885

Mr.T.F.Davis, of G'ville, and Miss Eliza Cocks, of Yazoo City, at the residence of the bride's father, Col. Phil Cocks, in Yazoo City, by Rev.Mr.McCracken. 11/10/1885

Mr.T.L.Skinner and Miss E.L.Newsom, at the residence of Mr.A.P.Watson, on Deer Creek, by Rev.S.Archer. 12/22/1885

Mr. Walter Johnson, of Iowa, and Miss Emma Peak, at the residence of the bride's father at Grand Lake, Chicot Co.,Ark., by Rev.S.Archer. The event was attened by a host of relatives and friends of the bridal couple, members of one of the largest and most popular family connections in the valley. Attendants were Misses Annie and Lydia Worthington, Lillie Elley, Linnie Johnson, and Fanny Valliant; groomsmen, Messrs. Sylvester Johnson, Leroy and Frank Valliant, Drs.Boisliniere and Beal, of St.Louis. 1/7/1886

Mr. Joseph Winston and Miss Emma Waldauer, at the Synagogue, by Rev.Dr.Bogen. 1/10/1886

Mr.C.J.Hodges and Miss Zilphia Shaw, in Arcola, at the residence of Mr.Chas.Bradley, by Rev.E.E.King. 1/27/1886

Mr. Britton L.Lee and Miss Jennie O.Swain, at the residence of the bride's father, in Stoneville, by Rev. S.Archer. 1/28/1886

Mr. Henry Dryfus and Miss Bertha Hirsch, at the residence of the bride's mother in G'ville, by Rev.Dr. Bogen. 2/7/1886

Mr. George Irwin, of Chicot Co.,Ark. and Mrs. Emma Crockett, at the residence of Mrs. Clifton, by Rev. R.M.Standifer. 2/10/1886

Mr.C.J.Bogrman, of Lake Cormorant, Miss. and Miss Maggie Quinn, dau. of Dr.Quinn, of Arcola, at Overby, Miss, by Rev. E.E.King, of G'ville. 2/23/1886

Mr.W.B.Powell and Miss Minnie Switzer, at the residence of the bride's mother, on Lake Lee, by Rev.Archer. 2/25/86

MARRIAGE RECORDS FROM THE GREENVILLE "TIMES"

Mr. Johnson Allen, of Lexington,Ky. and Miss Lily Ely, at the residence of the bride's mother,Mrs. Dudley, on Lake Wash., by Rev. Mr.Standifer. 3/18/1886

Mr.W.T.Harris and Miss Alice Grant, in G'ville, by Rev. E.E.King. 3/25/1886

Mr. Morris Rosenstock and Miss Minnie Peters, at the residence of the bride's mother, Mrs. Peters, by Rev. S.Archer. 4/9/1886

Mr. Louis Vormus, of G'ville, and Miss Celestine Mock, of Summit, at the Synagogue at Summit, by Dr. Bogen of G'ville. 4/7/1886

Mr.K.P.Attson and Miss Virginia Standeford, at the residence of Mr. Wm.Erwin, on Lake Wash., BY Rev.S.Archer. 5/6/1886

Mr.J.E.Vaughn and Miss Josie F.Scurlock, both of G'ville, in the Baptist Church, by Rev.E.E.King. 5/20/1886

Mr.C.W.Roche and Miss Mary A.Bennett, both of G'ville, at the residence of Mrs.McMurray, by Rev.E.E.King. 5/31/86

Mr.J.W.Thompson, of Paris,Tenn. and Miss Frances Harvey, of G'ville, in Memphis, by Rev.David Sessums. 6/8/1886

Mr. Wm.R.Harvey, of G'ville, and Miss Addie McCulloch, of Murfreesboro, Tenn. at Murfreesboro. 6/15/1886

Mr.Maurice W.Shaw, of G'ville, and Miss Mary Barsley, of Iowa, at the residence of and by the Rev.E.E.King. 7/8/86

Mr.Wm.Mercer Green,Jr. of G'ville, and Miss Drusilla Maria Billingsley, of Warrensberg, Mo., at the residence of Mr. and Mrs. Edward Billingsley, the bride's parents, in Warrenberg, by the Rev.S.H.Green, of St.Louis. The hearty congratulations of the Professor's many friends await his return home with his charming young bride, who is a sister of Mr.G.E.Billingsley. 7/24/1886

Mr. Charles A.Heard and Miss Mary Bell Watt, both of Wash.Co., at the residence of Mr. Hartson, the bride's step-father, on the Bogue, by Rev.E.E.King. 9/1/1886

Mr. Wm.L.Barkley, of Lexington,Ky. and Miss Pru Blackburn, of G'ville, at the residence of the bride's mother, Mrs. A.B.Carson. 9/22/1886

Mr.G.McD.Hampton and Miss Eloise Urquhart, both prominent and popular members of G'ville's young society, at the residence of Mrs.Urquhart, the bride's mother, by Rev. Wm.Cross. 11/10/1886

MARRIAGE RECORDS FROM THE GREENVILLE "TIMES"

Mr.A.K.Parker and Miss Minnie Vaughn, at Wayside, at the residence of the bride's father, by Rev.S.Archer. 11/18/86

Mr.W.H.Johnson and Miss Lizzie Ross, at the residence of Mr.A.B.Carson, the bride's Uncle, by Rev.S.Archer. 12/11/1886

Mr.W.L.Hay, of Texas, and Miss Mollie Swain, of Deer Creek, at the residence of the bride's father on Deer Creek, by Rev.S.Archer. 12/8/1886

Mr. Walter L.Sanders, of Rolla, Mo. and Miss Irene Gildart, at the home of the bride in Woodville (Ms) by Rev.T.W.Turner. Miss Irene is the sister of Messrs. W.K. and Thomas Gildart, and has many friends in G'ville. 12/23/1886

Mr.Thomas Canada and Miss S.E.Waters, at the residence of the bride's father in G'ville, by Rev.E.E.King. 1/9/1887

Mr. John Bernard Schulte, of Philadelphia, Pa. and Miss Mary Connell, of Bolivar Co.(Ms.), at the Catholic Ch. in G'ville, by Father P.J.Korstenbrock. 1/20/1887

Mr. Walter Lucy, of Helena, Ark. and Miss Bennie Hebron of Wash.Co. at the bride's home, by Rev.Archer. 1/26/1887

Mr.E.Kellner, Jr. of G'ville, and Miss Sallie E.Shines, of Durant, (Ms.) in Durant, by Rev.T.G.Ramsey.

Mr.J.Price Wright, of Frankfort, Ky. and Miss Mamie R. McGrath, of G'ville, at St.James Church, G'ville, by Rev. Wm.Cross. They will live in Henderson, Ky. 3/8/1887

Mr. Carl L.E.Dreschaw and Miss Maria K.Jobe, at the residence of Mrs. O'Conner, G'ville, by Rev.King. 4/30/1887

Mr. Walter Sillers, of Bolivar Co. and Miss Florence Warfield, of Lexa, Ark. at the residence of the bride's Uncle, Col.Graves, in Lexa, Phillips Co., Ark. by Rev. S.Archer. 4/28/1887

Mr. Baxter Thomas and Miss Pattie Connell, In Bolivar Co., by Rev.R.M.Standifer. 5/5/1887

Mr. John S.Ingram and Miss Mary C.Weilenman, both of Wash.Co., by Rev.R.M.Standifer. 5/17/1887

Mr. Joseph Addison Massey, of New Orleans and Miss Emma Belle Clary of Wash.Co., at the residence of Mr. M.L. Morgan on Silver Lake, by Rev.S.Archer...Mr.Massey was one of the volunteers who came to the relief of the suffering people in G'ville in 1878.(Yellow-fever) 7/18/1887

MARRIAGE RECORDS FROM THE GREENVILLE "TIMES"

Mr. W.W. Richardson and Miss Louise Rucks, dau. of the late Judge James Rucks, at the residence of the bride's sister, Mrs. Canfield, in Friar's Point, Coahoma Co. (Ms.) 8/10/1887

Capt. Daniel Williams and Miss Lovey Smedes, at Mississippi City, the ceremony was performed by Rev. Father Chevalier of Biloxi. The bride is the dau. of Gen. Chas. E. Smedes. The groom is a prominent planter near G'ville. 11/--/1887

Mr. John L. Griffin and Miss Anna Bell Stockman of New Orleans, at Trinity Church of that city, by Rev. Davis Sessums. 11/21/1887

Dr. William B. Martin and Miss Georgia Smith, at the church near Indianola, by Rev. S. Archer. 11/23/1887

Mr. Chas. Casey and Miss May Morson, at the residence of the bride's father, by Rev. S. Archer. 12/6/1887

Mr. C.M. Ozburn, of Atlanta, Ga. and Miss Sadie Taylor, of G'ville, Miss, at the residence of the bride's father. 12/15/1887

Mr. Edwin T. Carr and Miss Lilly B. Scott, at the home of the bride's father on Lake Lee, by Rev. J.A. Bowen. 12/--/1887

Mr. Robt. Reoche and Mrs. Lula Van Norman, both of G'ville, at the home of the bride's mother. 1/4/1888

Mr. S.W. Gidden and Miss Emma Hill, at the home of the bride's father at Lake Wash. Landing, by Rev. Archer. 1/12/1888

Mr. Orlando B. Crittenden and Mrs. Julia B. Finlay, at the home of the bride's mother in G'ville, by Rev. S. Archer. 1/12/1888

Mr. Basil B. Gordon, of Birmingham, Ala. and Miss Fannie Valliant of G'ville, at the St. James Episcopal Church, by Rev. Wm. Cross. 1/26/1888

Mr. John L. Hebron, Jr. and Miss Nettie Porter, of Florence, Ala. at the Presby. Ch. of that city, by Rev. M.L. Frierson. 3/15/1888

Mr. Jacob Laser, of Little Rock, Ark. and Miss Bertha Lemle, dau of Mr. D. Lemle of G'ville, at the Synagogue by Rabbi Bogen. 3/18/1888

Mr. Elijah Wray and Miss Leila F. Atkinson, at the residence of Mr. Barlow, in G'ville, by Rev. Archer. 4/12/1888

MARRIAGE RECORDS FROM THE GREENVILLE "TIMES"

Mr. Walker Percy of G'ville and Miss Mary Pratt DeBardleben dau. of Mr.H.F.De Bardleben, one of Birmingham's most wealthy and influential citizens; Dr.Beard of the Church of the Advent officiated. 1/--/1888

Mr.H.R.Wiggins, of Bolivar Co. and Miss Nellie Gray, of G'ville, at the St.James Episcopal Church, by Rev. Wm. Cross. 4/25/1888

Mr. J.A.Crawford of Los Angeles, Cal. and Miss Heathman of Sunflower Co., by Rev.J.S.Bowen. 5/15/1888

Mr. Alfred Ferguson and Miss M.L.Wilkerson, at Mrs. Herrington's in G'ville, by Rev.S.Archer. 5/26/1888

Mr.C.H.Florian, of San Antonio,Tex. and Miss Georgia Starling, of Lake Wash. at the Episc. Ch., by Rev.Cross. 6/20/1888

Mr.J.B.Hebron and Miss Nannie Burdette, at the home of the bride's mother, by Rev.W.Cross. 6/30/1888

Mr. Fred Rath and Miss Annie Muller, at the St.James Episcopal Church, by Rev.W.Cross. 12/19/1888.

Mr. Neville B.Scott and Miss Bessie Thomas, at Grace Episcopal Church, by Rev.W.Cross, in Rosedale. 12/20/1888

Mr. Hugh Alexander and Miss Polly Nurse, at the Methodist Church in G'ville, by Rev.E.E.King, ass. by Rev.R.M. Standifer. 12/20/1888

Mr. Lawrence T.Wade and Miss Lillie Gray, of G'ville, at the residence of Mr.S.T.Rucks, near Leland, by Rev.W. Cross. 1/15/1889

Mr.J.D.Lee, of Leesburg, and Mrs. Hattie Connor, of G'ville, Rev.E.E.King officiating. 1/15/1888 (1889?)

Mr.C.R.Wing and Miss Jennie O.Lashley, at the residence of the bride's mother on Silver Lake, Wash. Co., by Rev. S.Archer. 1/15/1889

Mr.M.Wood, of Hollandale and Miss Pink Bowles of this city, at All Sts. Church in Grenada, Ms. by Rev.T.B. Lawson. 2/28/1889

Mr. David Linnell, compositor on the TIMES, and Miss Belle Farmer, by Rev.E.E.King. 4/1/1889

Mr. Henry Gottlich and Miss Gussie Orgler, at the residence of Mr.and Mrs.M.Wachsman, Rabbi Bogen officiating. The Happy couple will make their home in Winterville. 4/13/8

MARRIAGE RECORDS FROM THE GREENVILLE "TIMES"

Mr. Jack Beardsley and Miss Lucy Paul, both of this city by the Rev.E.E.King. 5/5/1889

Mr. John Murphree, of Nashville amd Miss Lenore Seay, at the residence of the bride's father, by Rev.Archer.5/7/89

Mr.H.C.Anderson and Miss Emma Burdette, at the home of the bride's mother, Mrs.M.Burdette, Whitehall Plt., by Rev.J.A.Bowen.

Mr. John Crouch and Miss Lucy Ryalls, at the home of Mrs. Ryalls, Hollandale, Ms., By Rev.J.H.Shumaker. 6/1/1889

Mr.Thomas H.Collins and Miss P.Evy Metcalfe, by Rev. Wm. Cross. 6/12/1889

Mr. Robt.B.Sims and Miss Pattie C.Jones, both of G'ville, at the home of the bride's parents, by Rev.W.Cross.7/2/89

Mr.W.Mackall Dermott, of Baltimore, and Miss E.Corrine Sterling, of Lake Wash., at St.James Ch.,by Rev.Cross. 7/3/1889

Mr.H.C.Jolly and Mrs.Eliza Andrew, both of G'ville, at the residence of the bride, byRev.E.E.King. 7/4/1889

Mr. Thomas M.Sleator and Miss Annie Higgins, at the home of the bride, by Rev.Father Korstenbroek. 7/21/1889

Mr.M.W.Shaw and Miss A.Melville Love, both of G'ville, at the home of Capt. McBride, the bride's Uncle, by Rev. J.A.Bowen. 8/1/1889

Mr.J.A.Carmen and Miss Alice Turner, at the Dotson House, by Rev.J.A.Bowen. 8/4/1889

Mr.L.C.Dulaney and Miss Carrie Harris, at the residence of Capt.Harris in Issa.Co., by Rev.S.Archer. 8/5/1889

Mr. Wm.Connelly, of Talla.Co. and Miss Virginia Davidson of Wash.Co. at the home of the bride's father. 9/1/1889

Dr.Grainger of Paris,Tenn. and Miss Nellie Corrigan, of G'ville, at Monteagle, Miss.(?) 9/28/1889

Mr.W.H.Hall and Miss NoraK.Gravit, at the residence of the bride's father at Baird,by Rev.King. 10/3/1889

Mr.P.C.Chapman and Miss Cornelia Paxton, at the residence of Col A.J.Paxton, the bride's father. 10/23/1889

Mr.Frank Griffin and Mrs. Kate C.Champion, of Bolivar Co. at the residence of the bride's mother at Malvern,Ark. 11/16/1889

ABSTRACTS FROM THE "GREENVILLE TIMES":

DEATH NOTICES*

Elisha, eldest son of A.J. & H.M.Paxton, aged 14 years. 9/15/1868

Near Lake Washington, Kate R.,wife of Daniel A.Love and daughter of Jas.M.& Eliza Sutton, aged 34. 9/16/1864

On Mulberry Plantation Caroline, daughter of Samuel A.& Mary S.Holmes, aged 12. Sept. 1868
Henry H.Miller, deputy sheriff and formerly a Confederate soldier in a Texas Regiment. 10/10/1868

At the home of her father W.P.Montgomery, Mary Catherine, wife of W.L.Nugent. 10/24/1868.

On Black Bauou, William Bernard. 10/29/1868.

Body of Mary E., wife of A.G.Carter arrives by boat from New Orleans, where she died. Oct. 1868.

At home of her grandmother, Mrs. H.B.Theobald, Ruth Theobald Blanton, daughter of W.C. & Georgiana Blanton, aged 16. 11/7/1868

Sallie Trigg, Dau. of W.R.&Nancy Trigg, aged 4. 11/9/1868

MRS. Bettie A.Mears, wife of Dr.JohnL.Mears, at home on Deer Creek. Nov 1868.

Hon.Chas. S.Morehead, former Gov. of Ky. and a prominent citizen of Wash.Co. Resolutions were passed when the Probate court met on Dec. 27,1868 and signed by W.L. Nugent,J.H.Nelson,S.W.Ferguson. 12/22/1868.

At home of her son, M.R.Sanders, Mrs.M.A.Sanders, who was born in Ky. in 1818 and had come in 1866 from Hinds Co. to Wash.Co. 4/3/1869

At residence of G.P.Worthington on June 4 Aaron Wickliffe in his 73rd yr. Burial at home of Mrs. Amanda Worthington (Wayside) on Lake Lee. 6/5/1869

Mrs. Lucy A.Carter, aged 30 yrs.,leaving husband and 4 small children. 6/3/1869

Susie Hill, dau. of Dr.J.L.Griffin. 6/6/1869.

Bessie Howe, infant dau. of N.T.& Bessie Nelson. (Mr.& Mrs. Nelson later reared a child who was known as Jessie Nelson, probably 10 yrs. younger than their own child.

Indexed by Ms. Stockwell, from copies of the Times that are no longer available. "The Stockwell Papers".

DEATH NOTICES FROM THE GREENVILLE "TIMES".

James H. King, aged 34. 10/22/1869

Col. George R. Fall, 11/29/1869

W.J. Griffin, aged 28. 1/9/1870

George D. Prentice, aged 68. 1/9/70

Mary McLin Bryan, wife of E.J. Bryan, aged 20, at home on Lake Washington. 1/11/1870

Capt. Geo.T. Blackburn, leaving wife and children. 2/28/70

At Glenora Landing, Washington Co., Geo. Fearn, inf. son of P.A. & Lucy Strouecker.

At plantation of Mr. Archer, Mr. Hunsicker. Deceased was old, well-known and estimable citizen. 3/15/1871

At residence in Washington Co. Mrs. Elizabeth L. Carter, in her 64th year. 7/9/1871.

Mr. Harvell--he is the person who killed the negro man on Belle Aire Plantation some time ago. 7/13/1871

In Greenville, Mrs. Evie H. Comstock, wife of E.J. Comstock and daughter of Mrs. Myra Smith, aged 21. Lengthy obit by Rev. W.W. Drake. 3/6/1869

James Walter, inf. son of E.J. & the late Evie Comstock. 6/30/1969.

Princeton. Resolutions on death of Henry M. Muse signed by Thos. H. Johns & W.F. Shannon. 5/5/1869

Rev. Wm. Winans Drake. He was born in Jefferson Co., Ms. 12 Nov. 1843. During latter part of the War he was Chaplain in Darden's Battery. He came to Washington Co. in 1866 and settled in Greenville in 1867. 9/27/1870

On Black Bayou, Mrs Sarah A. (Brothers) Kirk, wife of Capt. A.M. Kirk. 12/15/1870.

Anna Hunter, inf. dau. of Mr. & Mrs. W.G. Yerger. 3/29/1871.

At Wildwood, Gen. A.W. McAllister, aged upward of 70, one of oldest residents of county, having been here over 40 years. 4/5/1871

In Greenville, Mrs. Lucy McMeekin, wife of Lawrence McMeekin, aged 26, dau. of Thos. B. Overton, of Louisville, Ky. 4/7/1871.

DEATH NOTICES FROM THE GREENVILLE "TIMES"

At Fredericksburg,Va., Wm.C.Blanton, aged 38, native & citizen of Greenville. Leaves wife,3 children, and widowed mother. 4/18/1869.

Wm.H.Hunter, formerly of Jackson, in his 32nd year. 7/24/1871.

At residence of Judge Trigg, Mr.McChain, a native of Va. 2/16/1871.

Alexander, Jonas, about 19 yrs. of age, and a native of Dinenger, Dept. Bas Rhin, France, of congestion. 10/3/1874

MEISNER,C.F., one of the original settlers. 10/3/1874.

Small,John, an old citizen of this neighborhood. 10/10/187

Pogle,Eliza G., aged 2 yrs.,dau.of F.A.&Julia A.Pogle. 10/9/1874

Heath,Willis,age 2 yrs.& 6 mo., son of John A.& Louisa Heath. 10/31/1874

Chotard, Mrs.Mary A., widow of the late J.C.Chotard, at Barnardiston, Washington Co. 5/6/1875.

Jackson, Hattie, dau. of Dr.D.C.(D) Jackson and granddaughter of Mrs. Ann Halsey. 5/16/1875.

Bott,Mrs. Elizabeth F., aged 52. The decd. was born in Chesterfield Co.,Va. March 25,1823, and resided in Tenn. until her removal with her husband to this state. 5/10/75

Randolph,Elizabeth Landon, aged 2 yrs.& 8mo., second dau. of Capt. Wm.F. & Nannie B.Randolph, at Woodstock Plt., Wash.Co. 12/10/1874

Brown,T.L., of Wetherbee & Brown Hardware Co. 1/9/1875

Kirkland,Mrs. T.A., of pnuemonia. 1/16/1875

Fox,Dr., a native of Warren Co. and son of Rev.J.Fox of that county. 6/9/1875.

MERRIL,N.,of Lake Providence, La. at the La Grange Plt. 6/8/1875

Comstock,Elisha J., aged 31, at the residence of his brother, L.J.Comstock, at Bergen Point, N.J. of consumption. 6/13/1875.

Beck,Mrs. Mary A., wife of J.G.Beck. 7/15/1875

DEATH NOTICES FROM THE GREENVILLE "TIMES"

Williams, Grant, at Glenora Place, of paralysis. 7/17/1875

Archer, Major Robt. H., near Wash. City, father of W.H. Archer and Mrs. Mary Brown of this place. 8/11/1875

Davis, Wm. J., aged 42, born Wellsburg, Va. He served through the War as a soldier of the Confederate Army, in the 21st Miss. Reg. & Rice's Battery. 9/28/1875

Estill, Nellie Virginia, age 1 yr, 10 mo. 24 days, eldest dau of J.C. & R.C. Estill. 9/29/1875.

Sutton, Mrs. Laura, wife of J.M. Sutton, for many yrs. a resident of this county. 10/15/1875.

Collier, Patton Knox, aged 23, eldest son of Col. J.N. & S.C. Collier. 10/7/1875

Peters, Dr., at his residence at Auburn. He was an old and highly respected citizen. 12/10/1875.

Estill, Mrs. R.C., aged 28, wife of James C. Estill, at the residence on Deer Creek. 12/10/1875.

McMurry, J.J., of this place. 2/7/1876

Moyse, Harriet, aged 20 yrs. neice of Leon Moyse. 5/24/76

Hammet, Capt. J.R., in Central Montgomery Co. Va. of pneumonia. 3/29/1876

Sanders, Carrie J. in Leota. 6/1/1876.

Mayer, Sigmund, aged 24, at Stoneville. 8/29/1876

Yager, Lula C., only dau. of Andrew & Margaret Yager. 8/30/1867.

Robinson, Cam M., son of Mrs. J.H. Young, of Riverton, Bolivar Co. Ms. 8/28/1876

Archer, Bettie, inf. dau. of Rev. S. & Anna P. Archer. 8/24/1876.

Trigg, Davis B., Inf. Son of W.R. Trigg. 8/31/1876.

Small, Wm. H., aged about 12 yrs. 8/30/1876.

Hudson, John S., of this county. 9/5/1876.

Quinlan, J.L., for several yrs. an officer of the wharf-boat. 9/9/1876.

Rucks, Mrs. S.J. 9/20/1876

DEATH NOTICES FROM THE GREENVILLE "TIMES"

Medley, Geo.B., at Hot Springs, Ark. of Liverpool & the Greenville Cotton Seed Mills. 9/24/1876

Melchor, Henry, of this county. 8/24/1876.

Kanatzer, John, for the past 10 yrs. a citizen of this neighborhood. 10/6/1876.

Montgomery, W.P., aged 77. He was born 1800 in the State of S.C. He came to this county in 1828, where he has ever since resided as a planter. He was one of the oldest citizens of our county, and leaves very few behind him who like himself participated in its earliest history. 10/4/1876.

Schlesinger, Isadore, aged 20 mo., inf. son of L.& H. Schlesinger. 10/20/1876

McNeily, May Percy, at Hot Springs, Ark. As a wife, dau., sister, & friend, her memory will be revered. 10/22/1876.

Schlesinger, Rachel, aged 3, dau of Louis & Huldah Schlesinger. 11/29/1876.

Mosby, John B. at his residence in Wash.Co. 12/11/1876.

McMeekin, Mrs. of pneumonia. 1/5/1877

Harrison,Wm.H. aged about 50, for 5 or 6 yrs past a resident of this place. 3/1/1877.

Forniquet, Col. E.P., at the Grand Central Hotel, of pneumonia. He was an old citizen of Miss; he resided in Summit, but he had landed interests in this portion of the state, to which he was attending at the time of his death. 3/6/1877.

Burt, C.H. aged 37, a native of new York, but for many years a resident of Miss., at the plantation of J.Q.Wills 4/16/1877.

Black, Moses B., founder and pastor of Mt.Horeb Colored Baptist Church. 4/26/1877

Frank, a French barber who had been living in Greenville for 5 or 6 years. 4/28/1877.

Brooks,Hon. Jos., a post master of this place, after a protracted illness. 5/5/1877

Beck, Cora May, aged about 7 yrs., dau. of J.G.Beck. 7/18/77

DEATH NOTICES FROM THE GREENVILLE "TIMES"

Brown, Tommy, little son of Mr. Sam Brown, drowned. 7/12/1877

Davenport, Robert, aged 67, a contractor and builder. He came to this county in 1855. 8/9/1877

Davis, Walter E., at Refuge. He came to this county from London, England, and has resided here for nearly 3 yrs. 8/20/1877

Goldstein, Leon, aged 21, at Skipwith, of congestive chill. 8/24/1877

McDowell, E.P., at the residence of his brother in Burlington, N.J. His remains were taken to Baltimore, his native city, for interment, under the direction of Odd Fellows, of which he was a past Grand. He was a citizen of Wash. Co. Ms. for many yrs., and of our town from its first settlement. 9/18/1877.

Alexander, Esther, youngest dau. of Jacob Alexander. 10/26/77

Montgomery, Charles, aged 19, at the residence of Dr. D.C. Montgomery. The deceased was the son of Eugene Montgomery of Bolivar Co. (Ms) and the grandson of ex-Gov. Chas. Clark. 11/29/1877

Clark, Charles, Ex-Gov. and Chancellor, at his plantation in Bolivar Co. 12/18/1877.

Courtney, Mrs. Jane E., at Oakland, Plantation on Deer Creek, a widow of the late John Courtney, an old and highly respected citizen of this county. 12/25/1877

Schmalholz, F.X., aged 48. 1/2/1878

Wilne, Geo. P., at his residence on Deer Creek, of pneumonia. 12/25/1877

Glidden, H.A., about 60 yrs. old, at Skipwith, Issaquena Co. He was a native of Malta, but had lived in Greenville for 20 yrs. No relatives or connections. 2/7/1878

Campbell, W.R., aged 37, at his residence in Rosedale, Bolivar Co. (Ms) of which county he was Sheriff. He was a native of this county, where his mother and sisters now live. He leaves a wife and 5 little children. 4/22/78

MORRISSY, John, at Albany, N.Y. 5/1/1878

Hampton, Anna Fitzsimmon, only child of Mr. Christopher F. Hampton, at Linden Place on Lake Washington. 5/3/1878

DEATH NOTICES FROM THE GREENVILLE "TIMES"

Gerdine,Mrs. Sallie West, at her residence on Deer Creek. She was married to Dr.Gerdine on Sept.2,1877. 6/17/1878

Montgomery, Kate, infant dau. of S.W.& M.A.Montgomery. 6/21/1878.

Worthington, Mrs. B.T., a resident of Leota, at the Peabody Hotel in Memphis. 7/6/1878

Mosby,L.H., at Loughborough Plt. on Williams' Bayou. 7/7/7

Morgan,Mrs., of Lake Washington, at Beersheba Springs. 7/4.

Worthington, Mark, an old and respected citizen of this place, at his residence near Egg's Point, of Intermittent fever. 8/8/1878

Montgomery,S.W. of this county, son of the late W.P. Montgomery, in Denver,Colo., of consumption. 8/17/1878

Rucks,James T. at his home near Friar's Pt. 10/5/1878

Sims, John Hampton, aged 17, a son of Mrs. Sims and a brother of R.L.Sims, formerly of Greenville, in New Orleans, of yellow fever. 11/16/1878

Rives, Orville C.,Sr., an old and respected citizen of Wash. Co., at his residence on Deer Creek. 11/23/1878

Mennfield, Caleb, mail agent, of Warrenton, Warren Co. Ms., but for the past 2 yrs. a resident of Greenville. 1/17/1879

Gilmore,Wm. a white man, pauper, said to be from Campbellsville, Giles Co.,Tenn. at Leesburg, on Deer Creek. 1/11/1879

Wingfield, Bowdrie, aged 18, at the residence of Capt. R.G.Sims, on Deer Creek. 2/28/1879

Farmer,R.A., of pneumonia. 2/8/1879

Bass, Council R., aged 31, at his residence near Leota. 3/13/1879

Peters,Bettie J., wife of D.G.Peters. 4/3/1879

Archer,Mrs. Maggie, wife of Wm.H.Archer, formerly of Greenville, in Clinton,Miss. 4/28/1879

Jackson, David, aged 20, son of Dr.D.D.Jackson, at the residence of his grandmother, Mrs.A.D.Halsey, near Greenville. 5/15/1879.

Warfield, Mrs. Carneal, in Memphis, wife of one of our most worthy citizens. 7/4/1879.

DEATH NOTICES FROM THE GREENVILLE "TIMES"

Elder, J.Llewellyn, aged 11 mos.,9 days, child of Wm.H. and Adele L.Elder. 2/21/1880

Ireys,Mrs.H.Mary, aged 73, in Minneapolis, Minn., widow of the late Henry T.Ireys, and mother of Mr.Henry Ireys of Greenville. 2/19/1880.

Perrice (Penrice ?) JohnS.,aged 69, in Brooklyn,N.Y. for over 50 yrs. a citizen of Wash.Co.(Ms). One of the earliest settlers in this portion of the state, there is little in its history before the War that he did not witness or participate in. He was widely known, and famous from the excellent character of the hotel he long kept, first at Princeton, then at old Greenville. It was the scene of nearly all the public gatherings of those who directed the destinies of the county intimes past. 3/27/1880

Cassino, Joseph, aged 3 yrs. 4/1/1880

Andrews, Wm.G.,of Salem,Ala., of abscess of the liver. He was a member of Oglethorpe Lodge, Columbus,Ga. and a Master Mason. He was buried by Greenville Lodge No. 206. 4/8/1880

Nelson, John Sharp, in Stormville, Bolivar Co.(Ms.) an old and respected citizen of this county. 4/12/1880

Reeves, Mrs. James, at Arcola, dau. (in-law?) of the late O.C.Rives. 4/16/1880

Able,Samuel, on Keystone Plt., near Egg's Point, son of an old and respected citizen of the county. 4/21/1880

Lee, Adedese Farrar,wife of John M.Lee, of this county, in New Orleans. 5/13/1880

Hood, David Hickman,son of Mr.Wm.N.Hood, of Wash.Co.Ms., in Cynthiana, Ky. 5/21/1880

Ede, Alice Maude Mary, aged 5 mos. and 1 day, only dau. of Joshua and Eliza Ede, at Northwood,Wash.Co.(Ms.)6/13/80

Collier, Levin Henry, 51, near Arcola. He was a native of Worcester Co.,Md., but for 34 yrs. a citizen of Wash. Co.Ms. 6/23/1880

Yerger,Mrs.E.B., aged 51 yrs.,11 mos.at Friar's Pt.,wife of Col.Alex Yerger, of Rosedale. She leaves a sister,Mrs. F.Valliant,and a brother,Mr.L.T.Rucks, both of Greenville. 6/16/1880

James, Frank,son of Mr.E.P.James, an old and respected citizen of Wash.Co., at his home near Egg's Pt., of dysentery. 7/6/1880

DEATH NOTICES FROM THE GREENVILLE "TIMES"

Feltus, oldest dau. of Major H.J.Feltus, on Deer Creek. 7/10/1879

Percy, Sam Ferguson, infant son of Harry Percy and Sarah Lee. 8/2/1880

Enos, Margaret Elizabeth, aged 6, dau. of Edward and M.F. Enos. 8/5/1880

Shute, Blanchard, aged 2 yrs. and 1 mo., son of J.D. & Anna E.Shute. 8/9/1880

Stone, Daisy, aged 18 months, dau. of Mr.&Mrs.W.W.Stone on Deer Creek. 8/11/1880

Randolph,Mary Thurston, aged 7, dau. of W.F. & Nannie B. Randolph. 8/14/1879

Stone, Carlile, formerly of Richmond, Ky., on London Plt at the residence of W.M.Worthington. 9/17/1879

White, Stuart,Dr., on of the first settlers of Greenville. 9/29/1879

Moore, and infant of W.H.Moore. 10/1/1879

Stone, Thos. at the residence of his brother, J.C.Stone. 10/9/1879

Walker, an old citizen of Richmond, Ky. and father of Dr. J.S.Swalker, of this place.

Davis, Augustus, who came here during the yellow-fever epidemic of 1878 in charge of the New Orleans nurses. 11/22/1879

Sterling, Bowman, of Stoneville, a suicide. He was a native of West Feliciana Parish (La.) where, and in Wilkinson Co. (Ms.), he leaves a large circle of friends and relatives. 12/2/1879

Heard, Nathan A.,aged 60, on Bogue Phalia in this county, of pneumonia. He was a native of Ga. but for nearly $\frac{1}{2}$ a century had been a citizen of this state. 1/5/1880

Love, W.Allen, aged 19 mos. son of D.A.Love, of congestion. 1/26/1880

Tutt,W.G.,aged 70, at Wildwood Plt. of Gen.Hampton on Lake Wash.,one of the oldest and most worthy citizens of Wash.Co.. He was the last of a family that has for several generations manifested devotion to duty and their country; he has been a trusted manager of Gen.Hampton's Mississippi property for 31 yrs. 1/14/1880

DEATH NOTICES FROM THE GREENVILLE "TIMES"

Worthington, Mrs. Geo.P., a most estimable lady of this county, at Louisville,Ky., of consumption. 6/27/1880

Morris,M., a merchant and excellent citizen, at his residence on Lake Lee. 6/8/1880

Carson,Matt F. aged 2 yrs. and 5 mo., son of Mr. & Mrs. A.B.Carson. 6/14/1880

Moore, Mary, aged 21 mos., dau. of Mr,& Mrs. John Moore. 6/12/1880

McCutcheon, Fannie Elizabeth, aged 10 mos. and 27 days, dau. of John M. & Maggie McCutcheon, at Panola Plt., Deer Creek. 6/9/1880

Montgomery, Eliza Burks, dau. of Mr.& Mrs.J.M.Montgomery. 9/3/1880

Joyes,Florence, aged 2 mos. and 10 days, dau. and only child of Clarence and Jenny Joyes. 9/5/1880

Alexander,Isidore, aged 5 yrs. and 1 day, son of Jacob and Fanny Alexander, of scarlet fever. 9/13/1880

Scott,W.A.Dr., at Rosedale, a brother of Charles and George Y.Scott. 9/19/1880.

O'Bannon,Wm.Percy, aged 5 yrs. 9/19/1880

Lashley,R.M., aged 40,at his residence on Silver Lake. 10/11/1880

Cahn,Eugene; who came here sick from Bolivar Co. 10/12/80

Foster,James Riggs; aged 12, son of Mr. James H.Foster, at Egg's Pt., of hematorrhoea. 10/15/1880.

Bradley,Mrs. Sarah;aged 51, an old citizen of this county, and wife of W.C.Bradley, of Sunflower Co.(Ms)11/3/1880

West, Aemiluis C.;a well-known and estimable citizen at Cletonia. 11/10/1880

Shelby, Isaac,Jr.;aged 8 yrs.,2 mos.,16 days, son of Isaac and Ella.P.Shelby, at his father's residence on Holmes Lake,Bolivar Co. (Ms.) 11/11/1880

Hunt, Mary Haycraft;infant dau. of Wm.E.& M.C.Hunt.11/30/80

Nelms, Nancy(Mrs.) wife of W.J.Nelms and dau. of W.W. Stark, of Marengo Co.Ala., at Oakland Plt. 11/9/1880

Bedon,Dr.; at his home in Bolivar Co.(Ms.) 12/12/1880

DEATH NOTICES FROM THE GREENVILLE "TIMES"

Huggins, Clarence E.; formerly of Cleveland, Ohio, at the residence of Chas.W.Clarke, in Greenville. 12/15/1880

Butler, Eli; aged 41, a jeweler and an old citizen. 1/20/81

Montgomery, Mrs. Frances S.; wife of Dr.D.C.Montgomery, and dau. of the late Judge Wm.L.Harris of Columbus, Miss. Her death is a severe loss to the entire community. 1/30/1881

Wilson, Jonathan W.Capt; aged 83, in Millstone, N.J., father of Mr.K.R.Wilson, formerly of citizen of Greenville. 1/24/1881

Gray, Mrs. Louise; wife of Mr.J.P.Gray, of consumption. 4/6/1881

Drake, Asa; drowned while bathing in the Miss.River. He was from Rising Sun, Ind. where his aged parents now live. He was a partner in the wagon manufactory here of A.Bedgood & Co. and highly esteemed. 6/8/1881

Kurtz, H.S.; formerly of Lancaster, Pa. and a resident of Greenville about a yr. in the employ of Weiss & Goldstein. 6/15/1881

Wyatt, Ed.; aged about 81, formerly of Somerville, Tenn. 7/23/81

Brennan; aged 27, a native of New Orleans; he was the engineer at the ice factory. 7/22/1881

Baer, Mrs. Rosetta; formerly Mrs. Kinstler. 7/28/1881

Sims, Mrs.; wife of Capt.Robt.G.Sims, at her residence on Deer Creek, of heart disease. 8/5/1881

Felker, Mrs. Caroline; aged 59, at the residence of her dau., Mrs.W.S.Clack. 8/19/1881

Joyes (Joyce), Clarence; son of the late Judge Joyes, of Louisville, Ky. 8/27/1881

Davenport, Adelia Gertrude; aged 9 yrs. 5 mos., 2 days. Dau. of Edgar D. & L.J.Davenport, on Deer Creek. 9/1/1881

Sanders, Martin R.; a resident of Wash.Co. for the past 15 yrs., at Leota, Ms. 9/15/1881

Baker, Judge Grafton; born in Va., July 12, 1807, moved to Ky., graduated as law student and came south at the age of 21, when he edited a paper at Rodney, Ms.; at 23 he formed a partnership with the late Judge Vanerson, of Natchez. At the time of his death, Judge Baker was the oldest practioner at the Miss. Bar, a leading Whig, and Chief Justice of New Mexico. He married a dau.of Col.Chas. I.Love, of Nashville, Tenn. 9/4/1881

DEATH NOTICES FROM THE GREENVILLE "TIMES"

Gildart,Mrs. Mary E.; wife of Town Marshall W.K.Gildart. 10/4/1881

Worthington,Mrs. Amanda;aged 76, Wayside Plt.,Lake Lee, one of the oldest and most respected citizens of Wash. Co.; mother of Messrs. W.M. and S.Worthington, Mrs.Jas. Stone and Davis Buckner. She was reared and educated in Washington City, where her father,Thos.Daugherty, was clerk of the House of Representatives. She made her home with her sister, Mrs. Robt.Tilford, of Ky.until her marriage to Saml.Worthington. She was beautiful, witty, and a gifted musician. She was a Presbyterian, as were her parents and grandparents. 10/5/1881

Moore,Jas.C.;at the residence of Mr.John McCutchen,on Deer Creek, a brother of Mr. John Moore, of the firm of A.B.Finlay & Co. 10/6/1881

Anderson,Ruby; aged 7, dau. of Mr.& Mrs. Lomax Anderson. 10/8/1881

Wright,Mrs.;wife of G.M.Wright, at Glenmary Plt. 10/7/1881

Green, Wm.P.;aged 24, in Gainsville,Tex. He was a native of Port Gibson(Ms.), and had but a short time removed from Greenville to Texas. 10/22/1881

Buckner, Davis;at Wayside Plt., an invalid for a long time. 12/15/1881

Flood,Ella; aged 9 mos. and 20 days, youngest child of J.W.& Laura V.Flood. 12/20/1881

Spencer,Rose;aged 13, dau. of Mr.& Mrs. Marshall Spencer, of Lake Washington. 12/24/1881

Hirsch, Clemence; aged about 2 yrs. dau. of Jacob & Henrietta Hirsch. 12/30/1881

Warfield,E.R.; accidentally killed when caught in the machinery of his gin. He was born in Lexington, Ky., the son of Dr.L.Warfield; he served during the war on the Staff of Gen. Wirt Adams. 1/20/1881

White,Mrs. Amanda B., wife of Chas.S.White, dau. of J.P. Gray, and a native of Georgetown, Ky. though she had lived in Greenville from her childhood. 2/14/1882

Dunn,Patrick;an old citizen of Port Gibson (Ms.), who came here some three yrs. ago to take a position on the railroad. 2/20/1882

Isenberg,Nathan;in New Orleans, a worthy and esteemed member of Greenville Lodge No.94 I.O.O.F. 2/10/1882

Lawson,J.B.M.; aged 58, for many yrs. a citizen of this county. 2/27/1882

DEATH NOTICES FROM THE GREENVILLE "TIMES"

Shields, Mr; aged 74, father of John W. Shields, at his home in Tallahatchie Co. (Ms.), an old and respected citizen of the state, residing formerly in Jeff. Co. (Ms.) 3/4/1882

Worthington, Mrs. Ann; at Leota. She was quite aged and had resided the most of her life in Wash. Co. She was the Mother of Mrs. L.B. Valliant of St. Louis, Mrs. Peak and Mr. Isaac Worthington of Chicot Co. (Ark.) and Messrs. B.T. and Thos. Worthington, of this Co. She was a lady of unusual strength of character and intelligence. 3/21/1882

Buckner, Willie; aged 15, only son of Mrs. Davis Buckner, a widow. 3/21/1882

Penny, Carrie; aged 16, dau. of the late Dr. B.F. Penny and Mrs. A.C. Penny, and has passed her whole life in Greenville. 5/30/1882

Robb, Mattie Thompson; aged 6 yrs., 7 mos. and 16 days, dau. of J.H. Robb, of Lake Lee, of congestion of the brain. 6/18/1882

Percy, Leroy Pope; aged 58, at Eureka Spr. Ark. 6/27/1882

Pace, Fannie Percy; aged 23 yrs., 5 mos. and 4 days, wife of Alfred Downs Pace and dau. of Col. and Mrs. W.A. Percy, at Eureka Sprs., Ark. 6/28/1882

Jenkins, Rev. S.G.: at Arcola, of brain fever. A young man of unquestioned piety, he was engaged in teaching a public school at Arcola. The family lived in Copiah Co. (MS.) 7/10/1882

Baker, Mrs. Grafton, widow of Judge Grafton Baker, and for 10 yrs. past a resident of Greenville, at Grand Junction, Tenn. 7/26/1882

Cleaton, Wm. A.; at Hot Sprs., Ark. Mr. Cleaton was for many yrs. a citizen of Yazoo Co. (Ms) and for 15 yrs. past a citizen of this county. 7/29/1882

Baugh, Augusta; aged about 18 mos., dau. of Capt. A.B. and Hallie Baugh, at their residence on William's Bayou. 8/3/1882

Lawson, Eugene W.; late publisher of the "Mississippian". Born in Vicksburg, where his widowed Mother now lives. 8/12/1882

Shields, Willie; son of Mr. & Mrs. John W. Shields, at Niagara Falls. 8/22/1882

Walcott, Mrs. T.G.: on Deer Creek. 9/3/1882

Gravitt, Rich. M.; aged 13 yrs., 1 day, son of Mr. & Mrs. W.H. Gravitt, at their home on Deer Creek. 9/12/1882

DEATH NOTICES FROM THE GREENVILLE "TIMES"

Gravitt, Mattie; aged 10 yrs.,6 mos.,11 days, dau. of Mr. and Mrs. W.H.Gravitt, at their home on Deer Creek. 9/15/1882

O'Connor, Kinnie; about 8 yrs. old, son of the late Tim & Mrs. Josephine O'Connor, in Cincinnati. 9/28/1882

Evans, Mrs. Emma E.; wife of Louis de N.Evans, and dau. of Mrs.S.F.Buckner, at her home in Claib.Co.(Ms.) 10/16/82

Robertshaw, Adele; aged 1 yr., dau. of Mr. & Mrs.James Robertshaw. 10/25/1882

Whitehead, Rennah; aged 12, dau. of Mr.& Mrs.Whitehead. 11/4/1882

Witkowski, Gustav; for many yrs. a merchant in the river counties of Ms. & La. 11/9/1882

Robb, Fannie Gwyn; aged 11 yrs.,11 mos.,dau. of Eugene A. & Carrie E.Robb, at their residence on Lake Wash. 12/3/82

Davis, Ben; formerly an engineer on the Greenville,Columbus, &Birmingham RR. He ran the first locomotive over this road. He was of English birth and had no relatives in this part of the country. 12/21/1882

Hammers, J.L.; aged 28, formerly of Hinds Co.(Ms.) near Cletonia, Deer Creek. 11/9/1882

BRITT,P.M.:for many yrs. a cit. of this Co., of pnemonia 1/3/1883

SMITH, DR. GEORGE:age 85,in active practice at the time of his death, at the home of his dau., Mrs. O.M.Blanton. He leaves a circle of Children, gr.children,gr.gr.children, He was a native of South Va. 1/4/1883

Metcalf, F.A.; age about 50, a planter of this Co. since his youth,at his home on Deer Creek. He was a man of unusual culture and literary attainments. He leaves a widdow and a large family of children. 1/15/1883

Kanatzer, Mrs. John; at her residence near G'ville.1/31/83

Williams, Merritt; age 3yrs.,11mos.,son of C.P.& Anna Williams, at Longwood. Mr.Chas.P.Williams was until recently a resident of this Co., and was on a visit with his little son to the home of his brother, Merritt Williams, Esq. 2/8/1883

Satterfield,Dr.W.E.:aged 40, at his residence on Deer Creek. He leaves a widow and 3 children. 2/22/1883

Foster,Jos.P.;a cit. of G'Ville for the past 10 yrs.3/2/83

DEATH NOTICES FROM THE GREENVILLE "TIMES"

Scott,Jefferson;aged 18, son of J.W.Scott,near Egg's Pt. of pneumonia. 3/8/1883

Lewy, Mrs.Ernestine; wife of B.M.Lewy. 3/6/1883

Tillman,Dr.; at his residence on Deer Creek, an old resident of the creek and a native of Ga. 3/21/1883

Hirsch, Jacob; aged 44. 3/28/1883

Gensburger,Saml.;aged 8 yrs. son of Mr.Marx and Mrs. Julia Gensburger, of protracted meningitis. 3/24/1883

Ousley, Harriet Byrne;dau. of the late Maj.Byrne of G'ville Mrs. Ousley passed her childhood and girlhood in G'Ville. She and her mother ceased to live here upon the death of Maj.Byrne and his only son, Erskine, of yellow fever in 1878. At the time of her death, she was residing in Chicago, of which city she married Mr.Ousley a few yrs. since. 4/7/1883

Head, Oliver J.;aged 38, a highly esteemed citizen of this Co. for several yrs., at Seauvia,Ga. of cancer.3/31/83

Cleary, Robt.; an old cit. of this Co. 6/2/1883

Champion, Mrs.A.M.:wife of Mr.Champion of the Ga.Pacific R.R., and a native of Ga., in Sunflower Co.(Ms.) She was buried on Mound,graveyard near Stoneville. 5/27/1883

Sowers,Chas.M.;at the store of Mr.Julius Landau on Deer Creek. 6/26/1883

Ward,Junius R.;aged 84, at Leota, at the home of his son, G.V.Ward. He was the oldest cit. of Wash.Co. and one of its most respected. 50 yrs.ago, with the late Capt.Henry Johnson, he came to this Co. from his home in Ky. and together they reclaimed from the wilderness,plantations near the present town of Leota. Up to the time of the close of the War, Mr.Ward was the possessor of large wealth in this county and in Ky. He was the father of Messrs.G.V. & Junius Ward and of Mrs. Johnson Erwin, all citizens of this county. 8/4/1883

Shorey,S.O.; a resident, we believe, of Kansas, before he came to G'Ville, where he has lived for 6 or 7 yrs.8/7/83

Finlay,Jas.Archer: aged 7mos.infant son of Mr.& Mrs. John P.Finlay, of G'Ville, at the residence of Mr.Jas. Archer, in Jefferson Co.(Ms) 8/11/1883

O'Neal,Mrs. Caroline; wife of R.T.O'Neal, on Deer Creek, near Overby Station. 9/10/1883

DEATH NOTICES FROM THE GREENVILLE "TIMES"

Sutton, Jas.M.;aged 79, one of our oldest and most respected citizens. He was a native of the state of Ill., but had been in this state more than 50 yrs. 9/21/1883

Shelby,Janora;only dau. of G.B.& Janie P.Shelby, who was born at Sardis, Miss.Mar.29,1879, at Sunny Side, Ark. 9/15/1883

Rives, Mrs. O.C.: aged 82, at her residence near Arcola, of pneumonia. 10/9/1883

Frid, Henry Herman; an honest,industrious man,city sexton,leaves a wife and large family. 10/12/1883

Nugent, Aimee; little dau. of Col.W.L.Nugent and Mrs. Nugent. 10/6/1883

James,B.F.: aged 25, of hematura, at the residence of his mother-in-law, Mrs. Nannette Switzer.

Wells, Willie B.;aged 10, only child of his mother,Mary Wells, at the residence of his grandmother, Mrs.Nannette Switzer, of hematura. 10/4/1883

Buckner, Dr.W.E.; aged 25, at Arcola, of dysentery. He was buried at Col.A.J.Paxton's. 11/24/1883

Dudly, Dr.Chas.; an old and highly esteemed citizen of Lake Wash. 11/30/1883

Thompson,Herbert; aged 26, son of Mr. Julius Thompson, of Deer Creek, at the residence of J.D.Britton, of this city. 12/28/1883

Bowen, Grant A.;aged 64, at his residence on Black Bayou. He was a native of Lebanon, Tenn.though he has lived in this county for near 50 yrs. He leaves a widow and 2 ch. and a sister, Mrs. Shall Yerger. 1/19/1884

Robb,Jos.H.Jr; aged 10 yrs.6 mos., only son of J.H.& Mattie B.Robb, at the residence of his parents on Lake Lee, of congestion of the brain. 1/26/1884

Rucks,Maggie;aged 24, dau. of the late J.T.Rucks and Sallie B.Rucks. 1/14/1884

Teidaman, Mrs. Rebecca, at the residence of her granddau. Mrs.D.A.Love. She was the oldest citizen of the county, having been here for more than 50 yrs. and had reached the unusual age of 92 yrs. 1/25/1884

DEATH NOTICES FROM THE GREENVILLE "TIMES"

Leavenworth, Noah Hunt; aged 58 yrs. a native of Ste. Genevieve Co., Mo., where his parents were taken for burial. He has lived here for the past 5 yrs. and with his brother, J.H.Leavenworth, has conducted a sawmill and lumber business of Leavenworth Bros. 2/5/1884

Dunn, Harriet Theobald, Infant dau. of Dr. and Mrs. S.R.Dunn. 2/17/1884

Archer, Helen; aged 15, dau. of Rev.& Mrs.S.Archer. 2/17/84

Smith, James Mosely; aged 4, son of Mr.& Mrs. J.D.Smith. 3/9/1884

Flood, the 12 yr. old son of J.W.Flood was drowned while attempting to jump on the Steamer Issaquena from the wharf-boat. 4/1/1884

Maury, James M.; a former popular citizen of G'ville, in Memphis. Burial in Somerville, Tenn. 5/8/1884

Walker, Orville Blanton; aged 27, wife of DR.J.S.Walker, and dau. of Dr.O.M.& Mrs.M.R.Blanton. 5/22/1884

Cahn, Barney; aged about 45, an old citizen of the town and one of the first to engage in merchandise here after it was established, and a native of Province of Lorraine. 5/20/1884

Craig, Francis Jerome; aged 57, on Bayou Granicus, of congestion of the brain. He was a native of South C. but moved to this state about 27 yrs. ago. 6/2/1884

Stone, Alfred Holt; infant son of Dr.O.W.& Mary H.Stone. 6/7/1884

Stone, Corrinne; aged 3 mos., 16 days, infant dau. of W.W. and Ella Stone. 6/7/1884

Rucks, L.Taylor; ex-mayor and judge, was killed in interferring in the cause of justice when certain lawless parties were menacing the hotel clerk. Rucks and 3 other men came to his aid and Rucks was killed in the interchange of shots. 6/7/1884

Paxton, Wm.Franklin; aged about 25, at the residence of his parents A.J.& H.M.Paxton, near Arcola. 6/14/1884

Slater, Mrs. Laura M., wife of Vastine C.Slater and dau. of E.V.& E.M.Barwick, formerly of Madison Co.Ms. at her home near Overby Station. 7/14/1884

Hammer, Mrs. Blanche; wife of Mr.Jos.Hammer, at the residence of Mrs. Mary James. 7/30/1884

DEATH NOTICES FROM THE GREENVILLE "TIMES"

Yerger, Mildred Humphreys, aged 11, dau. of Mr.and Mrs. Wm.Yerger. 8/9/1884

Miller, Maggie J., at Pass Christian, a native of Wash. Co.(Ms.) a dau of the late and sister of the present Mr.Harvey Miller, and of Mrs. Hal Yerger. 8/28/1884

Friley, David; aged 54, an old citizen of the Co., at his residence on Deer Creek, Warsaw Station. 8/29/1884

Pilcher, Fred Fielding; son of Mason Pilcher, of La., in Nashville (Tenn.) 9/6/1884

Rucks, Arthur; aged 28, at the residence of his aunt, Mrs. M.M.Rucks, of hemeturia. 9/13/1884

Shields, John W.; aged 36, at Roane Mountain, N.C. He came to G'ville from State University 10 yrs. ago, and was amember of the bar. 9/14/1884

Craig, Frank; infant son of the late F.J.& Mrs.M.A. Craig. 9/9/1884

Stone, Clarence;son of the late Dr.Stone, of Natchez, at Mound Landing. 11/1/1884

Tillman,Jeff.; an old citizen of Wash.Co. 11/1/1884

McCutchen, John M.; aged 43, one of the county's most public spirited and truest citizens, at his home on Leer Creek. He leaves a widow and 7 children. 11/3/1884

Hord,D.A.; aged 23, formerly of this Co.,in Panola Co. 11/3/1884

Lancaster, Dr.Alonzo; aged 63, for the past 35 yrs. a resident of Bolivar Co. (Ms.) 11/28/1884

Beck, Davis Buckner; aged 10 yrs, 9 mos. at the residence of his parents on Mosswood Plt. 12/7/1884

MaClennan, Emma;dau. of the late Rev. James MaClennan, formerly of Jackson, at the residence of R.E.Paxton, near Arcola. 12/20/1884

Gregory, Mrs.P.W.;aged 70, a native of Philadelphia and an old and much esteemed resident of this co., at the residence of S.R.Dunn. 12/19/1884

Satterfield, Mrs. Emma Ranaldson; aged 31, in Louisville Ky. 12/24/1884

Halsey, Mrs. A.D.;over 70 yrs. old, and for many yrs. a resident of this county. 1/17/1885

DEATH NOTICES FROM THE GREENVILLE "TIMES"

Williams, John; at the residence of his sister, Mrs. Craig on Silver Lake. 1/19/1885

Erwin, Victor Flournoy; aged 38, a native of Wash. Co., in New Orleans, of pneumonia. 1/29/1885

Jackson, Henry; son of Dr. David Jackson, at the Halsey Place. 1/29/1885

Watson, Hattie Sidney; aged 6 yrs. 7 mos. dau of A.P. & Mrs. E.D. Watson, at Avondale, near Stoneville, of congestive chill. 2/6/1885

Holmes, Leta Craig; infant dau. of Mr.& Mrs. John Holmes, at Ashland Plantation. 3/3/1885

Biggins, Mrs.; aged 65, wife of Mr. F. Biggins. 3/11/1885

Shanahan, Mrs. Mary O'Leary, aged 59, wife of T.M. Shannahan; born in Parish Skull, Co. of Cork, Ireland, Feb. 1827, for 29 yrs. a resident of Wash. Co. and 20 of the city of G'ville. 7/12/1885

Gravitt, Fannie Gordon; aged 4 yrs. 9 mos. little dau. of W.H.& M.E. Gravitt, of congestion. 8/13/1885

Shall, Mrs. M.C.; aged 62, after a long illness. Mrs. Shall was a native of Tenn., but has passed almost all of her entire life in this community. 8/24/1885

Goldsmith, Grover Cleveland; infant son of Mr.& Mrs. Sol. Goldsmith. 9/1/1885

Shall, Euella McCall; aged 30, wife of Jos.A.Shall 9/14/85

Head, Mrs.; aged about 68, Mother of Messrs. John C. and Dan Head of our town, at her home in Sinora, Ga. 9/15/1885

Finlay, T.P.; aged 26, of abscess of the side. 9/27/1885

Aldridge, Hannah; aged 5, dau. of Mr.& Mrs. Frank Aldridge at Arcola. 9/21/1885

Johnson, Mrs. Frances S.; wife of Mr. Jas.S. Johnson, at her residence on Deer Creek; born Aug. 11, 1833; Mother of 9 children, 7 of whom survive, as well as 2 grandchildren. 9/25/1885

Sanders, Norman; of Chicot Co. Ark. at the residence of Major O'Hea. 10/3/1885

Bates, Mrs. F.N.; at her husband's residence in G'Ville. 10/16/1885

DEATH NOTICES FROM THE GREENVILLE "TIMES"

Walcot, T.G.; over 50 yrs. old, an old and popular cit. of his neighborhood, at his home on Deer Creek, near Westburg, of congestion of the brain. 10/19/1885

Smith,Clark W.;aged 33, at the residence of his brother, Jas.D.Smith, of Arcola, of congestion; born Wash.Co. Feb. 26,1853, was buried 3 weeks from the day he was married. 10/6/1885

Kinkead,Jos.;19 mos. at Aldemar, the residence of Capt. W.H.Johnson. 12/26/1885

Vaughn,David C.;aged 13, son of Mr. JohnVaughn, at Wayside. 12/26/1885

Landau, Julius; aged 47, a native of Cracow, having lived in G'ville for 12 or 15 yrs. past. 1/19/1886

Bernard,Thos.;aged about 42, at his house on Black Bayou, of consumption. He was the son of the late Col. Bernard, of Adams Co.(Ms.), a gentleman of high character and reputation. 2/5/1886

Sims,Robert G.;aged about 45, at Ashley,Utah. Capt.Sims for many yrs. a popular and influential citizen of this county, had been in Utah in Government employment for only a few months. A native of Wilkinson Co.(Ms.), he was first Adjutant of the 21st Miss.Reg. of the Confederate Army. By all the survivors of the Griffith-Barksdale-Humphreys Brigade, Bob Sims is remembered as of its very flower. 2/7/1886

Kraunsopolski; at Arcola. 2/14/1886

Magoon,Mrs. Adeline; aged 73, at the residence of Mr. Geo.E.Billingsley. She was the Mother of Mrs.Billingsley. 2/27/1886

Gildart,John W.; aged 43, at Indianola. Mr. Gildart, who had for some months past been engaged in the Sunf. Court Clerk's Office, was a native of Wilk.Co., where his father and mother, sisters, and brothers reside, and was a bro. of Messrs. W.K. and Thos.Gildart of G'ville The news of John Gildart's death will be sadly received by his old comrades of the 21st Miss. Reg. 3/28/1886

Weatherbee,C.F.; of Atlanta,Ga. He had been only a few weeks in G'ville, where he had, with Mr.W.J.McCord, established an agency of the N.Y. Life Ins. Co. for the Yazoo Delta. 4/11/1886

Lundquist,Mrs. Clara;at Mr. Hood's on the Granicus,of consumption; a member of the Presbyterian Ch. 4/27/1886

DEATH NOTICES FROM THE GREENVILLE "TIMES"

Robinson, Mrs. Lucy; aged 57, a devoted member of the Episcopal Ch. The remains were carried to the former home of the deceased in ILL., accompanied by her bro. Mr. JohnW.Harrow, and her dau. Mrs. Hawkins. 5/26/1886

Weiss,Morris; aged 60, a native of Neustadt,Prussia, whence he came to America 35 yrs. ago. He was the Sr. member of the large merchantile house of Weiss & Goldstein, and in continuous business,G'villes' oldest merchant. 6/12/1886

Rowe,Jas. H.;aged 63, father of Mrs. S.Brown, from Fort Wayne, Ind. 6/6/1886

Hampton, Mr.C.F.; in Columbia,S.C. Mr.Hampton was a bro. of Senator Hampton and formerly owned and lived upon the Linden Plt. on Lake Wash. 6/7/1886

McGrath, Caldwell; aged 47, a native of Ky., but has been a resident of G'ville for 30 yrs. He was an old officer of the county before the War. He received a severe wound during the War, out of which grew the infirmities under which he has suffered ever since. 6/27/1886

McMurray,Mrs. E.B.;aged 47, a cit. of G'ville for 20 Yrs. 7/24/1886

Worthington, Dr.W.W.;aged 85, one of the oldest cit. of the co., at Georgetown, Ky. He is the last of several bros. who were among Wash.Co.s first settlers, and whose descendents constitute one of its largest families.7/23/86

Green, Annie; sister-in-law of Mr.Geo.Brown of G'ville, in St.Louis. 7/26/1886

Vaught,G.C.;aged 44, at Leland, of congestion of the brain. Mr.Vaught, a long time resident of G'ville moved to Deer Creek a few yrs. ago. On the incorp. of the enterprising town of Leland, he was elected Mayor, the duties of which office he discharged with vigor. 8/18/1886

Lacy,Mrs. Mary; an aged and respected cit. of this place, well known to the cit. of Leota, where she lived for yrs. before moving to G'ville, of heart trouble. 8/18/1886

O'Bannon,Mrs. Mary P.;wife of D.B.O'Bannon, a native of the community, dau. of the late N.C.Heard...9/3/1886

McCord,M.R.; Father of W.J.McCord, of this place, in Bennet,Neb. Born in Ky. Oct. 5,1808, being within a few days of 78 yrs. old. 9/13/1886

DEATH NOTICES FROM THE GREENVILLE "TIMES"

Mieure, Mrs. S.J.; a resident of Lakeland, on Silver Lake, Wash.Co., for 20 yrs., dau. of J.E.& L.B. Gayden, born near Canton (Ms.) April 10,1832. 9/18/1886

Bell,D.B.;an old cit. of G'ville...10/13/1886

Barefield, Aliena; youngest dau. of Saml. & Katie Barefield, on Deer Creek. 10/5/1886

Burrus, Mrs. Maggie; aged 38, wife of John Burrus, at the residence of Mrs. Judge Burrus, on Egypt Ridge, in Bolivar Co. 10/11/1886

Yerger, Hal; aged 44, at the residence of his mother, Mrs. Mary Yerger, son of the late distinguished Judge Shall Yerger. He served in the 18th Miss.Reg. in the War, was wounded in the battle of Malvern Hill;during the remainder of the War he was 1st Lt. of the Wash. Cal. During the past 20 yrs. he has been a Wash.Co.Planter. 11/13/1886

Bell, Mrs. Mollie A.;wife of Mr.Jas.B.Bell. 11/14/1886

Vaught,N.G.; aged 36, from the effects of an injury to his finger. 11/24/1886

Hill,Jas. Steward; aged 4 yrs, 10mos., son of Dr.Hill, and grandson of J.S.Johnson, of congestion of the lungs, near Arcola. 11/10/1886

Stone, Mary Worthington; wife of Capt.Jas.Stone and sister of Mrs. Amanda Buckner and Messrs.W.M.& S.Worthington, formerly of Wash.Co., at San Antonia, Tex. 1/4/1887

Salmon,Mamie; aged 6, dau. of M.Salmon.The little girl died of grief for the death of her mother some weeks ago. 1/27/1887

Erwin,Mrs.; wife of J.W.Erwin, at Ashland Plt. Her old home was Lexington, Ky. 3/16/1887

Lengsfield, Julius; aged 73, the oldest merchant and oldest Mason in G'ville. In the fire of 1875* the accumulation of yrs. of toil and care was swept away from him, but he bore his losses with fortitude. He retired from the merchantile business and occupied himself with the cultivation of his farm near town. He was a charter member of the Blue Lodge and Past Master. 3/31/1887

*The whole business section of G'ville burned, 1875.

DEATH NOTICES FROM THE GREENVILLE "TIMES"

Shields, A.Hunt; cashier of the Merchants Bk., of pneumonia. He was a native of Natchez. 4/18/1887

Enos, Mrs. Mary F.; 4/10/1887

Pepper, Freida; only dau. of Mr.& Mrs.S.Pepper, of congestion. 4/18/1887

Wall, George Alexander; inf. son of Mr.& Mrs.Joe Wall. 4/11/

Kerstine, Isadore; merchant at Hollandale, of hematura. 7/23/1887

Buck, Mrs. Elizabeth Stuart; wife of Dr.R.L.Buck, of congestion. 7/29/1887

Scott, Fannie; a sister of Mrs.H.P.Lee and gr.dau. of Abraham Scott, one of Miss's. early Gov., at Miss. City. 8/20/1887

Smith, Fannie Katie; little dau. of Mr.& Mrs. J.D.Smith at Castalian Springs. 8/26/1887

Wilmot; inf. son of Mr.& Mrs.Bowman Wilmot, in Sunflower, 8/27/1887

Johnson, J.Vernon; son of J.S.Jr. & Mrs.M.E.Johnson, in Canton, of typhoid malarial fever; burial in Arcola; born March 15, 1882. 9/11/1887

Stone, Mrs. Katie Hunt; aged 37, at the residence of her sister, Mrs. Rodman, of Frankfort, Ky.; a sister of Capt. W.E.Hunt and Mrs. Claude Johnson. 9/14/1887

Dubose, Mrs. W.P.; at Moffat, Tenn. dau. of the late Judge Rucks of Wash.Co.(Ms.) sister to Mrs.Henrietta Yerger of Jackson (Ms.) and Mrs. Valliant. 9/25/1887

Brotherton, Edward; at Pace Plt., an Englishman. 9/6/1887

Smith, Mrs. Myra; in this city, at the home of Mr. Robt. Somerville. 10/12/1887

Killerhouse, Jos.; in G'ville, aged 45. 10/26/1887

Sterling, W.H.; at his residence, on Lake Wash., an old citizen of this county, aged 65. 10/21/1887

Dabney, John; of Vaucluse, Cumberland Co.Va., in G'ville at the home of his son, Mr.J.B.Dabney, aged 63. 11/20/1887

Griffin, Miss Laura; at the home of her father, Judge Griffin. 12/1/1887

Smith, Dr.Jas.M., suddenly, in A.B.Finlay's Drug Store. 12/5/1887

DEATH NOTICES FROM THE GREENVILLE "TIMES"

Stone, Mrs. Kate Hunt; at her home in G'ville. 12/--/87(?) (See preceeding page for Stone,Mrs.Kate Hunt)

Richardson,Mrs.Patton; (Margaret Elizabeth), widow of the late Col.E.Richardson, in New Orleans. 12/18/1887

Meares, Dr.JohnLoudon; who for 11 yrs. was Health Off. for this city, passed away at his home, 1408 Calif. St., Fresno. Calif. The decd. was 65 yrs. old at the time of his death. He had practiced medicine, and raised thoro-bred stock in Wash.Co.(Ms.) many yrs. before moving to Calif. He served on the Staff of Col Bowen in the Conf. Army as medical director. After the War he returned to Miss. and represented his dist. in the Legislature. In Calif., Dr. Meares served several yrs. as Quarantine Officer in Fresno, and in 1876 was appointed Health Officer, serving in that capacity until his death. He was a gentleman of irreproachable character and a member of ante-bellum Deer Creek society. By his old friends here he is remembered with a warmth of regard undimmed by 18 yrs. separation. 1/27/1888

Davis,Mrs. Mary A.; an old citizen of West Carroll Parish, La., at the home of her dau.Mrs.A.V.Witkowski. 2/10/1888

Sale,Mrs. Jane A.; at the home of her son-in-law Mr. S.R.Swaine. 2/11/1888

Allen, Robt.; aged 32, in G'ville. The decd. was a nephew of J.B.Bell and was a native of Ky. 2/14/1888

Alfred; infant son of Mr.& Mrs. Sol Brill. 3/20/1888

O'Bannon, Columbus; at the home of his father, Mr.D.B. O'Bannon, aged 16 yrs. 4/7/1888

Cleaton,Mr.; at Deer Creek, by accidental gun discharge. 5/5/1888

McGraw,Mr.Chas.; at Bryan's store on Lake Wash., also by accidental gun discharge. Mr.McGraw was an old Confederate soldier, and a respected and worthy man. His home had been in Claib.Co.(Ms.) 5/1/1888

Crittenden, Col. John Allen; bro. of Ex-Gov Crittenden of Mo., and ½ bro. of Ex-Gov. Eli Murray, of Utah, died in Frankfort, Ky. The decd. was the father of Henry and Orlando Crittenden and Mrs.W.E.Hunt, of this city. 6/8/88

Taylor, Polydore; (colored) for several yrs. in the employ of the town and then of Mr.Theodore Pohl, aged 62. He was formerly a slave of Jas.R.Yerger, and has always enjoyed the respect of the white cit. of this community. 7/4/1888

DEATH NOTICES FROM THE GREENVILLE "TIMES"

Clifton, Mrs. Ellen; in G'ville, at her residence. She was a widow, had no ch., and was formerly from Water Proof, La. 7/31/1888

Yager, Mr. A.; in G'ville, of consumption. 8/18/1888

James, Mr. T.V.; near Egg's Point, at the age of 72. He was one of the oldest cit. of Wash. Co. 8/18/1888

Fryer, Mr. John; of this city. 8/--/1888

Tobin, Capt.; of the Steamer Paragould. He was 60 yrs. of age and was one of the last of the oldtime river admirals, a powerful and successful leader in his vocation. 9/15/1888

Anderson, Capt. T.S., in San Antonio, Tex. In G'ville he served as Engineer on the Levee Board for 6 yrs, from 1876 to 1882, and was a faithful and highly accomplished official. 9/15/1888

Perkins, Mrs. Jennie Sellers; wife of Capt. J.L. Perkins, at her home in G'ville. 10/7/1888

McCutcheon, Mr. R.B.: of heart disease. The deced. was weigher at the G'ville Compress and was very popular with his friends and associates. 1/4/1889

Craft, Gussie Lloyd; infant son of Mr. & Mrs. W.A. Craft. 1/9/1889

Hirsch, Sadie; little 6 yr. old dau. of Mr. & Mrs. Jacob Hirsch of G'ville, was run over by a freight train at Leland and fatally hurt. 1/12/1889

Kennedy, Clarence; infant son of Mr. & Mrs. W.L. Kennedy of Deer Creek, enroute home from Memphis, was taken suddenly ill and died at Shelby Station. 2/--/1889

Chew, Augustine; at his home on Deer Creek, at the age of 71. 2/21/1889

Mendelssohn, Herman; aged 17, at Los Angeles, Calif., at the home of his Uncle I.A. Newman. 2/26/1889

Goldsmith, Godfrey; at the home of his parents, age 6. 2/27/89

Vance, Mrs. Ida M.; at the residence of her husband, in G'ville. 3/--/89

Heard, Nathan; at the home of Mrs. Burdette, on the Bogue, aged 26 yrs. 4/30/1889

Hutchins, Dr. R.E. at his home in G'ville, formerly of Hinds Co. (Ms.) 5/14/1889

DEATH NOTICES FROM THE GREENVILLE "TIMES"

Gay, Mrs.C.A.: in G'ville, at the home of her son, Capt. W.L.Gay, aged 72. 5/15/1889

Hampton, Wade,Jr.;infant son of Mr.& Mrs. McDuffie Hampton, at his home on Lake Wash. 5/21/1889

Shongut, Aaron; in New Orleans, at Tours Infirmary, aged 31 yrs. 5/21/1889

Allien, Miss Sallie; at Wayside, Miss, aged 20 yrs. She was a dau. of Mr.Ben Allien of Jefferson Co. and a niece of Mr.W.W.Allien of Vicksburg. 5/28/1889

Riggs,Miss; sister of Mr. Frank Riggs and niece of Mr. H.E.Wetherbee, at the residence of the latter. 5/26/1889

Helm, Anna B.Eakin; wife of Geo.M.Helm,Esq. and dau. of the late Chief Justice of Ark., aged 25 yrs. 6/1/1889

Hebron,Wm.S., infant son of Mr.& Mrs.John L.Hebron,Jr. at his home on Deer Creek, near Leland. 6/12/1889

Wolfe, Charles W.; at Little Rock,Ark, who during the War, was Orderly Sergeant of Co.D.(Wash.Co.Calvary) 28th Miss. Reg. 5/30/1889

Franklin, Mrs. Rachel. 6/20/1889

Rucks, Marion Gray; dau. of Mr.& Mrs.Sam T.Rucks. 7/4/89

Solomon, Bertha; infant dau. of Mr.& Mrs. M.Soloman, at their residence in G'ville. 8/2/1889

Lewy, Mr.B.M.;at the residence of Mr.S.Pepperman, his son-in-law, aged 65. 7/30/1889

Sexton, Miss Jennie; at the home of her mother. 8/19/1889

Pond, Mr.T.E.; bookkeeper of Head & Co. 8.21.1889

Rogers, Mrs. Mollie, wife of Mr.W.B.Rogers, at Leland, Miss. 9/6/1889

Helm, Anna Eakin; infant dau. of Maj. Geo.Helm and his late wife, Anna B.Helm, at Waco.,Tex. 9/19/1889

Pohl, Florence;in this city, oldest dau. of Mr.& Mrs. Theodore Pohl, at the age of 12. 10/10/1889

Daugherty,O.R.; at Hollywood Plt. near Glen Allan, in the 51 yr. of his age. The decd. had been for more than 25 yrs. a citizen of this county. 10/13/1889

Harris,Audley Malvern;the infant son of Mrs. W.D.Harris, in G'ville. 10/28/1889

DEATH NOTICES FROM THE GREENVILLE "TIMES"

Scott, Mrs. C.S., of pneumonia, at Altheiner, Ark. The decd. was a sister of Mrs. J.H.Bowen and formerly lived in G'ville. 11/24/1889

Yerger, Wm.Jr.; at Biloxi, son of Mr.& Mrs. Will Yerger, at the age of 17 yrs., 11 mos. 11/30/1889

Feltus, Mrs. Eliza; at Hotel Dieu, New Orleans. For more than 10 yrs. this venerable and esteemed lady lived with her son, Capt.J.V.Feltus, on Deer Creek.

Vance, Rev.A.M., of typhoid fever. 12/11/1889

Wartski, Mrs. Minnie; at the age of 65 yrs. She was born in Kalisch, Russian Poland, and descended from a prominent Jewish family there. She came to this country over 30 yrs. ago, and resided in N.Y. and Cincinnati until about 18 or 19 yrs. ago, when she settled in G'ville. 12/10/1889

Other death records from "the Stockwell Papers"

Inscriptions on Stones in old Peters-Petit Private Cem. at Petit, Ms.
Dr.Matthew L.Peters; 25 Dec. 1821 - 11 Dec. 1875
Ann Garland Hooe; 1800 - 16 Dec. 1876
John J.Petit; 16 Dec. 1844 - 2 March 1899
Hallie Hooe, wife of M.L.Peters; 6 Apr.1836 - 18 Feb.1905
Clara Louise, infant dau of Morris and Minnie Peters Rosenstock; 12 Apr.1887 - 18 June 1887
Bettie T.(Peters) wife of Daniel G.Pepper; 15 Feb.1859 - 4 Apr.1879 and her babe.

A note on the bottom of this page : Minnie Peters, 1st wife of Morris Rosenstock, is buried on the plantation once owned by Mr. Rosenstock, now property of the H.N.Alexander estate at James, Ms. He is buried in the Jewish Cemetary in G'ville, Ms.

YELLOW FEVER IN 1878

A REVISED LIST OF THE DEATHS IN GREENVILLE AND THE SURROUNDING COUNTRY DURING THE EPIDEMIC

(From the files of the Greenville Times)*

For future reference, and as a record of our files, we publish a corrected list of our citizens who died during the epidemic. We have not been able to procure an exact statement of the number of cases, or per centage of deaths thereto. Though it will approximate 50% of the whites, the lesser mortality of the colored will reduce this to about 35% of the cases. We have made the list as complete as we could, though it doubtless omits some.

WHITE

August 23rd·Mobray, girl, 4 years old, white
" 30th. Perry, boy, white
" 31st. Pat Finnegan, man, white
Sept.1st. William Marshall, man, white
" 2nd. E.J.Byrne, young man, white
" " · John Simpson, man, white
" " · D.E.Brooks, man, white
" " · Mrs. D.Morris, white
" 3rd. Pryor, girl child, white
" " · Maria Winter, white
" 4th. C.Bathkee, white
" " . Mrs. FannieBrooks, white
" " . J.A.Chiesa, Mrs Shorey's child, girl, 5 yrs.
" " . Fred Perry, boy, white
" " . Mrs. James Perry, white
" 5th. Scott, girl,white
" " . Josephine Fox, girl, white
" " . Mrs. Thomas Mowbry, white
" " . Lyman Stowell, man, white
" " . Hiram Putnam, young man, white
" " . W.A.Haycraft, man, white
" 6th. Mrs. M.Morris, white
" " . Philip Barnet, man, white
" " . Miss Willie Scott, white
" " . Milton Jones, man, white
" 7th. Col.C.E.Morgan, white
" " . Mrs. A.Cox, white
" " . James Perry, white
" " . William Telfer, white
" " . Emma Duvall, white
" 8th. Charles Huntley, white
" " .Julius Ratchlitz, white
" " . Richard McCullough
" " . James Corney, white
" " . Mrs. Young, white

---

*
Taken from "The Stockwell Papers", Greenville Library.

Washington Co.Ms.
Yellow Fever in 1878; from the "Greenville Times"*

```
Sept. 9th. Edward Caffall, white
  "    "   Mrs. George Sanford, white
  "    "   Mrs. J.S.Ballard, white
  "    "   Mrs. F.P.Smith, white
  "    "   George Stream, white
  "   10th Mrs. Shorey, white
  "    "   George Bird, white
  "    "   Miss K.A.Ballard, white
  "    "   Fred Pryor, white
  "    "   Dr.W.S.Stafford, white
  "    "   Aleck, butcher, white
  "   11th Willie Caffall, white
  "    "   Mrs. Julia Pogle, white
  "    "   Unknown blacksmith, white
  "    "   Louisa Massey, white
  "    "   Mrs. T.P.Perry, white
  "    "   Abe Smith, man, white
  "    "   Eva Wetherbee, girl, white
  "    "   Elliot Dodge, man, white
  "    "   D.Dorman, man, white
  "    "   Steve Sutton, man, white
  "   12th.Louis Caffall, man, white
  "    "   Louis Radjesky, man, white
  "    "   Mrs. Beck, white
  "    "   Mrs. Flischer, white
  "    "   Mrs. Trammel, white
  "    "   Theodore Harbicht, man, white
  "    "   Mrs. L.P.Wetherbee, white
  "   13th.Mrs. B.Hasberg, white
  "    "   Walter Quick, man, white
  "    "   E.Steinberg, man, white
  "    "   Mrs. S.A.Platt, white
  "    "   Willie Ehles, child, white
  "    "   H.B.Putnam, man, white
  "    "   Mrs. William Ehlers, white
  "    "   Dr.V.F.P.Alexander, white
  "    "   Robert Cooper, man, white
  "    "   James McCann, man, white
  "   14th.Raphael Marshall, white
  "    "   James Minzies, white
  "   15th.Reverand D.C.Green, white
  "    "   Walter B.Butler, white
  "    "   Thomas McLean, white
  "    "   Frank Wagner, white
  "    "   J.Radjesky, white
  "    "   Bennie Diggs, white
  "    "   J.D.Taylor, white
  "    "   Charles Bigalow, white
  "   16th.Mrs. Ballard, white
  "    "   Charles Boswick, white
  "    "   James H.Buckner, white
  "    "   James Davidson, white
```

*Copied from the "Stockwell Papers", Greenville Library

Washington Co.Ms.
Yellow Fever in 1878; from "The Greenville Times".*

Sept.	16th.	James Connell, white
"	"	Thomas Kyle, white
"	"	Mrs. F.Pryor, white
"	"	Mrs. H.Bathke, white
"	"	Joe Badwick, white
"	"	Bigelow, child, white
"	"	Mrs. Habicht, white
"	"	Henry Laurens, white
"	"	Gus Forrester, white
"	17th.	Frank Gallagher, white
"	"	John Ballard, baby, white
"	"	Mrs. M.Sievers, white
"	"	Anna Platt, white
"	"	Unknown man, white
"	"	Gus Coughler, white
"	"	Helen Finlay, white
"	"	Frank P.Smith, white
"	18th.	Henry Freundt, white
"	"	Mrs. L.Pollo, white
"	"	William Ehlers, white
"	"	W.L.Porter, white
"	"	John S.Ballard, white
"	"	Willie B.White, white
"	"	John Ralph, white
"	"	Abe Wall, white
"	"	Tom Sylvester, white
"	"	Charles Williams, white
"	"	W,J,Manley, white
"	"	T.P.Perry, white
"	"	Nellie Warden, white
"	"	N.J.Nelson, white
"	"	M.Morris, white
"	"	W.P.Kretschmar, white
"	"	Fanny Diggs, white
"	19th.	Dan Shannahan, white
"	"	Mrs.J.S.Barnhurst, white
"	"	Dave Morris, white
"	"	M.Duffy, white
"	20th.	Albert Wheeler, white
"	"	Mrs. T.B.Shaw, white
"	"	Mrs. John Small, white
"	"	John Simpendorfer, white
"	"	L.Weitzenfeldt, white
"	"	Thomas Higgins, white
"	"	John Barnhurst, white
"	"	Julius Lochman, white
"	21st.	------ Tramble, white
"	22nd.	James McLean, man, white
"	"	J.Kinstler, man, white
"	"	A.B.Trigg, man, white
"	23rd.	Arthur R.Yerger, white
"	"	Anna Berry, girl, white
"	"	Adolphe Fleischer, white
"	"	L.P.Wetherbee, man, white
"	"	Amelia Kinstler, girl, white
"	"	Harry Vaughn, man, white
"	"	-----Perry, child, white

Washington Co.Ms
Yellow Fever in 1878;from "The Greenville Times"

Sept. 24th. Fanny Kelly, woman, white
" 25th. J.Gossett, man, white
" " Garrett Scott, man, white
" " A.Fleischer, man, white
" " Mrs. G.W.Elliott, white
" " John Manifold, man, white
" " Abe Hamburger, boy, white
" 26th. ------Pryor, child, white
" " C.F.Meisner, man, white
" " Rachel Radjesky, girl, white
" " Mrs. A.Ward, white
" 27th. Louisa Bodky, girl, white
" " Gus McAllister, man, white
" 28th. L.E.Morgan, man, white
" " Pat Burnes, man, white
" " Infant child of W.J.French
" " Sophia Yocum, white
" " George Brazier, man, white
" " W.Tilley,Jr. man, white
" " T.B.Speaks, man, white
" 29th. Mrs. L.Weisenfeldt, white
" " John H.Nelson, man, white
" " Eliza Kress, white
" " Helen Shaw, girl, white
" 30th. Wes.Wetherbee, white
Oct. 1st. L.M.Langley, white
" " Mrs. Mitchel, white
" " Minnie KLeiber, girl, white
" " Mrs. E.Stafford, white
" 2nd. Rev.T.Page, white
" " Lena Herman, girl, white
" " Jake Bier, white
" " Dr.J.S.McCall, white
" 4th. Madison Whitney Johnson, white, son of N.B.Johnson
" " Walter S.Berry, child, white
" " Mrs. James, white
" 5th. G.W.Elliott, man, white
" 6th. Dr.Archer, man, white
" 7th. Mable Wetherbee, white
" " Infant child of D.Morris
" 8th. Mrs. Greenfield, white
" 11th. William Myers, man, white
" " George R.Clark, white
" 12th. Frederick William Johnson, white, son of N.B.Johnson
" 15th. John Cotrell, man, white
" " Thomas Benjamin Johnson, white, son of N.B.Johnson
" 20th. Emma Childs, white
" 24th. Addaline Geinelle, white

Total in Town ------193

Washington Co., Ms.
Will Book 1: cont. from Vol. I

p. 411: Will of Cathaine Mundell; (Extract from Principal
Registry of the Probate, Divorce, & Admirality
division of the High Court of Justice.((England))
Of the town of Poole
Catharine Mundell is the wife of Joseph Hamilton
Mundell, Provision Merchant of Poole.
Exec; husband and Jane Daud of Wigton in Cumberland
Co. She (Catherine Mundell) states she has children
by Late husband and present husband, but does not
name them.
Will written; 6 Mar. 1876
Wit: by G.Baxton Aldridge, Soliciter, Poole
W. Mundell, Grocers Assistant, Poole
Proved: London 10 Apr.1876 by husband Joseph
Hamilton Mundell, who refers to articles of agreement of settlement dated 18 Aug.1858; Other exec.
is Jane Dade, widow.
Filed Washington Co. Ms 6 Feb. 1880

p. 412: Will of Ella Incisa de Cameranna
Names: Husband Alberto Incisa de Cameranna...gets
land in Wash. Co. Ms conveyed to her by R.C.
Brinkley...1900 acres or more;
To R.C.Brinkley for Trust for her mother,
Mrs. Eugenia Bertinatti;
Bro. C.P.Bass
Written: 1871, 2May
Wit: R.F.Brown, Jas. H.Bate, W.J.M_oor.
Codicil: Names Grand Mother Ann F.Bate
Will Prob. Sumner Co. Tenn Nov. Term 1872
Last document in series dated 28 Jan 1880, Gallatin,
Co. Tenn.

p. 413: Will of Council P. Bass:
Leaves "Riverside", Wash. Co. Ms (1570 acr.) to
Mrs. Eugenia P. Bertinatti (written in pencil
above her name - "his mother") If she dies, the
place goes to H.C.Bate;
In Sumner Co. Tenn, a plantation called "Reidmont"
to Ella Bass Bate & her natural heirs;
In Texas Counties of Ellis, Dallas - 1280 Acr. to
Leroy Valliant for interest of Elly Worthington for
her education; Should she die, proceeds go to Ella
Bass Conly now living Sumner Co. Tenn.;
States: Wants the body of his father, which is buried
in Wash.Co.Ms as well as Annie Bass (relationship
unexplained) as well as his body, shall be buried
near two sisters - Ella Ann Inchisa & Eugene Bass
on a certain Catholic Cemetary in Georgetown, D.C.
Written: Riverside Plt. 15 Mar,1879
Wit: Dr.Halbert, Charlotte x Jackson, Gen.X Jackson,
John Meyers, J.W.Atkinson
No recording date.

Washington Co.,Ms.
Will Book 1: cont. from Vol. I

p. 414: Will of J.B.Sterling (J.Bowman Sterling)
Wife: Penelope I. Sterling
Ch: by her (only one named)
Son: J.Bowman Sterling, Jr.
Sister-in-law: Mary McCausland, 1st w of bro.
Wm.F. Sterling.
No dates.

p. 415: Will of Wade Hampton, Jr.
Written at Wildwood Plantation; Wash.Co.Ms, res
idence of testator;
Wife: Kate
Names: W.G.Tutt
Wm. Goodwin, a servant, - a gun
Exec: L.W.Ferguson
Wit: W.G.Allen, L.M.Ball, Victor F.Erwin
"Wade Hampton, Jr. dec. 22 Dec 1879"

p. 416: Will of E.A.Eckhart: of Wash.Co.Ms "being in bad
health";
Will written in city of Dallas, Dallas Co., Texas
Wife: unnamed
Leaves the following property to his brothers and
sisters, whom he does not name: property in Boliv ar
Co. & Wash. Co. Ms; note from John Manifold, dec.
for "Onward" plt.; note from Wm.Summers; 65 acr.
in Wash. Co.Ms, part of "Forkland Plt.";
Exec: bro. Paul Eckhart
Heirs: children of Fillar(?) Smith - Wm & Henry;
Appoints Wm.Summers & Paul Eckhart Guard. of Wm.
& Henry Smith;
Written: 1 May 1879
Wit: F.M.Cain, Chas. W.Isham, W.L.Cummins, G.R.
Lear all of Dallas,Tex., D.C.Bosson, Bedford, Tar-
rant Co. Tex.
No Record. Date.

p. 417: Will of J.M.Standard
Names: Ginney Williams (who gets it all)
Written: 30 Jan 1880
Exec: friend P.M.Alexander
Wit: J.W.Collier, J.A.Stinson
No record. date.

p. 418: Will of Victor M. Flournoy of Fayette Co. Ky.
(written before the end of the war)
Names: his sister Betsy J.Johnson (gets int. from
Capt. Henry Johnson)
wifes's bros. & sis.
his brother
sis. Emily M.Ward gets amt. of R.J.Ward's
note;
Exec: wife Elizabeth J.
Written: 10 Jan 1865
Presented for Prob. Mar. Ct. 1866 Fayette Co. Ky
Later document dated 23 Jan 1878:Wash.Co.15 June 1881

Washington Co.Ms
Will Book 1, cont. from Vol. I

p. 420: Will of Patrick Dunn:
Wife: Fanny Dunn, land in Claib. Co.Ms he bot. from
  Henry S.Wheeless
2 ch: Willie Thomas Dunn
  Francis Leo "
Exec: wife
Wit: EdKenedy, F.Valliant
Written: 14 Feb. 1882
Codicil: "   "   "   left gold watch to son Willie
  Thomas when he becomes 15

p. 421: Will of Emory Clapp: Parish of Orleans, La. #1109
422 of Civil Court of Parish of Orleans
Will of Emory Clapp, dec. filed 5 June 1882
Exec: John J.Gidier, John I. Haidie
Wife: Pamela Starr Clapp, exec.
Mother: Mrs. Phineas Clapp Allen
½ bro. John Forsythe Allen
Namessake: Emory Starr Fry
  " : Emory Brown Thompson
Adopt. daus.: Lily Clapp, Sally Clapp
A second will of Emory Clapp filed 6 Nov. 1880
Changes from the first: gives Mother $30,000
Names Emory Fry of Marshall Co. Tex.
Grand ch. & namesake: Emory Clapp Day
Daus. Lillie Clapp, Sallie Clapp Day
Codicile annexed: adds name of John T.Allen
Ordered filed Maniton, Colc. 13 July 1880.

p. 423: Will of Wm.G.Tull of Wash. Co.Ms.,
Asks that he be buried between the bodies of his
wife, sons, and brother in Missouri.
Bro.-in-law: James W.Tate of Frankfort, Ky.
Wm.Tutt Baker gets his watch
J.E. Hauff Exec:
Wit: S.W.Ferguson & S.M.Ball
No dates.

P. 423: Will of Wm.Green (X) of Wash. Co.Ms.
Sons: Peter Green, Joseph Green, John Green, Lorenzo
  Green;
Exec: son Peter Green
Wife: Ellen Green
Written: 4 Aug 1880
Wit: A.B.Carson, Levi Moyse, Elijah (X) Hayes,
Alex (X) ___:
No record. date.

p. 424: Will of Jane E. Courtney, dec.
425: (owns a portion of Oakland Plt., Wash. Co.Ms, form
belonging to John T.Courtney, dec.) 160 acr.
Neph: W.L.Gay
Thomas Kelly (relat. unexp.)
sister: Caroline A.Gay
written: 7 July 1877; wit: W.A.Haycraft,
Mamie H. Bowen, Mary A.Yerger.

Washington Co., Ms.
Will Book 1; cont. from Vol I

p 426: **Will of Clarence Joyes:**
Greenville, Miss. 22 Aug 1881
Wife: Jennie A. Joyse
Wit: Geo. W. Platt, Edward Kennedy, F. Valliant
No record. date

p. 427: **Will of Mrs. Ann Worthington:**
Written 13 Feb. 1879
2 daus; James Ann Peak
       Tenie Valliant*
Thomas Worthington to receive 75 acres bought from
Ben Worthington
Step-son-Wm. Worthington
Names; Joel Johnson, Isaac Worthington
No record. date
*(Leroy B. Valliant marr. Theodosia Worthington
21 Oct 1862, Wash. Co. Marr. Bk A)

p 428: **Will of Leroy Percy:**
Written; 26 June 1873, Greenville, Miss.
Bro. W.A. Percy
No Record. Date

p 428: **Will & Codicile of Nellie (X) Thomas alias Nellie Kanatzor:**
Written; 16 Apr. 1877
Names children: Warren Davis, Cora Kanatzor, Joseph Kanatzor, Ada Kanatzor, Eno Kanatzor, Amelia Kanatzor.
Appoints as Guard. to ch. above - H.F. Kriger
Wit: Wm.G. Yerger, W.A. Ermman, W.A. Percy
Recorded: 5 Feb. 1883

p 429: **Will of Wm.E. Satterfield:**
430: Wife: Emma Kilgore Satterfield, exec.
Ch. Milling Marion Satterfield
    Vines John   "
    Emma Yeiser "
Advisors; Chas. R. Yeiser of Hinds Co. Ms.
       W.A. Pollock of Greenville, Ms.
our sisters: Elvie L. Yeiser
         Katie Yeiser
Written: 25 Nov 1880
Wit: Wm.G. Yerger, Jas. Robertshaw, W.A. Pollock,
    J.T. McNeily
No record. date.

p 431: **Will of Jacob Hirsch:**
Wife: Henrietta Hirsch, exec. & Guard. of ch. (minors)
Ch: Bertha Rosetta, Harry, Julia, Leopold, Sadie
Written: 28 Mar 1883
Wit: B. Caher, J. Wileizinski, D. Lemle
No record. date.

Washington Co. Ms.
Will Book 1; Cont. from Vol. I

p. 431: Will of Horace Scott:
    Written: 22 July 1882
    Wife: Margaret - part of Maeklenberg Plt.
    Ch: Mattie, Luey, Mary Anna, Evi Scott
    Wit: John T.Harris, Chas. F.Berry, Chas. W.Clarke
    Probated: 24 Jan 1883

p. 432: Will of Robert H. Walcott:
    Written: 16 Apr. 1883
    Father: T.G. Walcott, exec.
    Wit: J.N.Collins, R.L.Alves
    No record. date

p. 432: Will of James A.Tillman, dec.
    Written: Deer Creek, Wash. Co.Ms 20 Mar 1883
    Sister: Annie B.Tillman exec.
    Bro.: J.T.Tillman Exec.
    Mentions land he bought from Judge H.W.Foote*
    Wit: L.H.Wood, J.R.Johnson, Wm.Wood, Augustine Chew
    No record. date
    *(Judge Foote lived Noxubee Co., Ms. Was an early
    speculator in the Miss. Delta)

p. 433: Will of Saphrona Winn of Wash. Co. Ms.
    Written: 24 Sept. 1878
    Husband: Orsames (?) Winn, exec.
    Wit: Robt. Lusk, J.B.Winn, Margaret Jane Raney
    Later document shows it was wit.as authen. in Yazoo
    Co. Ms 28 Feb. 1883
    No record. date for Wash. Co.

p. 434: Will of John Wilson:
    Written: 19 Jan 1883
    Wife: Sarah Wilson
    2 ch.; Adelia Wilson, Eugene Wilson both under 21
    Guard. of 2 ch; Gen. L.W.Ferguson
    Wit: Harry W,Bell, W.APercy, Jr.
    No record. date.

p. 435: Will of Henry G. Saliziger :
    Written: 19 Oct 1883
    Wife: Anna Catherine Salizigior, exec.
    Ch.: Adolph R. Frey, Willie L. Frey, Louisa T.
        Saliziger.
    Wit: S.R.Dunn, D. Lemle, L.Hehcter, L.Hartman.
    No record. date:

p. 436: Will of James M. Sutton;
    Written 15 Sept. 1880
    Record. 19 Nov 1883
    Daus; Emeline T.Melchoir, has ch., 120 acr. on Black
        Lake, Wash. Co.
        Mary W.Vanoman, has ch.,but he excludes 2 of
        them - James Vanoman & Silas Vanoman "who are
    especially accepted and are to receive no portion
        of my estate"
    cont. next page.

Washington Co. Ms.
Will Book 1; cont. from Vol I

p. 437: Will of James M.Sutton, cont.
2 sons:Benjamin Sutton, Thos. J. Sutton
Mentions an agreement for working land with H.E.
Wetherbee.
Wit: Jno.H.Moore, D.C.Montgomery, R.A.Flanagan
Exec: 2 sons

p. 438: Will of Benhommie Cahn:(sp. also Cohn)
Written: 7 May 1884
Wife: Julia Cahn, sole exec. and G. of ch.
Ch.; Selig Cahn, Harry Cahn, Josephine Cahn, Julius
 Cahn, Joseph Cahn, Henry Cahn, Moses Cahn,
 Benjamin Cahn.
Wit: J.Wilezinski, W.H.Moore, Joseph Hirsch.
No record. date.

p. 439: Will of Francis J. Craig, decd.
Written: 16 Apr. 1874
Wife: Martha A.Craig
Wit: F.Valliant, W.B.Sullivan, A.W.Webber.
No record. date.

p 440: Will of Josephine M.Worthington:
Written: 16 June 1880
Husb.; Geo.P.Worthington, exec.
ch; unnamed
Wit: W.E.Hunt, D.F.Hunt, O.B.Crittenden
No record. date

p. 440: Will of Annie F.Hampton:DECD. State of La.
 441: Written: 2 Dec 1876
Est. in Miss. & La.
Names: father - Christopher F.Hampton
 aunts - Kate Hampton, Ann Hampton, Caroline
 Hampton
Wit: Rawlins Loundes, Jr., L.P.Loundes, ?Caroline
 M.Preston
No record. date

p. 442: Will of John Lees Wrigley: of Oldham, Co. of Lanc-
aster; Machine Maker, but lately of Woodris ing Hall
in Parish of Woodrising in Co. of Norfolk.(England)
Dated: 13 Sept 1873
Codicil: 19 Mar 1880
Prob. dated: 24 Sept 1884
Document states that he died 3 Aug 1884 - proved by
Edward Wright Wrigley & Henry Wrigley, the bros.
named within.
Will: Names bros. Edward Wright Wrigley of Abby Hills
 in Oldham - oil paintings
 Henry Wrigley of Holly Bank in Oldham - oil paintings
 cousin; James Collinge of Kinnerton Lodge in
 Co. of Fleming (?)
 bro; Geo. Wrigley
cont. on next page.

Washington Co.,Ms.
Will Book 1; cont. from Vol I

p. 443: **Will of John Lees Wrigley** (London) cont.
Thomas Henry Rushton, Benjamin Alfred Dobson, partners
with him in Machine Making business
States that he has property in United States
Sisters: Sarah Jane Wrigley, Caroline Wrigley
Wit: Alfred J.Riddle, J.F.Hansman
<u>Codicil</u>: Geo. Wrigley - of Melbourne, Aust. gets
#500 now - rest of est. div. into 4 parts
Bro. Edward Wright Wrigley - 1 pt.
Sis. Sarah Jane Wrigley of Remenham House,
Wraysburg - 1 pt
"   Caroline Wrigley   "   "   ", 1 pt
bro. Henry Wrigley of Oldham - 1 pt.
Wit: F.P.Thurston, 22 Gt. Marlboro St. W.
J.W.Rawlings, "   "   "   "   "
Given at London - 3 Oct 1884

p. 444: Follows: Hand drawn seal - Consulate of USA for Gr.
Briton & Ireland at London

p. 445: **Will of Robert H. Archer** of Ellicotts Mills, Howard
446: County Md.
Written: 28 day of ____ 1858
Ch: Robert N.Archer, Wm.H.Archer, Mary Archer
Stevenson Archer - trustee of sale of "Maidens
Bower" a farm in Harford Co.(Md.?)
States he is about to be married to Miss Mary Ruisold
Wit: Andrew McLaughlin, Saml. T.Houston, Stevenson
Archer
Prob.: State of Md., Howard Co. - 19 Oct 1875
Rec. Wash. Co. Ms 23 May 1885

p. 447: **Will of Charles Hill:**
Written: 18 Sept 1884
Wife: Sarah E.Hill
Ch: unnamed
Wit: W.B.Stewart, Geo.Reed, W.D.Hill, H.T.Stewart
No record. date

p. 447: **Will of Mary (X) Rives:**
Written: 8 Oct 1883 Arcola, Ms (Wash. Co.)
Dau.; Mrs. M.A.Murff & her ch. 2/3 of est.
John Orville Rives, Mary Leone Rives ch. of
decd dau Annie M.Rives - to share 1/3
Exec: A.W.Waddell
Wit: F.A.Bizzell, S.J.Phillips, B.T.Pearson
No record. date

p. 448: **Will of Emma K.Satterfield** of Hinds Co. Ms.
Dau. & only ch. Emma Yeiser Satterfield
Custody of this child to "my" mother Emma Yeiser, exec.
J.S.Niely & "my" 2 sis. as G. to ch. Emma
Wit: J.S.McNeily, S.M.Ball, H.W.Berkly
Written: 2 June 1884 - Prob. 21 Oct 1885

Washington Co.,Ms.
Will Book 1, cont. from Vol.I

p. 449: Will of Acinthea M.Cleaton:
Written 29 Apr 1885 - Prob. 9 Jan 1886
2 sons: Thomas Franklin Benson, Henry Calvin Benson
"Excludes other ch. because they have plenty of
worldy goods and these do not."
Wit: W.D.Ferris, J.A.Overby

p. 449: Will of H.V.(X) Price:
Written; 1 Feb 1885 - Prob. 9 Jan 1886
Wife: Ann Elizabeth Price, exec.
"her dau"; Elizabeth Price
Wit: Jas. A.Waring, Thos. Perkins

p. 450: Will of Wm.A.Haycraft:
Written: 8 Jan 1878 - Prob. 9 Apr. 1886
"my father" Dave V.Haycraft in Afton, Kans.
Wife; Mary Crittenden Haycraft

p. 451: Will of Morris Weiss;
452: Written: 17 May 1886 - Prob. 7 July 1886
453: Wife: Hannah Weiss
454: Merchantile partnership with Nathan Goldstein
    Ch.; Flora Wilkinski, Eveline Goldstein wife of
        partner, Jacob Weiss, Malinda Weiss, Ludwig
        Weiss.
    Wit: Sol Goldsmith, Jno.P.Finlay, Joshua Skinner
    Desc. of exten. holdings follow on pages 452,453,454.

p.454: Will of Mary E.G.Smith, decd.
Written: Live Oak - 22 Nov 1869 - Prob. 4 Oct 1886
Sis.: Jane Pryor Smith   (has other bros.& sis.)
Bro. James' wife - unnamed
Ida H.Blanton gets ivory comb, Fanny H.Smith - jewelry
Father; still living - unnamed

p. 454: Will of Jane Pryor Smith:
Written: 30 Apr. 1872 - Prob. 4 Oct 1886
Sis: Fanny Harriet Smith - est in Va. & elsewhere
Bro.: Harry Smith
* Widowed sis; Georgiana Blanton
Bro.; Dr. James M.Smith
Neph.; Geo Grenway Smith, s of Sr. Jas.M.Smith
Father: Dr.Geo. Smith
Friend: Dr. Alex Penny,
    "   Ida Hicks Blanton
Lizzie Gray dau of Jas.W.Gray of Vicksburg
Wit: R.Barnett, Lelia E.Donnellon, Ella Barnett,
Mary E.Wheeler

"Papers of the Wash.Co. Hist. Soc.";p.334 states that Georgiana
Smith married Wm.C.Blanton, and her sister Martha Rebecca
Smith m Dr.Orville M. Blasnton

Washington Co.Ms.
Will Bk. 1, cont.from Vol.I

P.456:Will of Mollie A.Bell:decd.
Names: son - Heddens Montgomery (under 21)
       Husb. - Jas.B.Bell, Exec:
       Mother - Josephine Harshe
       Sister - Annie Harshe
Wit:C.P.Montgomery,J.M.Montgomery,R.B.Campbell
Written: 6 Oct.1886 - Prob. 1 Dec.1886

P.457: Will of Peter Ellison of Greenville,Wash.Co.Ms.
To:Caroline Canbass (relat.unexpld.)
Wit:Annie (X) Gordon,D.L.Gordon
Written: 7 Sept.1886 - Rec: 11 Dec.1886

P.458-460: Will of Thomas J.Martin,Sr.,Decd:
Wife: unnamed - gets prop. and home on 3rd St.,G'ville,
      purchased from B.F.Guthrie.
Son: Thos.J.Martin,Jr.
Dau: Anna M.Blakemoore
Decd. states he owns property in Ark. purchased from Est.
      of H.D.Newcomb.
Exec: son T.J.Martin,Jr. and Alexander W.Blakemoore
Wit: H.M.Burford,Saml.Cassidy,Sr.,John B.Smith
Written: 5 July 1879
Will Probated in Jeff.Co.,Ky. 22 Jan.1883.Document states
that Thos.J.Martin owned prop. in Ky. and other states/
County Court accepts Will as valid.A.W.Blakemoore test.
No recording date for Wash.Co.Ms.

P.461-463: Will of Catherine (X) Egg:
Names: decd. Husband Joseph Egg
Bro: Thomas Reese - a lot in Louisville,Ky.
Dau:(surviving)Annie E.Cocks
Sallie Egg - last child of dau.Sallie C.Cox,decd.
Gr.son: John J.Cox, Exec.
Written: 5 Nov. 1869 - Rec. 26 Apr.1887

P.463-467:Will of Miss Mary Moore:(Mary Virginia Moore),
formerly of Mississippi but now of the state of N.C.
Names: Mother-Mrs. M.F.Moore,Exec:
Written: 19 Sept.1883
N.C.Currituck Co.:The Court to John Moore,L.H.Babb and
wife,Emma M.Babb heirs at law of M.V.Moore. Will has been
produced by Mrs. Martha Moore, exec."Service accepted"by
John H.Moore - brother of G'ville (Ms.) 15 Dec.1886;by
sister E.M.Rabb,L.H.Rabb - both of Brandon,Ms. - dated
18 Dec.1886. Will accepted in N.C. after examination by
M.H.Snowden,Mrs. Rosa Snowden, and Mrs.M.D.Baxter - bus-
iness acquaintances of the decd: N.C. verifies handwritten
Will - Rec.31 May,1887. No rec. date for Wash.Co.Ms.

P.468-472: Will of Harriet B.Theobald: Decd.
Son: Orville M.Blanton
Gr.Son:Willie W.Blanton (all things engraved Wm.C.Blanton)
She was concerned about moving the family graves in case
of encroachment by the Mississippi River, and asks that the

Washington Co.Ms.
Will Bk.1, cont. from Vol.I

Will of Harriet B.Theobald:cont.
bodies of her brother Augustus W.McAllister, and her
nephew A.W.McAllister be removed to a better site, if
need be.
To:Nellie Carrigan - lot in Paris,Tenn. & other things.
$1500 to Stewards of the Methodist Church.
Neice:Harriet B.Purser,now living near Carlile,Ark.
" :Mrs. Bettie Shelby & her daus.Kate Shelby,Hattie
    Shelby.
Alice Theobald,Annie Theobald(relationship unexpl.)and
their sister Ruth Langcape..all residing in Baltimore,Md.
Mentions Latting Family picture.
Gr.Dau:Ida Benoit
Exec:Wm.E.Hunt,Chas.H.Starling
Written: 18 May 1887
Codicil: concerns Mort. on D/T of Mrs. Amanda Dunn, wife
of Dr.S.R.Dunn, transferred "to me by W.A.Pollock".
Codicil written:June 1887
Filed for Probate:27 June 1888 at 12 o'clock.

P.472:Will of Samuel Harris:
Emma Passmore gets it all
Names "friend" S.H.King,Exec:
Wit:S.J.Willborn,Wallace Copeland
Written: 30 Sept 1883 Rec. 9 Mar.1888

P.472,473:Will of Andras Yager + Codicil:
Wife: Margaret R.Yager, Exec.
Ch.:Wm.Yager,Lula Yager,Geo.Yager,Leroy Yager,Goodie
    Yager,Maurey Yager.
Wit:L.Caffall,Albert Whiteway,M.Row.
Written: 14 July 1888 - Rec.29 Aug.1888

P.473:Verbal Will of Becky Powell: "made the Will on 23
Aug.1888, and died Sunday Aug.25,1888.
Wit:Maria (X) Orfut,Catherine(X)Overall,Ellen Robb,W.Glass.
Rec.11 Aug.1888.

P.474,475: Will of Lewis Thompson: Sharkey Station, Wash.Co.
Written: 23 Nov.1886
Wife:Unnamed - lot and house in Canton,bought from Chamber's
    heirs in 1865.
Dau: M.E.Chew - land on Deer Creek, Wash.Co.
Dau: (Decd.)Eugenia Torry and her ch. - land in Madison
    Co. Ms.
Son: Julius Thompson
Dau: Mary Ellen Britton - Deer Creek, Wash.Co.
 " : Hattie Baldwin
 " : Meta Moorman
Son:Lucuis Thompson
Son: (Decd)Herbert Thompson and his sd. widow Sally Thomp-
    son.
Exec:Son Julius Thompson and John D.Britton of New Orleans.
Rec: 30 Nov.1888

Washington Co. Miss.
Will Book 1; cont. from Vol I.

p. 476: Will of Julia H.Johnson, Decd.
Husb:Geo. G.Johnson - all prop. in Ms. & La.
Wit: H.K. Barwick, Jeff Connell, Eddie Barwick
Written: 26 Jan 1885 - Rec. 14 Jan 1889

p. 477: (Another !) Will of Lewis W.Thompson (see preceeding
478: page) Percy Station, Wash.Co.Ms
Written: 27 Nov 1886
Names Wife: Martha Ellen Thompson
Dau: M.E.Chew
Decd. Dau: Eugenia Torry
Son: Julius Thompson & wife & ch.
Dau: Mary Ellen Britton
" Meta Moorman & her ch.
" Hattie Baldwin
Son: Decd. Herbert Thompson - &widow Sally Thompso.
Exec: Son Julius & John D.Britton
28 Nov. 1886
Rec. 5 Feb. 1889 -(no expl. given for the 2 Wills.)

p. 479:Will of Martha (X) Axman of Greenville
Husb: Chas Axman, Exec.
Wit: O.Winslow, Mollie Smith, D.B.O'Bannon
Written: 4 Dec. 1888 - Rec. 7 Feb 1889

p. 479: Will of W.A.Percy
Son: LeRoy - to get law bks + other thgs.
W.Y.Yerger - law partner
Wife: Nannie I.Percy, Exec:
Ch: unnmd
Son: Wm.A. Percy,Jr. gets walking cane
Written: 17 Jan 1885 - Rec. 27 Mar 189_

p.480: Will of Celly (X) Turner of Greenville
Gr.Dau: Sarah Turner
Wm.Turner to be Guard. of Gr.Dau Sarah Turner
Wit: Elias Graves, Leonorah Wood, O.Winslow
Writ: ___May 1889 - Rec. 3 May 1889

p.480:Will of R.E.Hutchins; Decd.
Wife: Kate F.Hutchins, Exec.
Wit: W.H.Ballard, R.B.Campbell, R.S.Coombs
Written: 10 May 1889 - Rec.; %June 1889

p.481: Will of Wm.L.Vance:Decd. of Shelby Co., Tenn.
to (Huge Est.) Document subm. Prob. Court,Shelby Co.Tenn.
484: Nov. Term 1880 - Filed Nov.16,1880.
Names: sons -*Geo.T.Vance -Dresden Painting of "his
Mother and myself"
" * Guy P.Vance - watch,chain,& marble clock
Wife: Letitia H. Vance - homestead "Fernwood"
Dau.:Lulla V. - minature on Ivory of "Mother"
by Dodge.+ paint. of Bettie done in Paris.
" :Virginia - water-color painting of her
Mother made in N.Y. in 1849
" Bettie - "my mothers" minature by DOdge,
Old Family Bible, family papers, painting
from Venice.

Washington Co.Ms.
Will Bk.1,cont. from Vol.I.

Will of Wm.L.Vance:cont.
Dau: Sue - British Ency,Ebony Cabinet,Bk.Case,etc.and "her grandmother's old Family Bible dated 1816.
Son:Will - diamond pin
" :Otey, youngest, - cat's-eye button,Rosewood desk...
Sister: Elizabeth
Gr.Son:Wm.V.Martin - gold sleeve buttons
Dau:Virginia Vance Martin and her ch. - $16,450 already rec
Dau:Elizabeth V.Rutherford and her dau.Madge - $11,200 already received.
Dau: Sue -$10,950 already recd.
Dau: Lullie V. - $7,820 already received. (written beside this - "Lullie V.DuPass)
Son: Wm.L.Vance,Jr.
Decd. states that he has 8 children
Provided money for support and Ed. of Guy Balleran
Allowance for Horace Turner (colored)
Written: 30 June 1888
Wit: Orville Yerger, C.Kaiser, Wm.Lum
Rec: 16 Nov.1888 (all 9+ pages) Probated Memphis,Tenn.
    5 Dec.1889
Rec. Wash.Co.Ms. 21 Dec.1889
(Ed.Note: I have listed the artifacts inherited for their interesting types; there were many other things named.)

P.485: Transcript of the Will of Mrs. M.L.Dubose:Decd.
State of Tenn. Franklin Co. - Winchester
1st Monday in Nov.1888 (Nov.5)
Wit. to Will:P.S.Brooks,R.M.Dubose,S.C.Hodge.
Names:Husb. W.P.Dubose
Written: St.Luke 15 Sept.1885 - Final Doc. 16 Mar.1889

P.486,487: Will of Andrew P.Keisecker of Greenville:
To: Anna Clara Kenoye, dau.(only one) of Roxy Kenoye
    (female) nee Keener...$25,000 with his brother Chas.
B.Keisecker acting as her Guardian.
Names: Neph:Andrew Parker Keisecker - $5,000
       " :Frank Charles   "   - $2,500
       Bro: Chas.B.Keisecker - $10,000 - lives Dubuque,
            Iowa and has children
To:John Lewis Finlay and Mary Pelham Finlay, ch. of John
    P.Finlay - $5,000
To:young friend Willie T.Rhea to be held by W.F.Kriger
    of Greenville.
Decd. asks that $1500 be set aside for monument to be placed in family plot in German Catholic Cemetary at DuBuque,Iowa. Asks that Bro.Chas send his body to DuBuque to be buried with "my Mother and Father". If Anna Clara should die before she marries, asks that she be buried beside him. Requests that his bro. and his ch. not question his giving the bulk of his estate to Roxy and Anna Clara,"it is the right thing to do". If anyone tries to break the will, they shall be disinherited.
Mr.R.B.Campbell declared Attorney
Wit:J.H.Robb, Wallace Arnold, W.W.Toy
Written: 19 June 1888 - Rec. 8 May 1890.

Wahington Co. Ms.
Will Book 1; cont. from Vol. I

p. 488: Will of Minnie (X) Washington, Decd.
Widow of George Washington, decd. who decd 27 May 1888
intestate. "Having no ch. of my own" leaves all prop.
in Wash.Co. to neice Ellen Field
Wit: WmGriffin,H.Wilzinski,N.Wilzinski,Hy Saiden
Written: 21 Mar 1889 - Rec. 2 July 1890

p.487(2)(Duplication of page number)
Will of Frances George Perry of Greenville.Decd.
Sis: Ellen Whiteway
Bro: Thos.H.Perry
" : Sidney L.Perry
Exec: Albert Whiteway
Wit: Sam Brown, Geo.H.Stockwell
Written: 28 Feb. 1888 - Rec.: 23 Aug 1890.

p.488(2)Will of Minna Wartche (female)
489   Gr.Ch:Morris Bergman, Louis Bergman, Howard Bergman,
John M.Bergman,Lilly Bergman,Blanche Bergman;
Exec: Jos. Hirsch, Lee Hexter,Isadore Hexter
Wit:E.G.Marshall, Sol Brile, S.H.King
Written: 10 May 1888 - Rec. 14 Oct. 1890
Names also sp. Mina,Minnie Wastcki.

p. 490: Will of Caroline M.Skinner
Husb: N.C.Skinner
2 gr.ch. of "my 2sons " Joshua and Tristin L.Skinner
Gr.Child Caroline R.Skinner,dau of Joshua
"   "   Maria F.Skinner dau. of Tristan L.Skinner
To Mrs. Sarah Thompson "who formerly lived with me"
Exec: Husb., Joshua & T.L.Skinner, sons
Wit:W.G.Phelps, V.S.Phelps,James S.Marders
Written: 9 Mar 1885 - Rec: 27 Feb. 1891

p. 491: Will of Mrs. M.A.Barfield of Greenville
492:   Gives lot & house in G'ville, now occupied by Mrs.
B.P.Hughes, to Wm.G.Yerger in Trust for Wm.Given
Rucks and Sadie Maud Rucks, ch. of B.M. & Lee Rucks;
Lee Rucks is her neice and adopted dau.
Sister: Ann Hunter
" : Jennie Yerger
Wit: Stevenson Archer, W.E.Hunt
Written: __Aug 1891 - Rec: 7 Nov. 1891

p. 493: Will of Wm.E.Buckner, Dec.
Wit: A.J.Paxton,A.J.Paxton,Jr,A.J.Aldridge,A.G.Aldridge,
F.A.Bizzell
Witnesses state that on 24 Nov.1883 at Arcola, Ms.,
Wm.E.Buckner, at the dwelling of Dr.W .E.Buckner,
said he desired his sister Mrs. Mattie Wingfield and
her ch. to receive his estate.
Rec: 6 Feb 1892

Washington Co.Ms.
Will Book 1; cont. from Vol.I

p. 493: Will of Wm.W.Worthington, Decd.
    Written: 25 Mar 1884
    States he has already divided his Estate between his
    ch: 3 sons: Wm., Edward, Charles.
        Dau. Sallie Samuel & ch.
        Son: Thomas & his ch.
        Dau: Mary Nutt
    Mentions Wm.Hill, Harriet Place
    Wit: E.T.Worthington, E.P.Worthington,
    A Codicil, dated 26 Mar 1884 names his bro. Elisha, dec
    Rec: 13 May 1892

p. 494: Will of W.L.Jones, Decd. of Greenville
   495 To: Chas. H.Starling, Trustee of Est.
    Father: J.D.Jones
    Servant & Nurse: Ella Carter
    After Father's and Ella's death, all est. to go to
    the G'ville Library
    Wit:R.H.Spiers, W.S.Wright, B.Baer.
    Written: 13 Apr. 1892 - Rec: 30 May 1892

p. 496: Will of Matilda (X) Ross, Decd.
    Son: Laval Thompson of Louisville, Ky.
    Gr.Dau: Elizabeth Williams of G'ville, Ms.
    Exec: Dr. O.M.Blanton
    Wit:J.H. Robb,Jno.P.Finlay,Chas.H.Starling
    No dates

p. 496: Will of Mary H.Yerger,Decd. of Greenville
   497:Son: Wm.G.Yerger - land on Deer Crk., Wash. Co,
        leased at this time to Mr.Geo.Kittle (Reality PLT)
    Gr.Ch:Shall,Harvey,Wm &Bettie Yerger ch. of "my son"
        Harvey, decd.
    Neice: Mamie B.Helm
    Sis -in-law:Amanda V.Bowen
    Exec: Wm.G.Yerger
    Wit: W.E.Hunt, J.A.Shall, LeRoy Percy
    Written: 25 Mar 1892
   498:Codicil written 27 Sept 1892
    Added Gr.Ch: Mary Louise Wheatly
    Wit: Jno.P.Finlay,Geo.M.Helm,J.A.Shall
    Prob. 10 Oct 1892

p.499: Will of Sarah E.Buckner of Claiborne Co.Ms
    2 daus: Mrs. John M.Parker & Mrs. N.B.Anderson
    Gr.Ch: Robt. Lindsey Evans, Robt. Buckner Evans,
        Sarah Roberta Evans Le Bavon, Thos.Freeland
        Evans, Louis de N.Evans
    Names "Buckland Plt" in Wash. Co.Ms.
    Asks that graves of family on Winsdor Plt. or Daniel
    Place in Claiborne Co be put in order.
    Dau: Mrs. John M.Parker of N.O.,La. - land in Ark.
    Dau: Mrs. N.B.Anderson, wife of Dr.Lomax Anderson
    Cont. next page.

Washington Co.Ms.
Will Book 1; cont from Vol.I

p. 500: Will of Sarah F.Buckner, cont.
Exec: sons-in-law: John M.Parker & Dr.Lomax Anderson
Wit: H.C.Mounger,N.S.Walker,A.K.Jones
Written: 2 Jan 1892 -
Prob:Claib.Co.Ms, Port Gibson; 9 Feb 1892
" Wash. Co.Ms 17 Apr 1893

p. 501: Will of E.A.Fall (Eliza A.Fall) of Wash.Co.
502: To ch of Mrs. Sallie J.Phillips wife of S.F.Phillips of Virginia - land on Deer Crk.
To ch of Andrew Paxton, exec.
Wit: J.G.Paxton, S.B.Winn,W.E.Buckner
Written: 25 Sept.1878 - Reaffirmed 24 Mar 1892
Rec. 29 May 1893

p. 503: Will of S.L.Graham, Decd. Hickman Co. Tenn.
to Son: John M.Graham (custodian of family graveyard,
511: fenced in) - also Mills in Pinewood Village, Hickman Co.Tenn.incl. land purch. from H.Huddleston...lands border. on Bob Davis & Foster...Ld. bot. from A.G. Wilson, Cooper Place, Clarke Place, Phillips Place, & Mausion house "where I now reside"...ld. bot. from W,M.Phillips, Saml.A.Wilson,S.B.Lee,Ezra Peeler,A. Clarke from Jas. Clarke, also from Jones Collins & Campbell McEwen,& Hubbard...valued at $157,000.
Son: Harvey Hardman Graham (minor) land in E.Carroll Parish, La. #63,000 val.
states he has a wife and 3 ch.
Dau: Thomasella Hardman Graham (minor) - lots of jewelry - Plt. in Wash.Co.Ms "RedLeaf & "Wayside"+ others. $65,000 val.
Wife: Martha G.Graham - $40,000 + other
Bro-in-law: Geo. Helm
To: Miss Mollie E.Owen
To: Mrs. Marg. Clouston of Franklin, Tenn.
Ch's Uncle: Harden P.Figures of Columbia,Tenn to be G.
Exec: Jas.M.Meecham
Wit: A.C.Kuykendall, C.C.Meecham,J.H.hooper,R.H.Knight
Written: 23 July 1888
Codicil: adds land in La."Transylvania & New Translyvania", & "Stanbul" e.Carr.P. La. to Harvey
27 May 1891
Rec. Hickman Co.Tenn.:22 May 1893
" Was. Co. Ms. 15 July 1893

p.512: Will of Lewis (X) Lee, Decd.
Wife: Mary, exec.
Wit: Sam Raines, T.J.Williams
Written: 17 Oct 1893 - Rec. 18 Nov 1893

Washington Co.Ms.
Will Book 1; cont. from Vol.I

p. 513: Will of Nancy James, Washington Co.
Est. divided as follows:
½ to Rosa E.Glathry; ¼ to Nannie M.Glathery; ¼ to
Isaiah J.James
Nancy James signed by H.C.Watson
Wit: H.C.Watson, J.M.Scott,Ed.C.James
Written:14 Oct 1893 - Rec. 20 Dec. 1893

p. 514: Will of Virginia Dement, Louisville, Ky.
Written: 9 June 1893 at Burtonia, Wash. Co.Ms.
½ Bro: Stephen Castleman
½ Sis: Lucy Castleman
Lucy Jones
Adopt. daus: FlorenceBurton & Edna Burton; Exec.
Husb. J.R.Dement
Wit: J.S.Bowles, E.A.Bowles
Written: ___,___, 1893 Rec: 20 Dec. 1893

p. 515: Will of Sarah B.Allen of Greenville
Bro: Jas.B.Bell
Neice: Georgia Harbison
Ch. of Bro. Jas.B.Bell by his 1st marr, namely Alice
V.Bell, Sallie A.Bell,Archie C.Bell.
Asks for Exec. to send to Ky for copy of "my Mother's
Will"
Exec: E.N. Thomas
Wit: M.S.Smythe, L.A.Cappes, Va.G.Bell
Written: 10 Nov 1893 - Rec: 26 Dec. 1893

p. 516: Will of W.G.Phelps
Wife: Virginia T.Phelps - ld. in G'ville, Sunfl.Co.Ms
Bro: Alonzo J.Phelps & his heirs
Exec: wife and bro.
Written: 13 June 1890 - Rec: 21 Mar 1894

THE END

Washington Co.Ms.
Packet Gleanings

Many of the packets have been lost, but in researching the drawers of the earlier records, the following supplementary information has been noted:

Drawer 1 - 0/50

Pkt.#2. (Number corresponds with P. 2 in Will Bk.1) Est. of James Burns: Adm.Bd. Chas. Turnbull,Wm.W.Collins, Thos.W.Endecott: 22 Jan 1840: Final document Mar. 1851 toChas. Turnbull of Issaqueena Co.: No addit. info.

#3: Est. of Henry Rozier Dulany: (Rec. p.3,Will Bk.1) Adm.Bd. 27 Apr.1840 - Addison B.Carter, Alfred G. Carter, Thos.W.Endecott - $20,000: Packet contains will and adm. bd.

#8: Est. of Samuel W.(N?) Sullivan: (Will Bk.p.14) Pkt. contains Adm. papers of Nancy Y.Sullivan,now Nancy Y. Dodds and her husband Wm.Dodds. Petition for partition; John H.Farr & Mary Ann Farr of Issa.Co. claim 4/7 - Nancy Y. 3/7. The Farrs and the Dodds have entered into a contract to form a partnership for a period of 5 yrs. They own land in Issa. Co., + slaves. 4 May 1845 list of land in Chicot Co.Ark. assesed in name of Saml. N. Sullivan, heirs - 2,300 acres of "wild land".
Guardianship papers: Wm.Dodd appointed G. to Goldsmith Sullivan, Susan Ann Sullivan...Wit. by John H. Farr, Judge of Probate Issa. Co...States: Saml. Sullivan died intestate 26 Apr.1841 (of Claiborne Co.Ms) owned Plantation "Richland" in Issa. Co. G. papers 4 Jan 1846.
15 May 1841: Nancy Y. Sullivan pd $141 back taxes on land at Little Rock (Ark). Note signed by David Smart. Land transaction rec. Bk.J.p.14.
Adm.Bd.$10,000 signed by Nancy Sullivanm Jas.F. Jackson, Frederick P.Plant.
Est. closed out in Issa. Co.
(Census 1850 - Issa.Co. - lists: 15-15: Wm.Dodds, 34 bTenn, Nancy Y. 35 bAla,Mary A. 15 bIll,Cornelia 6 bMs, Eliz.T.3 bMs, Cecil E. 2 b Ms, Susan A. Sullivan 12 bMs.

#9: Will of Eliza Clara Dulany: Paper says recorded 27 Dec.1841 - but not where rec.
Written 24 May 1836 - Wit: John E.Dement,G. Briscoe, Edmund Briscoe.
Sons:Henry R.Dulany (see #3 above), Wm.Alfred Dulany
Son-in-law: Isaac B.Beall(Est. of Wash.Co.WBk.1,p.131
          June Term 1850)
Other ch:Benjamin, Cecelia J.Beall wife of Isaac, Virginia Dulany, Nora Dulany.
Only doc. in pkt. is the will.

Washington County, Ms.
Packet Gleanings, cont.

Pkt.#10:Est. of James S.Hardy: 30 Dec.1841 - Adm.Bd.by
Robt.S.French,Wm.W.Wilkins - $300. Not recorded.

#12: Est. of Thos.G.Percy: decd. 1841 (large packet)
Wife - Maria was Adm. for est. of decd, and replaced by
son Chas.B.Percy as Adm; Chas.B.Percy decd. by 1851 and
son J.W.Percy takes over.(Wife-Maria-decd. 1847)
1860: J.W.Percy,Adm. of Est. of Thos.G.Percy,names heirs
as follows: J.Walker Percy,Chas.B.Percy - decd;Leroy P.
Percy;Robt.H.Percy - decd 1853;Wm.A.Percy;Ellis Ware Percy
who decd.-1844.
Also included in this Packet is the unrecorded Will of
Chas.B.Percy: Written - 1850 - Feb.21: names: Wife Henri-
etta,decd;Children - Thos.G.;Eleanor N.;Joshua W.;Chas.B;
Henrietta; "my Mother" Mrs. Eleanor Nichols; Appoints Wm.
Nichols Guard. of Ch. "in Tenn."
(Ed.Note:Wash.Co.Will Bk.1,p.221,Vol.I of this series,Wm.
A.Percy of Wash.Co. is named the Guard. of Chas.B.Percy's
5 ch. named above in 1856)
(See Wash.Co.WBk.1,p.339 for Will of John Walker Percy:
Abstracted Vol.I of this series; Names Wife-Fanny E.;Dau.
Maria; 2 bros. - Leroy P.& Wm.A.Percy; Reco.Jan.1865)
(See Will of Leroy Percy: WBk.1,p.428, Abst. Vol.IIthis
series;Will written 1873; names bro. Wm.A.Percy.)
(Will Bk.1,P.479, this Vol. Will of Wm.A.Percy)

#16:Eof John Stowe: 28 June 1842 (Wash.WBk.1,p.26)

#18: Guardianship: James and Georgiania Tompkins, minors;
Guard.Bd. to Geo.N.Parks by Susan (x) his wife for her
ch. (WBk.1,p.51,Abst. Vol.I this series) Adm.Bd. for Est.
of Geo M.Tompkins, decd. Geo.N.Parks,Thos.Parks - Oct.1843

#20: Est. of John G.T.Prince:decd.1823 Ouachita P.La.
Adm.Bd. by David Blackburn,Secu. by Wm.Hunt,John G.Cocks
for $20,000 Dec.Term 1842. In 1846 Blackburn resigns as
Adm.stating "there is no est." No heirs listed.

#23:Est. of Wm.Ley;decd.(WBk.1,p.35-37,Abst.Vol.I) Adm.Bd.
by Wm.H.Taylor who is also Guard. of Ley's dau.Florida. Geo.
Croft, grandfather of Florida sends his son Benjamin to
Montgomery,Ala. for money from Wm.Ley's Est.for support
of Florida - 1844.

#24: Guardianship of Florida Ley:by Wm.H.Taylor. No new info.

#25: Guard. of J.R.Harvey:minor to J.M.Robertson, June 1851,
No add. infor. (WEk.1,p.59: Guard. of Evan J.Harvey,Belinda
Harvey,Jas.R.Harvey to Jos.W.Robertson.)

#27:Est. of Thos.Sellars:decd. Isaac Sellers,Adm. No add.
information.

#28:Guard. of Susan E.Penrice; minor - by R.A.Johnson,G.
(WBk.1,p.12,13) He asks for dismissal...she has married;
Doc. dated Feb.1846.

#34: Number matches Chan.Dock:Bk.1.Addit. infor:W.B.Shearer
& wife Letitia, sister of Ann L.Fitzpatrick - minor under
21. Letitia is of Madison Co.Ms. and they state their
mother was Ann L.Fitzpatrick and their father is J.E.
Fitzpatrick. Suit styled Shearer et ux vs J.E.Fitzpatrick.

Washington County, Ms.
Packet Gleanings, cont.

Pkt.#34,cont: J.W.Robinson of Hinds Co.Ms; Robt.W.Burney &wife Mary F; James S.Hampton & wife Octavia H; citizens of La; Jas.W.Phillips & w of Hinds.Co.; Chas.Buck & Alfred Murdock of Sunflower Co.Ms; Russell M.Williamson - heirs. Mary F.Burney, Octavia Hampton, ----Phillips. Suit dated 1857.

#35: Est. of John M.Tompkins; decd. Adm.Geo.Parks, No add.info.

#42: Est. of Jno.B.Holt; John R.Holt Adm. of John B.Holt vs Wm.L.Mills (WBk.1,p.72-Adm.Bd.25 Dec.1844) No.Add.Info.

DRAWER 2:50/113

Pkt. #50: Est. of George W.Clarke: decd. Adm.McLin Evans.

#55: Est. of Geo.Downing: decd. Adm.John F.Payne 24 Nov 1845 (WBk.1,p.76: Will of Geo.Downing, Adm.Bd.p.76-78) (See also WBk.1,p.80 - Jno.Downing to Edw.P.Johnson)

#62: Est. of Wm.F.Jeffries: decd. Adm.Bd.(Bk.A.p.341) by Thos.Endecott, Andrew Enos (Knox?), Robt.P.Shelby - $20,000 23 Apr.1838.
Dec. 1839 - Adm.Endecott "believes Est. to be insolvent" as debts outweigh assets.
Sale of Est. Rec.Bk.A,p.354,355: Buyers - Henry M.Lee, Jos.B.Penrice, G.G.Dromgoole, Chas.Turnbull, D.H.Threlkeld, Jas.B.Jackson, McLinEvans, C.R.Bass, L.H.Gish, A.M.Samuel - 30 June 1838, No heirs named.

#64: Est. of Joseph Wallace: Robt.M.Mccullough, Adm. of - 27 Feb.1837. Rec. Bk.A, 289,290; Adm.Bd.Robt.McCullough, secu. by T.E.F.Atchinson, Will E.Hale unto Orphans Court 22 Oct. 1833 who state Wallace left a Will. Inv. & Aprr. by Allen Wynens, John T.Georgain, Geo.W.Ward.
Will of Joseph Wallace: late of Wash.Co.Ms, being ill, called upon John Campbell, Wm.McFadden, S.B.Henagan. Wants the property brought to him by his wife, the widow of Isreal Matthews, decd. to go to the exclusive use of ch. of said marriage (1st) and all of Wallace's property to go to his own ch., all unnamed. Frances McFadden to get $100 per yr. as long as she is single; Exec. Robt.McCullough to be Guard. to his 2 ch. and also those of Isreal Matthews. Wit: Wm.McFadden states that Wallace decd.17 Aug. 1833. (Wife and ch. unnamed) Rec. Bk.A.p.123; Also Rec. 9 Jan 1834 Bk.E.p.341. (Does not say which series book)

#74: Est. of Allen Wynens: decd. Pkt. contains 2 doc. Adm. Bd. to Thos.T.Stevens - Dec.1847; Summons to Adm. 1850.

#76: Est. of Andrew McCormick: decd. Adm.Bd. by Council Bass, secu. by Jas.B. Jackson, Thos.Grimes - 26 Dec.1838 for $1200. Rec. Bk.A,p.362. Appointed John Saunders, Wm. W.Collins, Abraham W.Samuel to appr. Est. 1839. Bk.A,p. 374,375. Final a/c Oct. 1844. No heirs named.

#77: Est. of Wm.B.Wren; decd. Overseer of Council Bass who is Adm. of Wren's Est. 26 Dec.1838. Rec. Bk.A.p.372,373. Final settlement 1844.

Washington Co.Ms.
Packet Gleanings; cont.

Pkt. # 78: Est. of Dr. Edmund R.Bass, decd. Adms. Council R.
Bass & Jesse Bass.
Document states Dr. Ed.R.Bass decd. Madison Co.Ms
Intestate 9 July 1832 - DSP with bros. & sis.:
Bros. Isaac, Edwin, Giddeon, Jesse of Hinds Co.
Council is not listed as a bro. but probably is.
Gideon Bass's ch.: Eliz. m 1st Henderson Edwards,
m 2nd Jos. J. Holland; Anaskew; Alonzo T.; Louvenia,
wife of Sidney S.Sledge; Gideon R.;Charity Ann;Jno;
In Wash.Co.Ms. additional heirs - Penelope Willhite;
Jordan R.Bass; Louzanna Barrow wife of Josiah Barrow.
Final acc. Madison Co. 1846.

#81?: Est. of Philip A.Gilbert, decd: (1831) (Will Bk.1,79)
Documents incl.Inventory of Personal Prop.
17 Mar 1831 - Appraisal by Frederick G.Turnbull,
Andrew Knox, Wm.Penrice.
Feb. 1847 Final decree to sell land
28 May 1847 Proof of notice of publication
Jan. Term 1846: Heirs of decd. listed as follows:
Sarah Dromgoole, Alex Montgomery & wife Jane,
John G.Cocks - exec. 30 Dec. 1845 -, Philip
A.Cocks - exec. 9 Jan 1846 -, Seth Cocks,
Abram F.Smith and Myra his wife, William Scott
and Jane Scott. with A.W.Dunbar as Tenant in Possession.
Nov. Term 1845: Pet. of Thos. Endecott to become
adm. of Gilbert's est. since the appointed Adm.
Wm.Droomgoole has decd, who was a relative "by
intermarriage", being the husb. of Sarah.
Land squabble follows: Citations to Adams Co.Sher.
also Wash.Co...Endecott states there are many things
pending with the Est. that need attending. Court
grants his pet. for Adm.

#82: Est. of Soloman Phelps,decd. (name also sp. Salmon)
Adm. John Fulton: Summons - 1846. Appraisal $189.00
personal Est. 22 Sept 1838: No heirs named.

#85: Est. of Henry T.Irish, decd.Adm. Jethro Bailey of
New Orleans. Release signed by heirs of Irish;
H.Mary Irish, Mary B.Irish,Volney S.Irish, John
Irish - 20 Mar 1866. Only document. (See WBk.1,87)

#88: Est. of Patterson Rains, decd. Adm. Thos. S.Theobald,
(WBk.1,p94) No add. info.

#97: Est. of John C.Miller:decd. Guardianship of minor
dau. Laura Miller app. to her Uncle Harvey Miller.
Huge Pkt. contains detailed yearly crop yields, all
of Laura'a bills, copy of John C.Miller's Will
Recorded Bk.J,p.9,10,11. Names his widow as Jane H.
Miller. Final acc. 27 Feb. 1855

Washington Co.Ms.
Packet Gleanings:

Pkt. #98: Est. of Frederick C.Clark, decd. Adm. P.A.Cocks
(WBk.1,p109 - 111) Document in Pkt. ; Power of
Atty. - We: Henry Clark, Elizabeth Clark, Jane
Emaline Clark, George S.Clark, Robert S.Linsey
and Margaret Linsey his wife, all of Baltimore
Co.Md. give POA to Henry Clark to recover inheir-
itance from Est. of Frederick C.Clark of Wash.
Co.Ms.,dated 1850.
Final document 1852.

#104: EST. of Wm.H.Pope, decd. Adm.Bd. C.E.Percy (1848)
(WBk1,p.112,113)- Adm. Bd only .

#113: Est. of Wm.Flagg,decd. Adm. A.W.McAllister
(WBk.1,p.123 - Adm.Bd.) 28 Jan 1850.

DRAWER 3 -#114/145

Loose paper: Est. of Wm. Ley: Guardianship of his
dau. Florida Ley. Gd. Bd. signed by Wm.h.Taylor,
Wm.Laughlin,Nathan A.Ware, C.S.Tapley - 16 Jan
At this time Florida is living in Wash.Co.'s.
Through court proceedures, Wm.H.Taylor of Montgomery
Co.Ala. has liquidated Florida's est. and as she is
now living in Ala. with her grandmother, he wants
to terminate the G. in Miss., and put her funds
in Ala. In 1847 Florida is still under 14. Final
a/c 15 Feb. 1848 in Miss.

#114: Alonzo Lancaster is Adm of John W.Ward.
infor.

a 2nd #114: Mary Morris vs Henry N.Morris, divorce & alim.
(Chan.Ct. suit: States they were both from Wash. Co., & when
Doc.) they wed 9 July 1848, and both still live there.
She is suing for support, and begs to keep him fro
selling her dower. Bk.Q,p.66 for her dower share.
Wit: Sarah Glass of Golconda, Ill. Divorce granted
May 1862. No issue.

#118: Est. of W.M.Robertson, decd. by Eliz. M.Robertson
exec. WBk1,p. 143 for Will of: No addit. inf.

#119: Guardianship: James Rucks, Natural guardian to Maria
Louisa, Henrietta, Marion, Lewis Taylor, minor ch.
of Louisa V.Rucks who had a bro. J.F.W.Brown to whom
she owed $10,000. WBk1,p. 210 - pet. of G. for 2
of the ch.

#121: Est. of Starling Gorman, decd: WBk1,p.124, Wash. Co.
The following doc. in this packet: Notice in the
Vicksburg paper, listing heirs:
Petition of heirs for Partition of their bros. est.
dated 19 Dec. 1850 - Noxubee Co.Ms. Heirs are:
7 Brothers and sisters. 1.Terrel,2.Oliver,3.Mary,
4.Artimecy,5. Elizabeth G.,6.Felix,7.Sarah. cont.

Washington Co.Ms.
Packet Gleanings:

#121: cont. Gorman Est. (Starling Gorman died in Havana 1839/40) by 1850, when this document was probated in Washington Co.Ms, the following changes had occured in the family structure: Oliver had died, leaving no ch. but a widow, named Ann; Terrel had died leaving 5 ch. - Casendanah who marr. with David Hinds, now living in Noxubee Co.Ms.,Chalesta who marr. Pleasant Marion Mobley.,Mary Jane wife of William Marr,Felix, and _____ (cannot decipher his name) now in Marshall Co.Ms.; Mary Gorman who marr. Geo.W.Clement and had 3 ch. Oliver,Geo.Washington & Martha Clement, she m 2nd R.T.Payne in 1841, Nox. Co.Ms...her ch. living Hds. Co.Ms; Artimecy Gorman marr. E.L.Harrison who was dec. and she was living Wash.Co.Texas; Sarah Gorman had m Charles W.Allen and they had 3 ch. - Mary Margaret, Cynthia Williams Allen, and Chas. T.Allen, Sarah is now decd.; Felix is still living in Nox.Co.Ms; Eliz. Gorman marr. Wm.B.Reed:
Pet for Part: 1851 - Est. Divided into 1/7's.
Sale of Est. in Wash.Co. 6 Nov.1852 (Felix had bought out Artimecy & Ann)

Ed:(The desc. of George Washington Clement and Mary Gorman remained in the area around Hinds, and many are buried there.)

#125:Mary Morris vs Henry Morris: Henry still hasn't paid (Chan.Doc.)up, and she is trying to stop the sale of property.

#125:(cannot explain the duplication of numbers)
Green L.McCarroll, est. vs Jno.L.Finlay, states he departed this life 22 Feb 1851, leaving no wife, In 1846 G.L.McCarroll is G. of Andrew J.H.Crow, son of Henry Crow, decd.

#126:Guardianship: Ann D.Hill Halsey, G. of 3 youngest ch. of Stephen M.Jackson, decd. Names the slaves given to them by their grandmother Mary Jackson, Hds. Co.Ms 184_; States she has given them, 1851.
Ed.(She has since intermarried with Dr.Seymour Halsey of Vicksburg, Ms.)*

#127:Ward Sanders & Hunt vs James A.McHatton, et al:Civil suit over Mortage (very large pkt.)(Gen.Chan.Dock.p66)

#128:Dr.Wm.AHammet,decd; Est. of: Edward Hammet of Mont. Co.Va. appoints Walter R.Staples & Dr. Jas. P.Hammet of Montgomery Co.Va. POA for settling est of Bro. Dr. Wm.A.Hammet, decd. of Ms (Clerk of Court in Mont.Co. Va. is James M.Wade)..Doc. dated 3 Oct. 1865.
Doc.:E.M.Hammet vs Edw.Hammet, a commission app. to divide Lammermoor Plantation., Wash.Co.Ms.
20 Nov.1867: F.A.Metcalfe, sole heir of Evelina M. Hammet, widow of Wm.H.Hammet & the bro.Edw.Hammet. (Gen.Chan.Dock. Bk.1 p.66)

*(Ed.) Ann Dunn Hill and Stephen Mason Jackson had 4 ch.: David Dunn Jackson, M.D.,Joseph Littleberry,Laura V. and Henry. In 1851 Ann D.Jackson,widow, entered into a marriage contract with Dr.Seymour Halsey of Warren Co.

Washington Co.Ms
Packet Gleanings, cont.

Pkt.#/28(2):Est. of Geo.L.Yeagle;decd. Pet. for Adm.Bd.
by J.S.Small, who states that Yeagle was on Island 8⁻,
19 July1851,(he lived with "an old woman - Mrs.Brown")
and disappeared crossing the River (Miss.) His Est. needs
attention. Document settles a/c with Julian Brown. Pet.
Adm. granted.

#129:Est. of Thos.Endecott: (file stripped)

#129½: Indenture:Est. of Robt.P.MCconnell: 25 Feb. 1853
Mrs. Sarah Martin of Madison, Indiana and Mrs.Elizabeth
A.McConnell, widow of the decd. of Greenville,Ms.of the
1st part vs Joshua M.Craig of Columbia, Ark. Suit states
that Joshua Craig bought land in G'Ville previously bought
by Robt.P.McConnell "in his lifetime". J.M.Craig is Adm.
of Est. of R.P.McConnell - Adm.Bd. 15 Sept.1851: Craig
resigned his commission 1853, stating that the widow and
Mrs. Martin are "only heirs" of McConnell.

#31: (Misfiled) Est. of Wrenna B.Sellers: Isaac Sellers
is Guardian of Emily,Cornelia,Thos.Wm. and Erwin Ruthman
Sellers, infant orphans of Wrenna B.Sellers: Guard.Bd.
signed by Isaac Sellers, secu by Benjamin Sellers,Isaac
C.Hill - 24 July 1843.
Issaqueena Co.Ms: Isaac C.Hill and wife Emily C.Hill,
late Emily C.Sellers, heirs at law of Wrenna B.Sellers,
28 Nov.1848.

#65:Est. of Isreal Matthews:decd. Pkt. contains: Apprs.
of Matthew's Est.June 23,1827 by Phillip Gilbert,Wm.
Britton,Wm.Penrice: 1827 - John McFadden, co-adm. of
Matthews' Est. with Ruth Matthews,signs Adm.Bd.:Jos.
Wallace is appointed Guard. to Ely and Lavinia Berry
Matthews,minors. 1833 Robt.McCullough becomes Guard.
of Elijah and Lavinia Matthews (Wallace decd. 17 Aug.
1833) Jan.Term - Adams Co.Ms. - 1844: Elijah Matthews
and his "Next best friend" Lyra H.Glenn, who has married
Lavinia Matthews petitions for Part. of Prop.

#140:Guard: Emily M.Powell appointed Guard. to Sarah
Elizabeth Chaney,Thomas Y.Chaney,minor heirs of Thos.
Y.Chaney,Sr.,decd.late of Wash.Co.Ms. An earlier paper
also names Wm.J.(the oldest ch.) 24 Oct. 1836: Docu.
states that Thos.Y.Chaney decd.1835 Wash.Co.leaving his
widow,your petitioner, who has since marr.Mordecai Powell,
and 3 ch. - namely Wm.J. now 24 yrs. old,Thos.Y. 17,Sarah
E. 20 yrs. Filed 24 Jan 1853. Sarah Elizabeth Chaney
later marries Littleton P.Franklin. (For further records
of Mordecai Powell see Issa.Co.Ms.Rec.)

#143:Est. of Thos.J.Likens: WBk.1,p.179-181.No add. Infor.

#145:Est. of Daniel P.Marr,decd.James T.Rucks,Adm. states
Daniel Marr departed this life July 1853 Intestate, surv.
by a widow,Selina Jane Marr who refuses to act as Adm. Pet.
for Adm.Bd. filed 28 Nov.1853. Final decree 29 May 1860;
Named in some of the papers, but unidentified, are Geo.W.
Marr, N.L.Marr.

Washington Co.Ms
Packet Gleanings:
Drawer 4: 148/164A

Pkt. #148: Est. of Jeremiah Saunders Ward, Decd.: Wm.E.Daniels,
Adm.Appraisal & I. filed Dec. 1854:
Heirs and distributees: Evermont Ward; Essie P.Brasher
and wife Amy, formerly Ward; and Wm.Henry Wilburn,
Martha Alice Wilburn, Amanda Wilburn, Adelia Wilburn,
minor heirs of Adelia Wilburn, decd, formerly Adelia
Ward. The G. of the Wilburn ch. is Henry Smith.
Filed 7 Jan 1856: (Adm.Bd. WBk. 1, 195.
Paper of Joel Wilburn states he was in Chicot Co.
Ark when Henry Smith was declared G. of his 4 ch.

Extra Document in Pkt. 148: POA of Reuben L.Bohn &
Mary Ann Bohn, his wife, late Mary Ann Merclkeld
of Marion Co.Ms to Geo. Merclkeld of Boyl Co. Ky.
to collect from Est. of Joseph C.Merclkeld, decd.
Filed: 31 Jan 1851

#148½: Ellen A.Conway - vs James A.McHatton, et al:
Bill of Complaint; Ellen A.Conway & Charles Chinn,
her minor heir, with Richard Chinn as his agent
(relationship unexplained) vs Jas. A.McHatton,
Chas.G.McHatton (relat. unexpl.) with copies of
the document sent to Geo. W.Ward at Newport, Ky;
Wm.C.Graves at Georgetown, Ky; A.Edgar at Leesburg
Ky; J.M.Williams at St.Louis, Mo.; Jno.Viley at R
Roanoke Pt., Mo...Doc. dated 14 Nov 1866.
In one instrument Ellen complains that Richard
Chinn of La. and Jas.McHatton of La. are both in
Cuba and unable to attend to business.
1867 Fenelon McHatton also named, a non resident.
Suit over transference of notes; large sums of
money involved.(Gen.Chan.Dockt.1,p.77)

#150: Est. of Thos. J.James: Apr 1866 - Adm. Jno.L.Nelson.
Wm.Haycraft is adm of est of James Abel and Nannette
Able and has transf. notes over to Thos. James,
also notes on E.C.James. Small pkt.

#146½: Guardianship of S.R.Dunn to minor ch. of Thos.W.
Dunn, decd: Bettie Dunn, Jno.N.Dunn, Thos.W.Dunn,
Saml.R.Dunn, Chapin H.Dunn, Finlay M.Dunn; Appraisers
of Est.; Robert Carter, G.Mosby, A.Copeland, Russel
Montgomery. Dec. 1853.

#153: Hugh Barefield, decd: Adm. Susan Barefield
Large pkt. contains annual a/c, payments rec. from
Stephen Barefield, relationship unexpl.; Invent.
16 Dec.1854; School bill for their two ch. Eudora
and Thomas Barefield; Adm.Bd. for Susan Barefield
and Stephen Barefield dated 11 Dec. 1854; Pet for
final settlement. (wBk.1,p198..Adm.Bd.)

#153: WM.E.HUNT, GEO.B.HUNT et al vs Wm.F.Smith, et al.
-Many depositions; Sarah F.Walker only surviving
heir of Freeman Walker, decd. answers Bill of
Compl. of Wm.E, Geo.B. & Prudence B.Hunt, exec. of
the will of Wm.Hunt & Geo.T.Blackburn complt. by
Wm.F.Smith et al. Depos. of James S.Walker.
Filed: 14 May 1866; Rec. Gen.Chan.Dock.p.79.

Washington Co.Ms.
Packet Gleanings:

Drawer 4 - 148/164A
Pkt.#154: Est. of Eleanor Percy Lee, decd: Adm. Wm.H.Lee,
who is also Guardian of their ch. Adm.Bd. 25 Mar
1850; 1st Annual a/c 28 Dec 1852;
1850: Wm.H.Lee is app. G. to Kate, N.W., Harry P.
& Jno.M.Lee:
1862: following alterations: Kate Lee has married
L.W.Ferguson, N.W.Lee is decd, possibly leaving
heirs, Jno. Lee is still a minor. No mention here
of Harry P. (Rec. Wbk.1, p.200)

#159: Est. of Jesse Fields: Adm Bd 26 Mar 1855 to S.W.
Parks. Pet. of James W.Browder and Elizabeth his
wife, the former Elizabeth Fields; G.W.Faiso &
Ellen R. his wife the former Ellen R.Fields; Harry
and Henry C.Fields, minors by their Guard. James
W.Browder. Asks that James Browder be app. Adm.
Pet. granted.

Drawer Marked -52-66-67- whose numbers correspond with the
file numbers given in Gen. Chanc.Dockt.Bk.?,
are missing.

#52: Brown & Co. vs the Bank of Mississippi:
The Brown Bros. were from Liverpool, Eng. and
York. Many transactions are listed dealing
with varios planters of the Miss. Delta.
Two trans. show family connections; 1877 Exec. of
Will of Stephen Duncan were Stephen Duncan,
Duncan, Samuel Davis; Exec. of the Will of
R.Marshall were S.Duncan Marshall, and
Marshall.
2 of the Brown Bros. were Wm. & James

#61: Arnold Lashley vs James E.Zunts & Thos.
Mar. 31 1859 no addit. infor,

#60: John J.Penrice vs Robt. Marsh!
Suit over sale of slaves belonging to
Likens, Penrices' ward. 31 May 1859

#67: *Board of Police vs G.W.Robb, et al: Filed
Complaint against Gabriel W.Robb,
his wife, lately Mary Ann Evans;
Evans who is a minor under the age of
sole heir at law of said McLin Evans, decd.
*Later called the Board of Supervisors.
Wm. A.Haycraft is Guard. of Mary McLin Evans.

Drawer Marked
#85 - A,B,C. Est. of Henry T.Irish: Adm. J.B.Bailey of
New Orleans. Adm. a/c. Mound Pleasant Plantation
mentioned.

#74: J.R.WILLIAMS vs W.B.Wright: Exparte Partition for
sale of land 2 Apr 1860; Joseph R.Williams for minor
MyrtheB.Wright (no Guardianship stated - land to
be sold and ½ money to each.)

Washington Co.Ms.
Packet Gleanings,cont.

Drawer #52-#67: This Drawer seems to follow the numbers used in General Chancery Docket Bk.1, many missing.

Pkt.#58:May Minutes - 1859:
George H.Buford and Wife vs Annie Fulton,A.J.H.Crow:
Filed Mar.9,1859: John Fulton,decd in fall of 1852, leaving a Will which is in dispute; the relationships of the people involved are as follows;
John Fulton had 2 daus...Adelia Fulton and Sallie who was 10 yrs.old at the time of his death. John Fulton's wife and mother of Sallie is Annie Fulton who was the former wife of Henry Crow. Annie Crow Fulton had 3 ch. by Henry Crow - Andrew J.H.Crow;Mary Crow now married to John James; and Eliza Crow who married Edward C.James and they had a son Edward James.Of these 3 ch.Eliza Crow James has decd and Ed.C.James is Guard.to their minor - Edward James of Ark.(Pkt.#21),Annie Crow Fulton has decd: 7 July 1859)By Jan.1861. - Sallie Fulton has married (1858) Geo. H.Buford.(Gen.Chanc.Dock.Bk.1,p.30)

#76:R.H.Hord,et al vs John A.Miller: Robert H.Hord and wife Mary I,Hord (Formerly Mary I.Jackson) were to furnish John A.Miller slaves to work on the road and they are in dispute over the arrangements for this.

#77:Thomas Kershaw and wife vs John P.Cunningham:Gen.Chanc. Dockt.Bk.1,p.39: lists suit as Thomas Kershaw vs Anne Kershaw, et al...Geo.Kershaw: In this document Thos.Kershaw's wife is named as being Mary Jane Kershaw.(Ed.Note: she was the former Mary Jane Cunningham sister to John Peavey Cunningham - see John P.Cunningham's Will WBk.1,p.203,Abst. in Vol.I. of this series)Affidavit of A.F.Smith..."John P. Cunningham, at the time of his death left Mrs. Mary Jane Kershaw, wife of complainant; Richard Cunningham,Miller. Cunningham and his sister whose name, I think, was Frances C., all of whom have since died...Richard, Miller, and his sister Frances without issue". 1860.

DRAWER #128-152-seems to be from Gen.Chan.Dockt.

#129: Nannette Abell vs W.A.Haycraft, et al: Filed 29 Oct. 1861. Nannette states she is widow of James Abell,decd. and that she was formerly Nannette James, one of the heirs of Theodorick James,Sr.decd. She further states that she marr. James Abell 1850, at which time her father, Theodorick James Sr. gave her 4 negro slaves - and at his death she received more slaves and some land. James Abell, decd. 20 May 1861 leaving his widow and Mary Abell, James Wm.Abell,Frances Abell,Saml.Abell,Susan Abell, and Nannette Abell, all minors. Wm.A.Haycraft is the Adm. of Abell's Est. and the Guard. of the minor ch. Nannette, the widow, wants her property separated from the Est. of James Abell. Thos.J.James certifies he "managed the plantation for Mr. and Mrs. Abell 1860 - 1861" and her property is as she claims. Commissioner complied - Nov.1861

Washington Co.Ms
Packet Gleanings:

#130: **Robert B.Carter, Exec. vs Robert H.Carter, Adm.**
Filed 12 Nov 1861; Robert B.Carter is Exec. of
Landon F.Carter, decd. - States; On 10 Oct 1853 an
agreement entered into by brothers Alfred G.Carter
and Landon F.Carter. Alfred G.Decd. 1854 -55 without
paying Landon F. his share. Robt. H.Carter is Adm
of Alfred G.Carter, decd.
Document dated 10 Oct 1853: Agreement between Alfred
G.Carter, Robt. G.Carter, Landon F.Carter, by his atty
Robt. G.Carter. Also Wm.G.C.Mann...all heirs at law
of Wm.G.Carter of 1st part & Isaac Shelby Adm. of sd.
Wm.G.Carter, decd. and his wife Susan S.Carter, wido.,
both of the 2nd part. Isaac Shelby had sold land in
Ark. from the Est to John A.& Silas Craig. Isaac
Shelby pays the heirs; Doc. signed by A.G.Carter,
R.G.Carter, Landon F.Carter, by his atty. R.G.Carter,
W.G.C.Mann, Isaac Shelby, Susan S.Carter;
There was land in Ark., and Carter Co., Ky; and Fayett
Co.Ky.

#131: **Victor F.Wilson Vs Joseph Lovell, et al:** Filed 5 Dec
1861: Bank Firm of Victor F.Wilson, Shepherd Brown,
Jos.H.Johnston, J.J.Thomas, Jas.Shirley, E.G.Cook, E.
Pendleton, Geo.R.Fall - - on Credition of late Benet
A.Crawford (decd. 1860); Edmund Crawford, Richard
Crawford, Elizabeth Crawford, Nancy Crawford, & Benj.
B.Taliaferro and Judith A. his wife (former Judith
Crawford) heirs at law of sd. Bennet A.Crawford &
citizens of Va. complainants (in his own right as
Adm. of Est of Jno.A.Geatman, decd) against Jos.
Lovell & Louisa G. His wife - Wm.L.Lovell & Antonia
his wife, & F.Henry Quitman, M.Fredericka Quitman,
M.Rosalie & Elizabeth T.Quitman all of Ms. the last
3 minors....Land in Coahoma Co.Ms. & Wash, Co.Ms.
A document states: "Natchez - Dec.12,1851" 1041 +
1357 acres in Wash.Co. conveyed by Bennet A.Crawford
to Gov. John A.Quitman.

#133: **Aramus Winn et ux vs Tecumseh F.Royall:** Filed 25 Sept
1862: Sawmill contract. Aramus ' wife is Ereline S.
Winn.

#134: **Case & Colburn vs John Norwood:** Filed 7 Feb,1863:
Suit states; T.B.Case and Saml. Colburn Pet. the
Board of Police (Later called the Board of Supervisors)
for a license to operate a ferry across the Bogue
Phalia on a road leading from Deer Creek to Indian
Bayou in Sunflower Co....dated 1858. Case then bought
land on points on which the ferry landed. The Military
blocked the road and ordered them to secure the boat,
which they did. Later the boat turned up on John
Norwoods' land, and Case wants it back. Handwritten
note enclosed in Packet:"Notice - Forewarn any person
interfering with my boat. I want it to stay where it
is - John Norwood": The Court ordered the Sheriff
to return the boat to Case.

Washington Co., Ms.
Packet Gleanings:

#136: John J. Smith vs Chas. Vernon- Writ of Seques.;
Filed 25 Dec. 1865:
Suit states: John J. Smith of Vicksburg, Ms. agreed to
"furnish" Chas. Vernon of Wash. Co. who had a contract
to work land for Mrs. Martha A. Blanton, near Greenville,
owned by C.M. Blanton, Esq.... Plantation called "Belle
Air"... to be worked on ½'s.

#137: Jas. Cammack (of New Orleans) vs Walter L. Campbell
(of New Orleans) & Wm. F. Smith (of Wash. Co. Ms.)
Filed 29 Dec. 1865: no addit. infor.

#138: Austin F. Alexander, Adm. vs Wm. F. Smith: a Bill to
enforce Lien   Filed 30 Jan 1866:
Austin F. Alexander, Adm. of Amos Alexander, Decd.,
states that Amos departed life Adams Co. Ms 1860 intestate. Documents incl. in Pkt.: Final decree...1869.
In May 1868, V.F.P. Alexander is Adm. for Amos Alexander; Nov. Term 1868 - Bankruptcy of Wm. F. Smith declared;
D/Conveyance - 15 Feb. 1856 - between Amos Alexander
and Louisa F. Alexander his wife of Adams Co. Ms to
Wm. F. Smith of Wash. Co. Ms.

#142: Jas. T. Rucks, et al vs Benj. Hardaway, et al: Filed
28 Mar 1866: Jas. T. Rucks and Sallie B. Rucks, his wife,
of Hinds Co. Ms. 1st part & Ben Hardaway and Franklin
White of Vicksburg, Ms. Doc. Incld....3 June 1858...
between Benj. Hardaway & Franklin White and Emily White
his wife of Warren Co., Ms & Thos. G. Stocket of Wilk. Co.:
Summons...28 Mar 1866 - for Ben Hardaway, Emily White,
Jesse White, Lucy White, Emily White minors - to answer
charge of Rucks: Guard. Bd...signed by Emily White and
VanDyke White.

#143: Bartly Johnson & Co. vs T.A. Elliott, John Woodburn
Filed 1868: Aug. 1868 - Jno. R. Woodburn only heir of
John Woodburn, decd.

#144: Thos. H. Johns vs R.C. Kershaw, et al: Filed 16 Apr.
1866: Thos. H. Johns states that Mary Jane Kershaw has
decd. intestate, and "leaving issue of her body, to-wit;"
Annie Kershaw who was married to (blank) Montague,
Rose Sarah Kershaw who was married to Chas. F. Turnbull,
Richard C. Kershaw, John T.C. Kershaw, Geo. T. Kershaw,
Mary Kershaw: Letters of Adm. of Est. of Mary Jane
Kershaw to Thomas Kershaw, 27 Feb. 1860. Thos. H. Johns
states that he is an Architect and head mechanic who
drew up elaborate plans for a dwelling on the Kershaw
Plantation known as "Palmetto Plt." and had delivered
some of the materials, etc....but process was interupted by the War. Seeks reimbursement for expenses.
from Mary Janes's Est. saying Thos. Kershaw has nothing.
in his own name.

#147: Inv. of Est. of D.Y. Stamply, decd. Filed 28 Nov. 1854
Adm. - Chas. L. Robards. No heirs listed.

Washington Co.Ms.
Packet Gleanings:

#149: Est. of Patrick Garry: Decd. of Ark. Documents incld.
in Packet: Will of (see WBk.1, Wash.Co. p.80):
Will was written Jan 1852 - and filed 29 Nov. 1855:
Left everything to his Father, if still living.
P.O.A. of John Garry,(in Ireland) Patrick's Father,
to Most Rev. J.B.Purcell, D.D. of Cincinatti,Ohio
to act in his stead - dated 25 May 1857(Ed.Will also
named bros. Thos.,Bernard,John)

#149: Benjamin Roach vs V.F.P.Alexander & others: Filed
23 Apr. 1866. Benjamin Roach states he has plantation
known as "Roach's Plt." fronting on the River (Miss.)
V.F.P.Alexander & others are parking their "wharfboat"
and conducting business on his plantation, and he wants
it stopped.

#150: Jeremiah S.Robinson vs Christopher Gillespie of Sunf.
Co.Ms.; and Margaret H.Walker, widow and Adm. of Peter
M.Walker, who has 3 minor children: Filed 25 Apr. 186.
Adm. Papers for Est of Peter M.Walker dated 20 Apr.186.
1860 - Christopher Gillespie and Melissa D.Gillespie
his wife of Wash.Co.Ms 1st part vs Peter M.Walker of
New Hanover, N.C. 2nd pt.

#151: Pamelia B.Swan of Phillips Co.ARk. vs John M.Bott, et al
Filed 26 Apr. 1866: Elizabeth F.Bott, wife and Adm.
of Est of Jno.M.Bott, decd. - - - Bill to foreclose
Mortg.: Heirs at law of Jno.M.Bott - Arabella Bott,
Josephine M.Worthington (formerly Bott) wife of Geo.
T.Worthington - 25 Oct. 1867: Guardianship of Arabella
Bott to W.L.Nugent 1868. (Elizabeth F. is Arabella's
and Josephine's mother)

ABELL: Fannie 81;Frances 150;Jas.67,148,150;Jas. Wm.150;Mary 150;Mary E. 73;Nannette 148,82,70,150; Saml.150,101;Susan 150.

ABERCROMBIE:Chas. 61.

ABY: L.H. 22.

ACKER; A.W.50.

ADAIR:Robt. 38.

ADAMS:D.A.9;F.A.S.75; Gen.Wirt 105;Randall 9; Rev.Bishop 80,82;Rosine 85;Wirt Jr.22;

ADEN:H.B.9.

AIKENS:Anna 18.

AINSWORTH: L. 61.

ALDER; Sarah 82.

ALDRICH:Lyman 70.

ALDRIDGE:A.D.73;A.G.137; A.J.86,137;Andrew 80;Frk. 112;Frk.S.80;G.Paxton 125; Hannah 112.

ALEXANDER; Isadore 103; Amos 61,152;Austin F.152; D.H.9,46,47,60;Daniel 47; Esther 99;Fanny 103;Geo. B.83;H.N.120;Hugh 92;J.81; Jacob 99,103;Jas.W.47; Jonas 96;Louisa F.152; Mollie 47;P.M.126;Rachel 84;Dr.V.F.P.122,152,153;

ALFORD:T.F.60;Wm.A.74.

ALLEN;Alice Van 77;C.W.61; Chas.T.146;Chas.W.146; Cynthia W.146;Dr.W.G.78; Henry 5;John B.44;John F. 127;John T.127;Johnson 89; Marg.5;Mary 5;Mary Marg. 146;Mrs. P.C.127;Robt.117; Saml.19;Saml.N.30;Sarah 5, 18;Sarah A.44;Sarah B.140; W.G.126.

ALLIEN:Ben 119;Sallie 119; W.W.119.

ALLISON:Wm.73.

ALSOBROOKS:W. 61.

ALSTON; P.G.9.

ALVES;R.L.129.

ANDERSON:Alex 9,51,80; Capt.T.S.118;D.N.43;Dr. Lomax 74,105,138,139;F.W. 54,57,58;Frank 32;Frank W.19;H.61;H.C.93;Harmon 9; Lorenzo B.3;Mrs. N.B.138; N.R.45;Ophelia 9;Rev.79; Ruby 105;Wm.53.

ANDREW :Mrs. Eliza 93.

ANDREWS:C.G.68,69,71,87; Jas.51;Wm.G. 101.

ANTHONY: Mary R. 78.

ARCHER:Bettie 97;Anna P. 97;Dr.124;Helen 110;Jas. 108;John G.83;Maj.Robt.H. 97;Mary 131;Mr.95;Mrs. Maggie 100;Rev.S.(Marr. Sec.pgs.67-93)110,97,131, 137;Robt.H.131;Robt.N. 131;W.H.97.

ARMSTRONG;JOS.L.9.

ARNOLD:Madison M.75; Wallace 136.

ASHFORD:Wm.T.,M.G.67,71,73,74.

ATCHINSON: E.F.61;T.E.F. 143.

ATKINSON:J.W.125;Leila F. 91.

ATTSON :K.P. 89.

AULDER; Sarah 86.

AUSTIN:E.A.4;H.R.4;Shall- Ina C.5;Wm.J.3.

AVERY: Fleta 86;John 86.

AXMAN:Chas.135;Josephine 85;Martha 135.

AYDAM: Emile 84.

B
BABB:Emma M. 133;L.H.133.

BACON:L.61;Wm.61.

BADWICK: JOE 123.

BAER:B.138;Mrs.Rosetta 104.

BAGLEY:Dr.W.M. 87.

BAILEY:J.B.149;Jethro 144.

BAINS:Patterson 144.

BAKER:E.W.87;H.L.72;Jos.9;

BAKER: Judge Grafton 20, 104,106;Mrs.106;Wm.T.127.

BALDRIDGE:Calvin W. 71.

BALDWIN:Hattie 134,135.

BALFOUR: ChAs.E.41;Rosa 17,41;C.C.17,27,41.

BALL:G.W.61;L.M.126;Rev. L.83;S.M.127,131.

BALLARD:John 123;John S. 123;K.A.122;Mrs. 122;Mrs. J.S.122;W.H.135.

BALLERAN:Guy 136.

BANKS:John O. 78;Marg.61; C.R.9;Sue 78;Aaron 9.

BANKSTON:G.M.44;Isaac 67; M.J.44.

BANNISTER: Monroe 75.

BARBEE: Benj.17

BAREFIELD:Aliena 115; Eudora 148;Hugh 148; J.H.73;Katie 115;Mrs. Jane 75;Mrs. K.F.73;Saml. 77,115;Stephen 148;Susan 148;Thos.148.

BARFIELD:J.H.71;Mollie J. 71;Mrs. M.A.137.

BARKLEY:Wm.L. 89.

BARLOW:Frank Jr.53;Frk. 9,54;G.W.61;Indiana C.53, 54;Lydia 61;Mr.91;N.61.

BARNARD:Eliza 42;Endora C.L.17,34,35,39;Henry 3,8, 55;Henry C.9,15,42;J.L. 35,55;Jos.8,55;Jos.S.(L) 8,42;Jos.L.Jr.42;Mary E. 42,55;Mary J.5;Mrs.J.L.35; Rebecca F.8,55;Sarah 5; Sarah L.5;Thos.61;Wm.3; Wm.B.5,18,72;Wm.H.42,45,55; Wm.T.3,4,5,8,17,18,20,21, 29,34,35,37,38,39,42,50,55;

BARNES:H.M.43,48;Henry 9.

BARNET:Ella 132;Phillip 121.

BARNETT:R.132.

BARNETTE:J.W. 2.

-155-

BARNHURST:John 123;Mrs.J.S. 123.

BARNOW: W.L.9.

BARRETT:J.E.9.

BARROW:Absolem 31;Absolem H. 1;Jos.J.1;Josiah 144;Louz-anna 144;Wm.1.

BARSLEY:Mary 89.

BARTON:Wm.P,M.G. 68,69.

BARWICK:E.M.110;E.V.110; Eddie 135;H.K.135;Mary E.78.

BASKETTE:Matilda K. 18.

BASKINS:Frank 9.

BASS:Alonzo T.144;Anaskew 144;Annie 125;Charity Ann 144;Council 61,144;Council R.100,125,143;Dr.Edm.R.144; Edm.61;Edwin 144;Eliz.144; Eugene 125;Giddeon 144;Isaac 144;J.R.61;Jesse 144;John 144; Jordan R.144;Louvenia 144.

BATE:Ann F.125;Ella Bass 125; H.C.125;Jas.H.125.

BATEMAN:Joe 30.

BATES:Mrs.F.N.112;

BATHKE:Mrs.E.123;C.121.

BATZ:Berry 87.

BAUGH:Archie 73;Augusta 106; Capt.A.B.106;Hallie 106.

BAXTER:Mrs.M.D. 133.

BEACH:Wm.84.

BEAKER:Heirs 9.

BEAL:Dr.88;Geo.61;M.R.61.

BEALL:Cecelia J. 141;Isaac B.141.

BEAN:Martha 24.

BEARD:(BAIRD): Eliza M.43; Cornelius 43;Benj.9;Dr.92; Jas.1;Nancy 1,24;Rich.2,3;

BEARDSLEY:Jack 93.

BEAVER:Henry N.19;John M.19; Wm.19;Wm.H.19.

BEAVERS:Henry 5;John 5;Marg.18;Marg.M.5;Wm.5.

BECK:Cora May 98;Davis B.111;Ida A.86;J.G.78,98,96;Mrs.122;Mrs.Mary A. 96.

BECKMAN:A.17.

BECKWITH:J.W.69.

BEDGOOD:A.104.

BEDON:Dr.103;Nannie 82.

BEIN:Fannie M. 41;Hugh H.41;John D.41;John S. 41;Lawrence G.41;Mary S.41;Rosina C.41.

BELCHER:C.M.35

BELL:Alice V.140;Archie C.140;Carrie 83,86;D.B. 85,115;Fannie 80;Harry W.129;J.B.117;J.S.9;Jas. B.115,133,140;Mollie A. 133,115;Mrs. E.T.47; Sallie A.140;Tenie 85; Va.G.140.

BENNETT:E.61;Mary A.89.

BENOIT:Aug.79;Ida 134.

BENSON: H.C.132;J.B.75; T.F.132.

BERGMAN:Howard 137;John M.137;Lillie 137;Louis 137;Morris 137;Blanche 137.

BERKELEY:Col.E.82,85;M.M. 82;M.W.85.

BERKLY:H.W.131.

BERNARD:Col.113;Thos.113; Wm.94.

BERNSTEIN:E.9,52;

BERRY:Anna 123;Chas.F. 129;J.G.61;Walter S.124.

BERTINATTI;Mrs. Eugenia 125.

BEVELL:Sarah V.7.

BEVERIDGE:Mrs. N.50.

BIBB:G.B.61.

BIEN:Dr. 83.

BIER:Jake 124.

BIGALOW:Chas.122.

BIGELOW:(child)123.

BIGGINS:F.112;Maggie 77;Mrs. 112.

BILLINGSLEY:Drucilla M.89; Edw.89;G.E.89,113;

BINDER:Leon 9.

BINNEY:Martha 9,46;

BIRD:Geo.122.

BIRDSONG:D.M.17;Frank 9.

BIRMINGHAM:Ben 61.

BIRNEY:Matthew 46.

BIZZELL:F.A.131,137;

BLACK:Andrew 61;E.Jr.61; E.Sr.61;J.61;Moses B.98; R.61.

BLACKBURN:Capt.Geo.T.95; D.F.17,34,39,40,50;David 142; Dr.Henry B.83;G.T.67,68,70,148; Julia 83,85;Loula 87;Pru.89.

BLACKMON:Thos.149.

BLACKWELL:Annie 46;Soloman 46.

BLAIR:M.L.9.

BLAKE:Edw.C.43;W.P.34.

BLAKEMORE:Alex.W.133;Anna M.133

BLAND:Eliz.9;Ella 70.

BLANTON:Dr.O.M.77,80,110,138, 132;Mrs.Georgia 81;Georgie 77; Georgina 94,132;Ida 79;Ida H. 132;Irmgards 54;Lola 80;Mrs.M. R.110;Mrs.Martha 152;Mrs.O.M. 107;O.M.152,71;Oliver 9,54; Orville 79;Orville B.133;Ruth T.94;W.W.61;Willie W.133;Wm.C. 94,96,132,133;

BLINCOE:Jas.D.67.

BODKY:Louisa 124.

BODLEY:W.S.61.

BOGAN:Rabbi 83,84,86,92;

BORGMAN:C.J.88.

BOHMERT:Rev.F.C.80,82, 85.

BOHN:Mary Ann 148;Reubin L.148.

BOISLINIERE:Dr.88.

BOLLING:J.H.15.

BOMAR:Rev.Mr.79.

BONHAM:D.W.C.6,41;Judge 24;Mary T.41,

BONLEY:Leila 9.

BOOKER:R.L.61.

BOOKOUT:B.F.39;Ben 61.

BOOTH:Rosewell V.22.

BOSSON:D.C.126.

BOSWELL:Anna 51;Anna H. 50;Wm.51.

BOSWICK:Chas.122.

BOTT:Arabella 153;Belle 74;Eliz.F.153;John M. 68,153;Josephine 153; Josie M.68;Mrs.Eliz.F.96.

BOURGES:Capt.E.82;Nana 82.

BOWEN:Amanda V.138;Col. 117;Grant A.68,109;John 82;Mamie H.127;Mannie 82; Mrs.J.H.120;Rev.J.A.91, 92,93;

BOWERS:Jacob 19;Marg.19.

BOWLES:E.A.140;J.S.140; Pink 92.

BOYCE:F.H.70.

BOYD:A.P.9,43;J.L.9,19, 43,48;J.W.9;Wm.B.43.

BOYER:F.H.69;Miss C.32.

BRABSTON:T.61.

BRADFORD:Malekiah 16; Wm.8;Wm.B.16.

BRADLEY:Chas.88;Mrs. Sarah 103;W.C.103.

BRADSHAW:Harrison 46; Wm.46.

BRANCH:H.T.9,35,45; Hester J.45;Lon 32; Martha 45;Thos.Anne 45; W.P.60;Wm.H.45.

BRANTON: K.C.27.

BRASHEAR;Horace C.87;

BRASHER:Amy 148;Essie P.148.

BRAZIER:Geo.124.

BRAZIL:Albert 9.

BREELAND:M.61.

BREHM:Rebecca 9.

BREHUR:J.H.9.

BRENNAN:(blank)104;T.J.52.

BRICKELL:H.B.2.

BRILL:Alfred 117;Sol 83, 117,137.

BRINKLEY: R.C.125.

BRISCOE: Anne 8;E.C.61;Edm. 141;G.141;Jas.M.8,15,55; Mary 8;Mason 8;Wm.8;Wm.P. 8,9,55;

BRISCONNET:S.61.

BRITT:P.M.107.

BRITTON:Fanny I.39;Hester 45;John D.109,134,135; Mary Ellen 134,135;Wm. 147;Wm.J.39.

BROMA:Fluer 9.

BRONSON:M.B.9.

BROOKS:Rev.A.D.75;A.W.46; Anna 68;D.E.121;Hon.Jos. 98;Isaac 46;M.J.6;Mrs. Fannie 121;P.S.136; Va.L.69.

BROTHERTON:Edw.116.

BROWDER:D.W.31;Eliz.149; Jas.W.149;

BROWN:Geo.H.9;Alice V.32; C.T.50;Chas.9;Eliz.69; Emma 9;Family 149;Gabe 50; Geo.114;J.F.W.145;Jas.149; Jas.H.73;Julian 147;L.M. 72;Lucy 9;Mrs.147;Mrs.Mary 97;Mrs.S.114;Peter 50;R.F. 125;Rebecca F.Barnard 42, 55;Rich.61,67;S.B.9;Sam 99, 137;Shepherd 151;T.L.96; Tommy 99;W.32;W.D.31,32,45; W.W.42,55;Wm.149;

BROWNING:J.61,Wm.61,67.

BRUCE: Rev.81.

BUCKWAY:Jas.80.

BRUIN:Daniel 42.

BRUM:Alex 9.

BRUMLEY:J.C.87.

BRYAN:E.J.21,95;Mary M.95.

BRYANT:E.J.72;W.P.61.

BUAN:B.9.

BUCK:Chas.143;Dr.R.L.116; Mrs.Eliz.S.116;Rich.S.20; Saml.H.20.

BUCKNER:Mrs.Amanda 115; Davis 70,71,105;Dr.W.E. 109,137;Emma E. 70;J.H. 75,122;Jennie 72;John 67;Mamie A.79;Mattie 75; Mattie D.79;Mrs.Davis 106;Mrs.S.F.107;Robt.H. 61;Sarah F.139;Sarah E. 138;W.E.137,139;Willie 106;

BUFORD:G.H.67,150;Sallie C.150.

BUGG;Sam F.1.

BUNN:Alex 55,60;Burrell 34;Burwell 55;Eugenia 55; J.Z.55;Jos.19,55,60;Rich. G.55;W.H.55;Wm.55.

BURDETTE:Fannie 84;Emma 93;Mrs.118;Mrs.M.93; Nannie 92.

BURDITT:Mrs.Eldora 53.

BURFORD:H.M.133.

BURKE: Cataline 36,37. Nellie 80.

BURNES:Pat 124.

BURNEY:Mary F.143;Robt. W.143;

BURNLEY:Albert T.40; Francis A.40;Lucy V. 40;Martha A.40.

BURNS:Jas.141.

BURRETT:Sallie R.77.

BURRUS:John 115;Maggie 115,Mrs.Judge 115.

BURT:C.H.98.

BURTON:Edna 140;Eliza 50; Florence 140.

BURWELL:Armistead 40.

BUTLER:Cynthia Jane 1; Eli 72,74,104;J.61; John E.6,16,25;Noble 61; Walter B.122.

BUTTERFIELD:Mary M.78.

BUTTERWORTH:H.J.17.

BUTTS: Bettie 57;Edw.57; Eva 57;J.M.57;John 34; Mary 57;Mary B.34;Mary T.57.

BYRD:Geo.61;John 61.

BYRNE:E.J.121;Erskine 108;J.B.61;Maj.108.

CAFFAL:Lula 84.

CAFFALL: Agnes 81;Edw.122 L.134,122;Willie 122.

CAGE:Henry C.39;Martha W.39

CAHER:B.128.

CAHN(COHN):Julia 130;B. 130;Barney 110;Benj.130; Eugene 103;Harry 130;Henry 130;Jos.130;Josephine 130;Julius 130;Selig 130.

CAIN:F.M.126;Jas.61.

CALDANIS:Peter R.61.

CALDWELL:Isaac 61.

CALHOUN:John C.9,47;

CAMERANNA:Alberto I.125; Ella I.125.

CAMMACK:Jas.152;N.B.6; R.B.1,2,3,8,33,28,30,40;

CAMP:Rev.Wm.F.68.

CAMPBELL:A.W.57,58;Alex. 3;Beasley 61;C.R.61;J. 61,143;J.C.61;Maggie 76; Mattie G.71;R.B.133,135, 136;W.R.61,71,99;Walter L.152.

CAMPION:Pat 76;

CANADA:Thos.90.

CANBASS:Caroline 133.

CANFIELD:Mrs.91;W.L.81.

CANNON:J.A.85.

CAPERTON:A.C.70.

CAPPES:L.A.140.

CAREY:Catherine 20; Geo.W.20.

CARMEN:J.A.93.

CARNAHAN: Rev.Wallace 74.

CARNES:G.61;W.61.

CARPENTER:Rev.A.C.70. H.61;J.M.61;W.T.80.

CARR:Edwin T.91;Eliz.20.

CARRIGAN:Nellie 134.

CARROLL: P.W.73;

CARSON:A.61;A.B.85,87, 90,103,127;Andrew 69, 70,71,72;Mary I.67; Matt F.103;Mrs.A.B.89; Susanna 26.

CARTER:A.B.141;A.G.94, 141,151;Ann B.73;Ella 138;Francis C.75;H.C. 9;Jane P.24;Landon F. 151;Louisa 9;Lucy A.94; Martha 73;Mary E.94;Mrs. Eliz.L.95;R.M.73,74;R.T. 9;Robt.148;Robt.B.151; Robt.G.151;Robt.H.151; Susan S.151.

CASE:Jas.47;Mary 47; T.B.151.

CASEY:Chas.91;John T.79.

CASSIDY:Saml.133.

CASSINO:Jos.101.

CASTLEMAN:D.F.6,28;Lucy 140;Stephen 140.

CATCHINGS:Dr.6;Nora 35; T.C.58;W.W.47.

CHAMBLISS:P.C.61.

CHAMPION:Mrs. Kate C.93;Mrs. A.M.108;Wm.7.

CHAN:Moses 130.

CHANDLEY:D.H.61.

CHANEY:Ann L.9;Ann S.6,15; Bailey 37;Bailey D.16,61; Bailey I.6,16,25;Bailey J. 16;Bailey Y.60;C.A.9;Catherine A.20,37,16;Jas.I.61; Jas.J.16;John F.4,9,16,20, 26;John F.Jr.4,16;Marg.9; Marg.A.6,15;Martha A.25; Mary J.18;Michael 16;Sarah C.15;Sarah E.16,39,147; Susan 16;Susan H. 4,9,15; T.Y.9,15,18,39,147;W.I.(Y) 39;Wm.J.15,18,39,147;Wood 6,15;Wm.45.

CHAPLAIN:W.R.T.61.

CHAPMAN:Atty.51;Isabella 9; John L.42,55,9,52,54,57,58; P.C.93.

CHARNLEY:Amelia A.70.

CHASE:Alex 9,54;Andrew 54.

CHEATHAM:John 9.

CHEVALIER:Rev.91.

CHEW:Aug.71,72,73,118,129; M.E.134,135.

CHEWNING:J.J.61.

CHIESA:J.A.121.

CHILDS:Emma 124;Mary 82.

CHILTON:H.R.9;J.M.61;Mrs. Alice P.9;St.J.9.

CHINN:Chas.148;Rich.148.

CHISHOLM:John 38,39;Nancy V.38.

CHOTARD:J.C.96;Mrs.Mary A. 96;Rich.19.

CHRISTMAS:Ann D.39;Henry 39,40,45;Henry Hill 9,40; Jas.Y.40;Mary E.40,45;Rich. 1,16,28,61,39,40,41,45; Thos.H.39,40;

CHURCH:John 79;Laura L.79.

CLACK; Mrs.W.S.104; R.Lee 85.

CLAPP:Emory 127;Lilly 127;Pamela Starr 127; Sally 127.

CLARK:D.45;E.D.20,28,29, 42;Eliz.145;Eunice Mayfield 18;Fred C.145;Geo. R.124;Geo.S.145;Gov.Chas. 99;Henry 145;J.M.24;J.S. 18;Jane E.145;John H.2; John M.2,16;Jos.S.18; Mary 32,75;Mary J.18; Matilda Jane 18;W.H.54; J.S.9.

CLARKE:A.139;Chas.W.104 129;Geo.W.143;Jas.139;

CLARY:Emma B.90;Thos.61.

CLEARY:Robt.108.

CLEATON:Acinthea M.132; Mr.117;Wm.A.106.

CLEMENT:Geo.W.146;Martha 146;Oliver 146.

CLEMENTS:E.C.45.

CLIFTON:Mrs.88;Mrs.Ellen 118.

CLOUSTON:Mrs. Marg.139.

CLOY:M.61

COALTER:Geo.4,9,15; John 6,4.

COBB:Henry 9,15;Leonora S.15;Mary A.15;Olivia T. 15;R.E.15.

COBURN:Jas.M.73.

COCHRAN:D.J.74.

COCKS:Annie E.133;Col. Phil 88;Eliza 88;John G.144;P.A.145,144;Seth 144;Susan A.61;John 142.

COFER:C.H.84.

COFFEE:Addie 42.

COFFIELD:Amanda 9,52,30; Dr.Horatio D.47,9,30,52, 53;Dora 53;Lee 53;R.N.52.

COHN:John W.9,16;Robt. 22,54,49.

COKER:H.B.16;J.45;John H.9.

COLBURN:Saml.151.

COLE:Eliza G.1;Wm.T.71.

COLEMAN:Angelina 9,16; Nancy 9;Sarah Ann 16; Thos.H.16;Wesley 9.

COLLIER:Col.J.N.97;J.C. 72;J.N.73,77,78,129; J.W.126;Levin H.101; Patton Knox 97;S.C.97.

COLLINGE:Jas.130.

COLLINS:Abe 9;Agnes E. 2;J.M.71;J.N.129;Jones 139;Mary 51;Mary M.20; Mrs.Mary E.51;Thos.H. 93;Will E.51;Wm.20;Wm. A.9,51;Wm.W.141,143;

COLLUM:E.71,73.

COLTER:John 3.

COMPTON:Jeff 67;W.H.61.

COMSTOCK:E.J.72,95,96. Jas.Walter 95;L.J.96; Mrs.Evie H.95.

CONER:Mrs. Mattie M.57.

CONLY:Ella Bass 125.

CONNELL: Jas.123;Jeff 135;Mary 90;Pattie 90.

CONNELLI:D.W.61.

CONNELLY:Sarah J.1; Wm.93.

CONNER:John A.9;Mrs. Hattie 92.

CONVERSE:J.B.9.

CONWAY:Ellen A.148.

COOK:Caroline 8,18;E.G. 151;Frank 9;G.9;John H. 75;Mary J.9;W.B.61.

COOLEY:G.W.50.

COOPER:Jos.J.67;Jas. 61;Robt.122.

COPELAND:A.148;Parolee M.67;Sarah V.72;Wallace 134.

CORNELL:M.J.32;N.S.32.

CORNEY:Jas.121.

CORRIGAN: Nellie 93.

CORTRIGHT:I.G.52.

COTRELL: John 124.

COUGHLER:Gus 123

COUNCIL:Eliz.16;F.S.16; Martha Ann 16;Mrs.Permelia 16,17;Serena 16; Wash.S.9,16,17;Evalina 16.

COURSER:Chas.60.

COURSEY:D.9,15,53,56.

COURTER: J.61.

COURTNEY:Jno.T.69,70, 99,127;Mrs.Jane E.99,127.

COWAN:Tarleton B.9 58.

COWDRAY:W.C.61.

COX:A.61;J.G.61;J.H.9; J.S.61;John 74;John J. 74,133;Kate 77;Mrs.A. 121;Phillip A.61;Sallie C.133.

CRAFT:Gussie L.118;J. 61;Maj.61;W.A.118.

CRAIG:F.J.84,111,110, 130;Frank 111;John A. 151;Joshua M.147; Martha A.111,112,130; Mrs.Mattie A.87;Silas 151.

CRANDLE:E.S.70

CRANE:Jas.8;Wm.C.68.

CRAWFORD:Benet A.151; Edm.151;Eliz.151;J.A. 92;Judith 151;Nancy 151; Rich.151.

CREATH:Albert G.17,61; Alberta 17,34,39;D.H. 17,35,39;Endora 34,35; Henrietta 60;Minors 9; Mary B.17;Shalline 17,34, 39.

CRICHLOW:Sarah 7.

CRISLER: J.W.69.

CRITTENDEN:Col.John A. 117;Gov.117;Harriet B. 40;Henry 83,87,117;Hy. 85;O.B.87,130;117,91; Robt. H.40.

CROCKETT:L.61,Martha 61; Mrs. Emma 88.

CROFT:Benj.142;Geo.142

CROSS:Rev.Wm.83,87,88, 92,93.

CROUCH:Annie E.47;John 93;Peter W.9,3,16; Walter V.47;

CROW:Andrew J.H.67, 150,146;Annie 150; Eliza 150;Henry 61, 146,150;Mary 150.

CROXTON:Anthony 46.

CRUMP:W.E.2.

CRUTCHER:G.B.61.

CULLEN:E.W.9;Irene 32; R.J.32;Dr.Elijah W.17

CUMMINGS:N.69

CUMMINS:W.L.126.

CUNNINGHAM:Belinda 61; Frances 150;John P.9, 150;Mary J.150;Miller 150;Rich.150;

CURD: David 9;Eliza P.9

CURELL:(CUTRELL) Kate 81.

D

DABNEY:J.B.116;John 80,116;

DADE:Jane 125.

DALGREEN:Chas.G.43.

DAMERON:Bessie 79;Lewis 24;Lewis S.8;Robt.C.21; W.H.16.

DANGERFIELD:Thos.60.

DANIEL: Jas.W.10;Mary 36.

DANIELS:Wm.E.148.

DANKS:Catherine 41.

DARDEN:D.M.61;J.61.

DART:C.62

DASH:Cecelia C.76;

DASHEAR:Geo.62

DAUD:JANE 125.

DAUGHERTY:Belle 54;
Lucia 54;Mary F.54;
Nora 54;O.R.54,59,
119;Thos.105.

DAVENPORT:Adelia G.104
E.V.10;Edgar D.104;
Jos.9,18;L.J.104;Luke
18;R.G.62;Robt.67,99;
Sarah 18;Sina 18.

DAVIDSON:Christopher
62;Jas.122;Va.93;W.L.62.

DAVIS:Aug.102;Ben 107;
Bob 139;Daniel 62;Fielding 9,17,27;Henry H.28;
J.E.62;J.M.70;Jos.G.44;
Josephine 10;Laban 62;
Letitia M.28;Lewis R.46;
Lucinda 17;Mrs. Nellie
72;Mrs. Mary A.117;Robt.
A.74;S.62;Saml.81,149;
Sarah 52;T.F.88;Taylor
17;Tom F.87;Walter E.99;
Warren 128;Winchester 10;
Wm.J.97;Yancey 10.

DAVISON:G.S.86.

DAWSON: Henry S. 62

DAY:Emory C.127;Sally C.
127;W.T.62.

DEAN:James Ann 10.

DEARING:Thos.62;Wm.62.

DEARMAN:SJr.62;

DEBARDLEBEN:H.F.91,92;
Mary P. 92.

DECOIN:R.L.62

DEESON:A.G.18,10;Elisha
24;Eliza V.24;Henry L.
24;M.J.10,18;Matilda J.
18;Thos.W.5;W.A.5;Wm.M.
1,24.

DEHART:John 62

DELOACH:Madison P.3,9,15;

DEMENT:J.R.140;John E.141;
Va.140.

DENHAM:Simp.62

DENNETT;E.A.80

DENTON:GAB. 62.

DERMOTT:W.Mackall 93.

DESAULLIS:Louis 62

DETERLY;M.M.72

DICKENS:David 62;E.B.10;
Jas.C.62.

DICKINSON:John 62

DICKSON:J.C. 62

DIGGS:A.R.10;Alfred 10;
Bennie 122;Cornelius 53,56;
Fannie 123;John 53,56;

DIRKER:John B.46.

DIXON:Frances E.77;J.B.2;
R.L.68.

DOBSON:B.A.131.

DODD:Nancy Y.1;Wm.1;

DODDS:Cecil E.141;Cornelia
141;Eliz.T.141;Mary A.141;
Nancy Y.141;Wm.15,28,35,141.

DODGE:Elliott 122;

DOLLAR:Jas.C.55;Mary J.55.

DONNELLON:Leila E. 132.

DORMAN:D.122.

DORSEY:Mary 10;Z.H.5.

DOSWELL:Jas.62

DOUGHTERY:Belle 10;Nora 10.

DOUGLAS:Wm.H.69

DOUGLASS:Katrude 72

DOWNING:Alex.62,Geo.143;
John 143.

DOWNS:A.C.62;T.D.62;

DOZIER:J.D.62

DRAKE:Asa 104;Rev.Wm.Winans
70,71,72,73,74,95;

DRESCHAW:Carl L.E.90

DREYFUS:Albert 10;D.A. 56;Henry 88.

DRIDY:Mary 75.

DROMGOOLE:G.G.143; Sarah 144;Wm.62,144;

DRUMMOND:Mary A.71; Sarah J.70.

DUBOSE: Mrs.M.L.136; Mrs.W.P.116;R.M.136; W.P.136.

DUDLEY:C.W.72;Mr.68; Mrs.89;Mrs.M.A.68.

DUDLY:Dr.Chas.109.

DUFFY:M.123

DUKE:Simeon 62

DULANY:Benj.141;Eliza C.141;Henry R.141; Nora 141;Va.141;Wm.A. 141.

DULANEY:L.C.93

DUNBAR:A.F.82;A.N.62; A.W.144;Jos.43,62;

DUNCAN:Henry P.149; Jesse J.73;R.55;Steph. 23,60,149;

DUNLAP:Hugh W.62

DUNN:Annie F.70;Bart. 62;Bettie 148;Bettie M 69;Chapin H.148;Dr. John A.53;Dr.S.R.21,76, 83,110,111,129,134,148; Fanny 127;Finlay M.148; Francis Leo 127;Franklin 53,9;G.L.73;Harriet T.110;Jas.S.73;John N. 148;Mary R.70;Mrs.Amanda 134;Patrick 105,127; Sallie R.76;Thos.J.53; Thos.W.148;Willie Thos. 127;Wm.62;Wm.B.69.

DUPASS:Lullie V.136.

DUPREE:Mrs.35

DURFEY:Robt.W.67

DUVAL:A.D.8,18,9,10; Claiborne 8,18;Gwinet S. 8,18;Marg.8,18,41;Mary C.8;Matilda 8;Emma 121.

DWYER:P.T.79

E

EAKINS:S.J.60

EARLY:David 48

EASLEY:Edw.T.40;L.I.40; Tandy W.40.

EASTMAN:Emerson C.19;R.F. 10,19;

EASTON:Gwinnet S.18 T.J.Jr. 18.

ECKFORD:H.P.70;Mattie A.81

ECKHART:E.A.126;Paul 126.

ECKSTONE:Mark 79;Sarah 84,86

EDE:Alice M.M. 101;Eliza 101;Joshua 101.

EDERSON:H.11

EDGAR:A148;Bettie M.85; W.E.3.

EDRINGTON:B.T.62

EDWARDS:Arthur C.7;E.W. 62;Dan.62;Henderson 144; Jas.82;John 62;

EGG:Catherine 133;Chas.62 Jos.62,133;Sallie 133.

EGGLESTON:Dr.Wm.M.82

EHLERS:Wm.123;Mrs.Wm.122 Willie 122;

ELDER:Adele L.101;J.Llewellyn 101;Wm.H.101

ELDRIDGE:Ann E.40;Hallam 40

ELIOTT:J.S.10

ELLEY:Lillie 88;Lois 72;

ELLIOTT:Ann G.79;Belle V. 75;Chas.10,74;Chas.S.59; Eliz.45;G.W.79,124;J.S.45; Mrs.Emma 10,59;Mrs.G.W.124; S.C.10,44,54,59,73;T.A.152; T.D. ,57,58;Walter 10,59.

ELLIS:J.W.50

ELLISON:Peter 133

ELLY:Mary D.73

ELMORE:Mrs.Mary E.72

ELWELL;Saml.O.74

ELY:Lily 73

EMBRY:W.T.74

ENDECOTT:Thos.141,143,144,147;

ENGLESSING:F.C.17

ENOS:Edw.73,102;Marg.E.102;Mrs.Mary F.102,116.

EQUIN:Jonte 87

ERMMAN:W.A.128

ERSKINE:Alex 62

ERWIN:Emma 71;J.W.115;Lillie J.68;Mrs.115;Mrs.Johnson 108;V.F.112,126;Wm.89;

ESTES:Arch.H.62;J.E.62

ESTILL:Jas.C.74,81,97;Nellie Va.97;R.C.97.

EUSTIN:Hannah 58;Wm.58

EUSTIS:Cath.C.19;H.S.10;Haratio 19.

EVANS:L.A.57;Louis 70,107,138;Mary A.149;Mary M.72,149;McLin 62,143,149;Mrs. Emma E.107;Robt.B.138;Robt.L.138;Thos.F.138.

EVERETT:R.H.P.62;T.T.62

EVERHART:M.10

F

FAISON:Ellen R.149;G.W.149.

FAKE:Henry 62

FALL:Col.Geo.R.95,151;Eliza A.139;

FARES:A.87

FARISH:A.W.56;Dr.R.D.10,43,76;F.P.10;Minors 10;T.H.10;W.S.10,57;

FARMER:Belle 92;G.P.73;G.R.74,75;Mary 73;R.A.100.

FARR:Elias 1;Eliz.J.19;Jas.18;John H.1,2,10,18,19,30,141;Mary Ann 1,2,18,19,141;Robt.10,19;Wash.B.2,6,8,10,19,21,23,30,34,35,38,55;

FARRAR:A.P.80;Chas.F.78.

FARRISH:R.D.48;W.S.52.

FAULKNER:J.W.62;Saml.C.62

FELKER:Mrs.Caroline 104

FELTENBERG:Henry 43

FELTS:D.W.62

FELTUS:Capt.J.V.120;Char.80;J.A.V.80;Maj.H.J.102;Mrs. Eliza 120.

FENTRESS:Jas.36

FERGUSON:Alfred 92;Gabrell 10;Gen.88,129;Jas.62;Jos.20;L.W.126,149;Saml.W.69,94;127;Wm.20;

FERRISS:Annie B.47;Annie M.10,20,47;Annie Marie F.20;Dr.St.Clair 10,20,47;W.D.86,132;

FIELD:Ellen 137

FIELDS:D.10;Eliz.149;Ellen R.149;Harris 149;Henry C.149;Jesse 149.

FIEST:L.84

FIGURES:Harden P.139

FINLAY:A.B.105,116;Eliza B.77;Helen 123;J.P.75;Jas. Archer 108;John L.69,136,146;John P.108,132,136,138;Mary Nelson 76;Mary P.136;Mrs.A.B.85;Mrs.Julia B.91;Pricilla W.83;Saml.D.77;T.P.83,85,112;

FINNEGAN: Pat 121

FIRRANO;Manuel 62

FISCHEL:A.L.10;M.10;Albert 48;Babette 48;Leon 47,48;Leopold 48;Lyon 10;Maurice 48;Saml.45,48;

FISHER:Alex.66.

FISK:Alv.62;Francis M.41.

FITLER:Chas.A.56;Theo.28.

FITZ:Gideon 20,21,62;John W.10,20,21;Martha 20,21; Robt.J.20,21;

FITZPATRICK:Ann L.142; J.E.142.

FITZSIMMONS:Ann 23

FLAGG:Wm.145

FLANAGAN:R.A.130.

FLEISCHER:A.123,124;

FLEMING:K.10;Nathl.10; Rev.79.

FLISCHER:Mrs.122

FLOOD:Ella 105;J.W.105, 110;Laura V.105.

FLORIAN:C.H.92

FLOURNOY:Eliz.J.126;Matt. 62;Victor M.126.

FLOWERS:Jennie 84

FLY:A.D.10

FOLEY:B.J.73

FOOTE:Georgia A.27;Judge H.W.27,129;Sybelia A.27.

FORD:Edna 10;Jas.C.62;Manly 10;West 10;Wm.G.40,62; America 44;B.B.10,44;C.J. 10,44;D.J.3;G.C.68;Jesse 44;John 44;Martha 44;Mary 44;Milton 44;Peter 44; Rebecca 44;Simen 44;Wiley 44;Wm.44.

FORNIQUET:Col.E.P.98

FORRESTER:Gus 123

FOSTER:Ann M.20;Caroline 26;Earnest 20,47;Frances 26;Isaac H.20;Jas.H.103; Jas.R.103;John 43,47,62; John Tillman 20;Jos.P.107; Josephine E.69;Leila 10,20, 47;Levi 20;Mary 20;Minors 10;Mrs.Sarah 26;Nancy 26; Nannie 10;Sarah 8,10,20, 25;Thos.20,26;

FOWLER:E.10;Sarah 10.

FOWLKES:Ella H.79;Saml.66.

FOX:Rev.J.96;Augusta C. 55;Dr.96;Henry 10,55; Josephine 121;Julius 52, 53,55,56;Mrs.Rosalie 55; Saml.52.

FRANK: (no other name)98

FRANKLIN:Herman G.86; Littleton 147;Mrs.Littleton 15;Mrs.Rachel 119.

FRAZER:Wm.62

FREELAND:Thos.62

FREEMAN:Martha 27

FRENCH:Isadore 79;John 46;O.C.79;Robt.S.142; W.J.124.

FRESHWATER:Peter 10;

FREUNDT:Henry 123.

FREY:Adolph R.129;Willie L.129.

FRID:Henry H.109

FRIERSON:Rev.M.L.91

FRILEY:David 67,76,111.

FRY:Emory S.127.

FRYER:John 118

FULTON:Adelia 150;Annie 150;Annie Crow 150;John 144,150;Mrs.Allison 52; Nelson 52;R.N.10;Sallie 67,150;Z.X.62.

FURLOW:Amanda J.19;Martha Sue 19;Nancy 19;Paralee 19;R.A.58;Robt.J.19;Robt. N.10;Ruth Ann 19;Wm.19.

FUSELL:Sherwood 66;Wm.66

FUTRELL:Rev.J.L.80,81.

G

GADDIS:Thos.33

GAINS:Abner 24,Sally 24;

GALLAGHER:Frank 123

GALLOWAY:Rev.Chas.B.78

GAMBLE:J.T.10;John L.21.

GAMMETER:Albert 70.

GANO:Robt.10

GARGARO:Angelo 74

GARLAND:Burr 62

GARNER:H.C.10

GARRETT:J.10,21,60;Lizzie 21;M.R.10;

GARRY:Bernard 153;John 153;Patrick 153;Thos.153

GARY: Adolphus 48;Mary Ann 48;Rose 148;

GATES:John 62;John B.62; Rev.Mr.82.

GAY:Capt.W.L.119;127; Caroline A.119,127.

GAYDEN:J.E.115;L.B.115

GEARY:Ida 74;

GEATMAN:John A.151;

GEINELLE:Addaline 124.

GENSBURGER:Marx 108;Mrs. Julia 108.

GEORGAIN:John T.143

GEORGE:H.P.10;Jas.M.10

GERDINE:Dr.78,100;Mrs. Sallie West 100

GIBBONS:Frances A.E.73.

GIBSON:Claudius 62; Constine 7;Wm.62.

GIDDEN:S.W.91

GIDIER:John J.127

GILBERT:Phillip 144,147; Webster 62;Wm.62.

GILDART:Irene 90;John W.113;Mrs.Mary E.105; Thos.90,113;W.K.83,90, 105,113;

GILKEY:Lloyd L.53;A.J. 54;A.S.10;Ada L.10,52, 53;Andrew J.53;Anna G. 53;Eva 10;Loyd 10;Laura 10;Ida C.53;Laura H.53; Mary Eva 53;Rolf W.53.

GILL:R.D.15

GILLESPIE: Christopher 69, 153;M.22;Melissa D.153; R.72.

GILMORE:Wm. 100.

GINSBERGER:Saml.108

GISH:L.H.143

GIVENS:Wm.137;Alonzo 25.

GLASS:Cornelia 42;G.J.42; Joel 23;Nellie 23;Saml.42; Sarah145;W.134.

GLATHERY:Nannie M.140

GLATHRY:Rosa E.140

GLEMSER:Helen 70

GLENN:Lyra H.147

GLIDDEN:H.A.99

GLOYD:Spencer 62

GOLDMAN:Bertha 84;J.A.74; Rowina 74.

GOLDSMITH:Godfrey 118; Grover C.112;L.E.84;Sol 112;

GOLDSTEIN:Evaline 132;Leon 99;Nathan77,132;Sarah 83;

GOOCH:J.S.62

GOODWIN:Jas.W.86;John L. 10;Wm.126.

GORDON:Annie 133;Basil B. 91;D.L.133;Nancy 62;

GORMAN:Ann 146;Artimecy 145, 146;Cassendanah(?)146;Eliz. 145,146;Felix 145,146;Mary 145,146;Mary J.146;Oliver 145,146;Sarah 145,146;Starling 62,145,146;Terrel 145, 146;Chalesta 146.

GOSHEA:Liz 10

GOSSETT: J.124.

GOTTHELF:Rev.Dr.76

GOTTLICH:Henry 92

GOWAN:Wm.62

GRACE:C.A.18,54;Eva 10,54,55, Louis 10;Geo.C.10,54,55; Harriet B.54;Harry Louis54, 55;J.C.10,18,47,54,55;T.C.55;

GRACE:(cont)T.E.54; Virginia C.54.

GRAFTON:Allen 20

GRAHAM:Harvey H.139;John M.139;Martha G.139;S.L. 139;Thomasella H.139.

GRAINGER:Dr.93

GRAMBLING:Heirs 10; A.D.44;

GRANT:Alice 89;Amos 10; Bettie 60;Gen.50;Heirs 10;Jas.10;Lawrence 10; Lenora 10;Martha 60; Mary 10;T.J.10.

GRAVES:Col.90;Geo.10; Nancy 66;Tabitha 33; Wm.33;Wm.C.148;Elias 135;

GRAVIT:Nora K.93

GRAVITT:Fannie G.112; Jennie 87;M.E.112;Mattie 107;Rich.M.106;W.H.106, 107,112;

GRAY:Alice 87;J.P.104, 105;Jas.W.132;John H. 10;John M.20,37;John W. 10;Lillie 87,92;Lizzie 132;Mrs.Louise 104;Mrs. E.D.J.83,84;Nancy 20,38, 37;Nannie 82;Nellie 87, 92;Rev.Arthur 82,85;Saml. B.10;Stephen 3,4,10,21;

GREEN: Abner 20;Annie 10; Bishop 76;David 62;E.H. 10;Eliza O.83;Ellen 127; Ely 47;Henry 10;J.10,69, 127;Leonard 62;L.S.62;Lorenzo 127;Mrs. Annie 114; Mrs. Eliz.47;Oscar P.47; Peter 127;Rev.Duncan C. 77,78,79,76,122;Rev.S.H. 89;S.F.6;Sarah 10;T.B.40; Taylor 10;Thos.Jr.47;W. 47,127;Wm.Mercer 89;Wm. P.105;T.B.47.

GREENFIELD:Mrs. 124.

GREENLEY:J.C.79.

GREGORY:Geo.G.10,21;Mary 10;Mrs.P.W.111;Peter 10, 21;Pricilla W.21;

GRIER:Mary E. 76

GRIFFIN: Alf.10;Dennis 62;Dr.J.L.94;Eliz.62; Francis 62;Isabella 68; Frank 93;John 10,83;John L.75,91;Judge 116;Laura 116;Mary 10;Susie H.94; W.J.95;Wm.137.

GRIMES:Thos.62,143.

GRISSOM:Frances A.67

GROOMS:Jake 46;Louisa 46; Paul 10,46;Viney 10,46.

GRUBBS:F.62

GUBBS:W.G.10

GUTHRIE:B.F.133

GWIN:A.J.41;Alex.M.3,8, 19,31,33,21,41,4,10,18; Eliza C.2,21;Frank 21; Ida 21,51;Jas.41;Lizzie 51;Marg.21;Mary E.H.41; Saml.41;Sarah C.21;Thos. 41;Thos.W.21;Wm.L.53;Wm M.41,62;

GWYN:Hugh 72

H

HABICHT;John 74;Mrs.123.

HAGAN:David 2;Henry 2; Hiram 2;Hiram,Jr.2;John 2;Martha 2;Stephen 2;

HAIDIE:John I.127

HAILBURTON:Robt.11

HAILE:Calhoun 82

HAIR:Jas.

HALBERT:Dr.125

HALE:Will E. 143

HALL:John B.62;S.L.Barnard 18;W.H.93

HALLADEN:J.C.45

HALLBERG:Chas.J.46;Ida 46;Robt.Lee 46.

HALLORAN:Jas.11

HALSEY:Dr.Seymour 146;
Mrs.Ann D.Hill 96,146,
100,111.

HALSTEAD:Rev.Mr.80

HAMBERLIN:Marg.V.71;
Mary 62

HAMBLIN:Henry 3

HAMBURGER:Abe 124.

HAMEL:Jas.H.22;Kate A.
11,22;Lavinia E.22;
Mary E.22;Patrick 11,22,
60;Wade H.11,22.

HAMILTON:Nash 46;Rachel
50.

HAMMER:Jos.110;Mrs.
Blanche 110.

HAMMERS:J.L.107.

HAMMET:Edw.146;Capt.J.R.
97;Dr.Wm.A.146;E.M.146;
Dr.Jas.P.146.

HAMNER:J.81

HAMPTON:Ann 23,130;Anna
F.99;Annie F.23,130;C.F.
23,99,114,130;Capt.Wade
Jr.119;Caroline 130;
Caroline L.23;Catherine
M.23;Col.Wade 23;Frank
23;G.M.89;Gen102;H.19;
H.R.26;Harriet 23;Jas.S.
143;Kate 23,126,130;Maj.
Wade 80;Mary H.23;McDuffie
119;Octavia H.143;Senator
114;Wade 11;Wade Jr.23,
126;Wade,III60;Wm.H.28.

HAMS:Milton H.28

HANEY;Mrs.Mary J.67

HANNUN:Fisher A.62

HANSMAN:J.F. 131

HANWAY:John 78

HARBICHT:Theodore 122.

HARBISON:Georgia 140

HARDAWAY;Benj. 152

HARDEN:Nancy 11

HARDIN:Alma11,22,23;Geo.
23;Ida 11,22,23;Ira 11,
23,51;Nancy 22,23,51;

HARDING:Geo.40,41;Ira 41

HARDY:Anderson 48;Jas.
S.142;

HARMON:Archer 88

HARPER:J.D.72;Jas.T.62;
Jesse 62;

HARRELSON:A.W.62

HARRINGTON:Rev.Whitfield
67,68.

HARRIS:Audley M.119;
Buckner 22;Capt.93;Carrie
93;Eliza 22;Eudora 22;
Ezk.62;Geo.C.45;J.L.53;
Jas.R.11,22;Jas.R.Jr.22;
John 11,22,129;L.B.22;
Mrs.W.D.119;P.22;Robt.22;
Saml.134;Sarah 22;W.T.89;
Wiley P.22;Wm.L.104.

HARRISON:A.G.62;E.L.146;
Gilson P.62;Wm.H.98.

HARROW:John W. 114.

HARSHE:Annie 133;Josephine 133;

HART:Anna M. 11

HARTMAN:L.129:Lee 78

HARTSON:Mr.89

HARTY: John J.86

HARVELL:Mr. 95

HARVEY:Belinda 142;E.Jones
20,26,31,37,40,55,60,8,142;
Eliz.44;J.R.142;John 62;M.I.
20;Martha J.37;Mary 63;Wm.
R.89;

HARWOOD:Agnes 11,50,51;
Anna E.50,51;Lowry E.51;
Mary E.50,51;S.B.50.

HASBERG:Mrs. B.122;Nancy 80.

HASSBERG:Fannie 76;Pauline
76.

HATCH:Benj.63.

HATCHER:Cath.J.67

HAUFF: Eddie 57;J.E.127.

HAWKINS:H.P.83;Mrs.114; W.P.74.

HAY:Thos.W.22;W.L.90.

HAYCRAFT:Dave V.132;Mary C.132;Wm.A.121,71,67,127, 132,148,149;

HAYS:Elijah 127;Ellen E. 22;Jack P.11,22;Sue H.22; Thos.W.11,53,46;Thos.45.

HEAD:Dan 112;J.C.79,112; Mrs.112;Oliver J.108.

HEARD:C.72,73;Chas.A.89; Mary P.74;N.74,118;N.C. 114;Nathan A.102;S.C.60.

HEATH:J.P.52;J.W.11;Jas. A.45;John 11,45,72,96; John W.45;Louisa 96;Thos. 11;Jas.11;Thos.A.45; Willis 96.

HEATHMAN:J.M.69;Miss 92.

HEBRON:Bennie 90;J.B.92; John L.Jr.91,119;Wm.S.119

HEHCTER:L.129

HEIDINGSFELDER:Jacob 74.

HEISON:Ida W. 35.

HELM:Anna B.Eakin 119; Geo.M.119,138;Mamie B. 138;Walter 82;Geo.139.

HENAGAN:S.B.143

HENDERSON:Geo.11;Harmon 45;Hester 45;John 66; Wm.53.

HENNESSY:Adaline 11; John 11.

HENSHAW:Col.80;Miss 80.

HERALD:J.J.63

HERBERT:Lizzie 51

HERMAN:Henry 74;Lena 124; Lucein 41.

HERRING:Benj.F.2,18;Mary Ann 2;Mary Ann Farr 18; Redding B.63.

HERRINGTON:Mrs. 92.

HESTER:Annie Loyle 50;C.A. 11,50;David 50;E.63;H.O.G. 50;John 11,3,4,23;Marshall J.50.

HEXTER:Isadore 80,137;Lee 137.

HEYMAN:(HEIMAN):Hannah 52; Henrietta 52;Saml.52;A. 11,52;Amelia 52.

HICKS:Frances 75;M.S.54; W.P.11.

HIGGINS:Annie 93;Brand 22; Joel 22,63;Joel G.22; Randall G.11,22;Rich.22; Sally 22;Thos.123.

HIGHES:Mary Agnes 50

HILL:Dr.115;A.P.2;Alice G. 3;Amelia 3;Ann 3,6,33,34; Ann Dunn 146;Caleb 63;Chas. 131;Edw.B.3;Elb.A.3;Emily C.3,23,60,147;Emma 91;Eva L.23;F.B.23,53,54;Frank,J.C., Lizzie - Minors 11;Glenora Ann 23;H.R.W.11,21,38; Henderson 11;Henry C.3;I.C. 3,6,8,28,33,29,23,34,147; Isaac 3,6,11,55;Isaac F.3; J.D.44,60;Jas.F.3;Jas.S.115; John A.2;Lizzie S.23;Mrs. Tina 51;Orren 63;Parley 63; Sallie E.71;Sarah E.131;Thos. H.69;Thos.W.2;W.D.131;W.R. 2;Wm.138.

HINDS:DAvid 146;Howell 63; Thos.67.

HINES:Rev.Rich.81;Wm.B.67.

HINTON:Wm.H.40;Susan 40;

HIRSCH:Bertha 88;Bertha R. 128;Clemence 105;Harry 128; Henrietta 105,128;J.52,75, 105,108,128,130,137,118; Julia 128;Leo 128;Sadie 118, 128;Sam 84.

HOBSON:Jos.79;

HODGE:Ed.H.74;S.C.136.

HODGEDON:Morrell 5.

HODGES:C.J.88

HOFF:Moses 63

HOFFMAN:Danl.63;Deliah 63

HOGAN:Wm.11

HOLLAND:Clara 11;Jos.J.144.

HOLLBERG:Robt.11;Ida 11.

HOLLIDAY:Thos. 63

HOLLINGSWORTH:H.J.76.

HOLLY:P.B.73

HOLMES:Angeline 11;Caroline 94;Chas.11;Hinds 76;John 84,112;Leta C.112;Mackley 11;Marg.H.11;Mary S.94;Peter 46;R.B.11;Saml.A.94.

HOLT:Dr.A.C.82;John B.143;John R.143;Jos.H.20;Mary 82.

HOOD:David H.101;Dr.Dedrick 85;Mr.113;Wm.87;Wm.N.101.

HOOE:Ann G.120;Hallie 120.

HOOPER:J.H.139;P.63.

HOPKINS:Rev.W.A.72.

HOPPER:J.D.72;Louisa 27.

HOPPIN:F.M.73.

HORACE:Turner 136.

HORD:D.A.111;R.H.67,150;Mary I.150;

HOUGH:Jos.63.

HOUSTON:Saml.T.131;Wm.63.

HOWARD:Arthur 63;L.11;P.25;S.D.2,11;

HUDDLESTON:H.139;Jno.66.

HUDSON:John 16;John S.97

HUGGINS:Clarence E.104.

HUGHES:Archie 50,51;B.63;Benj.F.83;Jas.50;Jas.H.2;Jeff J.2;Lucia L.50;Mary 51;Mary Agnes 50,51;Mrs.B.F.137;Robt.50,51;Timothy 24.

HUNDERMARK:A.27.

HUNSICKER:Mr.95.

HUNT:Alice 81;Capt.W.E.116;David 2,4,45,63;Katie B.73;M.C.103;Mary Haycraft 103;Mrs.W.E.117;Prudence B.148;W.E.81,130,103,134,137,138,142,148,63;D.F.130;Geo.B.148.

HUNTER:Ann 137;Jennie 71;Lee B.86;Mrs.Belle 76;W.B.74;Wm.H.96.

HUNTINGTON:Geo.W.66.

HUNTLEY:Chas.121.

HURST:Nannie S.69.

HUSSEY:S.L.54.

HUSTON:F.63.

HUTCHINS:Kate F.135;R.E.118,135;

HYDE:Ezek.63

I

IGNACE: Oscar 87

INCHISA:Ella Ann 125

INDENTURES:Benj.60;Chaney John 60;Thos.Dangerfield 60;Dixie 60;Edw.60;Esq.Harvey 60;Milly 60;Phillis 60;Bettie Grant 60;Eugenia 60;Florence 60;Hal 60;Henry Hamilton J.60;Martha Grant 60;

INGRAM:Jas.63;John S.90;Robt.82;Sally Ann 48;W.S.54;Wm.63.

IREYS:Henry T.101;Mrs.H.Mary 101;

IRISH:Geo.63;Henry T.63,73,144,149;John 144;Mary B.144;Mary H.144;Volney S.144;

IRVIN:Arch.63;

IRVING:J.51;John 11.

IRWIN:Geo.88;John 44.
ISENBERG: I.86;Nathan 105.

ISHAM: Chas.W.126.

H

JACKSON:Andrew 11,48;

JACKSON:(cont.)Ann D. 146;Anna 56;Ben 63; Charlotte 125;D.D.8, 26,55,100,96,112,146; Gen.125;Hattie 96;Henry 112,146;Henry Hamilton 60;J.A.56;Jas.B.141, 143;Jos.L.146;Laura V. 146;Mary 146;Matthew 11; Melissa C.6;Mary I.67, 150;Posey 11;Sally 48; Stephen M.146;Wm.75.

JAFFREY:Robt.63

JAMES:Mrs. Mary 110; Annie C.72;B.F.109; Belinda J.68;Benj.82; E.P.101;Edw.C.140,150, 148;Eliza C.150; Frank 101;Gab.63;Isa.J. 140;John 150;Laura 70; Mollie 84;Mrs. 124. Nancy 140;Nancy J.68; T.I.63;T.V.118;Theodk. 150;Theodl.J.63;Thos. 148;Thos.J.148,150; Nannette 150.

JAMISON:G.60

JARRETT:Thos.R.66

JEANS:Wm.11.

JEFFERIES:Sallie 38.

JEFFORDS:C.S.21,54;E. 18,50,53,54;Judge 48; Mrs. N.P.11;

JEFFRIES:Wm.F.63,143.

JELKS:Dixon 63;G.W.63.

JELLEY:W.E.43,44;

JENEEN:J.P.81

JENKINS: Baley 63; Crittenden 63;Geo.11; John 63;John P.57; Mary E.22;Rev.S.G.106.

JENNINGS:Josephine 74; Loujenia 74.

JINKINS:Eliza 11.

JOBE:C.M.81;Maria K.90.

JOHNS:Thos.H.95,152;

JOHNSON:A.G.11;Albert 75; Bartly 152;Benj.72,45; Betsy J.126;Bryant 45; C.M.81;C.S.11;Capt.Henry 83,108,126;Capt.W.H.113; Col.Matt F.78;Cyrus 67; Daniel 48;Edw.P.66,143; Edw.P.Jr.68;Fred.W.124; Geo.78;Geo.G.135;Helen S. 39;Henry 11,48,63;J.R.129. J.S.115;J.S.Jr.116;J.V. 116;Jacob Y. 78;Jas.11, 51;Jas.S.112;Joel 128; Julia H.135;Lance 63; Linnie 88;Lucy 83;Matt F.67;M.Belle 67;Madison W.124;Moses 11,56;Mrs. Claude 116;Mrs.Frances S.112;Mrs.M.E.116;N.B.124; R.A.142;Rachel 48;Roseanna 60;S.S.33;Sam 11;Sarah 83; Sarena 60;Sylv.88;Talfour 60;Thos.B.124;W.H.90;Walter 88;Wesley 11;Wm.11,63;

JOHNSTON:C.11;Chas.W.70; Geo.P.2,3,4,23;Harris H. 68;Helen S.39;Jos.H.151; Wm.36,37.

JOHNSTONE:S.G.39;

JOLLY:H.C.93.

JONAS:Alex.96.

JONES:J.N.8;Rachel 11;A.K. 139;A.L.79;Caroline 75; Chas.H.6;E.D.75;G.P.6;J.D. 138;J.P.11;Jas.47;Jos.20; Lewis 39;L.P.11;Lucy 140; Maria H.6;Martha H.6;Martha P.6;Mary S.6;Melissa 47; Michael 17,37;Milton121; P.11;Pattie C.93;S.A.79; Saml.63;Susannah 63;Thos. 63;W.L.138;Z.63;Marg.16.

JOOR:Geo.1,2,11,35;John S.2,11,22,34,35,39;

JORDAN:York J.11;

JOYES:Clarence 103,104,128; Florence 103;Jennie 87,103, 128;Judge 104;

JUDON:Mollie 75

JULIENNE:L.11,22.

JUNY:Rev.Dr.80,81.

JUSTICE:M.53.

K

KAISER:C.136.

KANATZER:Cora 85;John 98; Mrs. John 107;

KANATZOR:Ada 128;Amelia 128;Cora 128;Eno 128; Jos.128;Nellie 128.

KANSLER:J.29.

KAUFMAN:W.59.

KEDDELL:Jas.P.20

KEEN; M.66

KEENE:Anna 53;Jacob 53; Jas.53;Wm.F.53,56.

KEENER:Roxy 136.

KEEP:Anna L.11;H.V.11, 19,57,58;Mrs. Sallie B. 11;

KEIGLER:Frances 42,43, Issac 43;

KEISECKER:Andrew P. 136; Chas.B.136;Frank C.136.

KEITH:Miss 86;S.N.86.

KELLNER:E.Jr.90.

KELLOG:M.B.11

KELLUM:Nathl.K. 63.

KELLY:Fanny 124;Ida B.81; Jas.A.17;Mary C.18;Rachel 73;Thos.127;

KENNEDY:Clarence 118;Edw. 77,127,128;W.L.118;

KENNY: Arch.S.63.

KENOYE:Anna Clara 136;Roxy 136.

KERSHAW:Anne 150;Annie 152;Geo.150;Geo.T.152; J.P.54,59;John T.C.152; Mary 152;Mary J.150,152; R.C.152;Rosa Sarah 69,152; Thos.69,150,152;

KEYS:Jos.72

KIGER:G.41;C.I.21,50; Caroline E.41;Mrs.B.G.51.

KILLERHOUSE:Jos.116.

KILLIAN:Mark 86;Mary 86;Max 11,52,18;Va.11.

KILPATRICK:Eb.63;Elihu 63

KINCAID:John 63;Peyton S.83.

KING:Caroline O.44;Jas H.95;John H.17;Maggie 69;Rev.E.E.88,92,93; S.H.134,137;

KINKEAD: Jos.113

KINNEY:Ellen 75.

KINSTLER:Amelia 123;J. 123;Mrs. 104.

KINTER:D.M.29.

KIRBY:Soloman 66;

KIRK:A.M.81;Capt.A.M. 95;Mrs.Sarah A.(Bro.)95.

KIRKLAND:J.71;Mrs.T.A.96.

KIRSHNER:Abraham 83

KRISTINE:Isadore 116.

KITTLE: Geo.138.

KLEIBER:Minnie 124.

KNATZER:John 72

KNIGHT:Geo.11;Mary 11; Geo.M.50;George May 50; John 50;R.H.139;Wm.63.

KNOX:Andrew 38,63,143, 144;Mary B.34;

KOBER:Henry 69.

KORSTENBROCK:Father P.J. 90,93.

Koufman; Aline 84

KRAUNSOPOLSKI:(no other)

KRESS:Eliza 124.

KRETSCHMAR:W.P.77,123;

KRIGER:H.F.85,128;W.F.136

KUHN:Julia 81

KURTZ: H.S.104

KUYKENDALL:A.C.139

KYLE:Thos.123.

L

LABUZAN:Chas.A.63

LACEY:Eliz.J.74;Mrs. Mary114;Robt.85.

LACHS:S.W.53;T.W.54;

LACKS:Audora 46;Winfield 46;

LACY:F.63;Thos.63.

LAFOE:T.E.86

LAIRD:Arch.63;G.W.63

LALLIEN:John 11,42;

LAMBETH:Thos.L.40;

LAMIE:Father 80

LAMPKIN:Annie 84

LAMPKINS:Edw.O.67

LANCASTER:Dr.Alonzo 111; 145;G.B.82.

LANDAU:Bertha 84;Julius 108,113;

LANE:J.A.27;John 1; Mary A.27;Nancy 27; Sarah 27.

LANGCAPE:Ruth 134.

LANGLEY;L.M.124;W.S.19.

LARSEN:Morris 11.

LASER:Jacob 91.

LASHLEY:Alex 63;Arnold 149;H.63;Jennie O.92; John 63;R.M.103;

LASSITER:Martha V.7

LATHAN:Lorenzo 63

LATTING:Family of 134.

LAUGHLIN:Wm.145.

LAURENS:Henry 123.

LAWS:Gertrude 69.

LAWSON:A.J.70;Eugene W. 106;J.B.M.105;L.E.11; Mrs.85;Rev.T.B.92.

LAWSTE:Chas.A.63

LAX:Aaron 11;Aurora 46;Winfield 46.

LE BAVON:Sarah R.E.138.

LEA:T.D.67

LEAKE:Fredreka 80.

LEAR:G.R.126.

LEATHERMAN:5;Frank 23,42, 43;Geo.W.4,23,42,43;John 23,42;John Jr.42;John W. Jr.23;Mary S.42,43;Peter R.23,42,43;R.H.43;Rich. 42;Robt.23,42,43;Saml. 11,23,28,42;Saml.B.23,42; T.3;Z.23,42,47;

LEAVENWORTH:J.H.110; Noah H.110.

LEDBETTER:A.C.R.24;H.C. 24;Homer V.M.1,11,24; Jane 24;Jas.W.24;Wm.B.24.

LEE:Sarah 102;A.M.11; Adedese F.101;Britton L. 88;Cath.S.69;Eleanor P. 149;Harry P.72,149;Henry M.143;J.D.92;J.L.84;Jas. D.63;John D.56,57;John M. 80,101;149;Kate 149;Lewis 139;Lizzie B.11;Mary 139; Mary L.88;Mattie 79;Mattie M.56;Mattie T.C.57;Mrs.H.P. 116;N.W.69,149;Permelia 72;Rev.Mr.79;S.B.139;Sam 11;Wm.H.149;

LEIGH:Thos.J.1,3,4,5,8; Thos.C.24;

LEIGHTON:Sarah 24;T.J.11.

LEMAY:S.T.60

LEMLE:Belle 87;Bertha 91; D.91,128,129;

LEMLER:Max 84

LEMMON:Jas.L.52

LENGSFIELD:Benj.F.76;J.L. 72;Julius 115;Julius J.74;

LENNAN:Father 86.

LEONARD:A.R.78;Hattie 78.

LEPPARD:Harriet 71

LERIEMONDIE:Mrs.H.C.74.

LEVERETTE:Johanna 74

LEVINGSTON:C.E.84

LEVY:Daniel 29;H.84;
Katie 83;Kaufman 56;
Mrs.Charlotte G.55;
Pauline E.87;Rachel
86;E.87.

LEWIS:C.W.76.

LEWY:B.M.108,119;Lep.
86;Mollie 84,85;Mrs.
Ernestine 108;

LEY:Florida 142,145;
Wm.142,145;

LIGHES:Rial 11

LIKENS:Endora C.35;Kate
Knox 149;Thos.J.35,147;

LILES:Chas.63.

LIMMELL: T.L.41

LINDER:Danl.63

LINDSEY:Mrs.Martha 23

LINNELL:David 92

LINSEY:Eph.63Marg.145;
Robt.S.145.

LINVILLE:John R.56.

LIPONSKY:Henry C. 73.

LLOYD:Spencer 63

LOCHMAN:Julius 123.

LOFTIN:E.W.S.28;Eld.28;
Walter C.28,63;Wm.B.28.

LOGAN:Mary 11.

LONG:Green B.3.

LONGELY:A.63.

LORD:W.W.68,69.

LOUNDES:L.P.130;Rawlins
130.

LOVE:Chas.I.104;D.A.72,
94,102;Dave 11;Kate R.94;
Mary 87;Melville 93;Mrs.
D.A.109;W.Allen 102.

LOVELL:Antonia 151;Jos.
151;Louisa G.151.

LOWE:E.2

LOWRY:Agnes 3;J.Wm.2;
Lucia Cornelia 2,3;Sue 51;
Susanna L.2;Wm.Jr.3;Wm.T.
2,4,3,51.

LUCAS:Silas 38.

LUCUS:I.11

LUCY:Walter 90.

LUDLOW:Ben A.63

LUHM:A.G.11;Augusta G.59.
Mary F.59.

LUM:Erastus 63;Wm.63;136.

LUNDQUIST:Mrs. Clara113.

LUNEY:Ephraim 63

LUSK:Robt.129.

LYNCH:J.C.11;J.P.11;
Mattie T.11.

LYONS:Rich.J.66;Wm.H.76

LYPSCOMB:Ben11

M

MACLEMAN:Jas.73

MACLIN:J.H.71;
MADDOX:Wm.C.76.

MAGEE:Willie 12,27;

MAGOON:Mrs.Adeline 113

MAGRUDER:H.S.85;R.W.85.

MAHOFFEY:J.T.66

MAITLAND:Robt.L.12,58.

MALLARY:John 3.

MALOY:Fannie A.69.

MANDEVILLE:Henry D.20.

MANFIELD:Chas.P.80.

MANIFOLD:John124,126;
Lelia 83.

MANLY:W.J.123.

MANN:Wm.G.C.151

MANNIFEE:Robt.C.63

MANNING:Lucy 12.

MARALIS:A.12

MARDENS:Bettie 80.

MARDERS:Jas.S.137.

MARKS:Rev.Alex76.

MARLOW:Jos.63

MARR:Daniel P.147;
Geo.W.147;N.L.147;
S.C.23;Selina Jane
147;Wm.146.

MARSH:Lizzie D.70;
Robt.29,149.

MARSHALL:E.G.84;137;
Geo.63;Henry 12;L.R.
66,149;Marcella 78;
Mrs.Sarah 149;Raphael
73,122;Reubin 66;S.
Duncan 149;Wm.76,78,
121;

MARTIN:Bettie 41;D.D.
41;Dr.Wm.91;H.G.1;
John 63;Mrs.Sarah 147;
Thos.J.Jr.133;Thos.J.
Sr.133;Va.V.136;Wm.V.136.

MASON:P.L.12

MASSEY:Jos.Addison 90;
Louisa 122.

MATTHEWS:Ely 147;Isreal
143,147;Lavinia B.147;
Mrs.Ann 59;Ruth 147.

MAURY:Jas.M.110;Dilly
F.22;Mrs.C.L.22.

MAXEY:Walter 12.

MAXWELL:L.P.63;Mary 32;
R.Y.31,32;

MAY:John 63

MAYER:David 45,48,57;
Henry L.12;Mrs.M.B.12;
Sigmund 97.

MAYES:J.D.22

MAYFIELD:E.66;F.E.1,2,8,
15,17,27,28,31,34,38,33;
J.L.8,18,21,23,27,29,31,
33,34,38,46,50,30;Jos.L.
33;M.H.1,12,27;Mary 63;
N.P.27;Saunders 63;T.E.
12;Thos.W.27;Virgil H.27;
Wm.J.27;Wm.S.27.

MAYNARD:Eliz.S.41;John
C.41.

McALLISTER:A.W.134,145;
Arch.63;Aug.W.63,134;
David 63;Gen.A.W.95;Gus
124;Harriet 73;John 63;
Louisa M.77;Marg.38.

McALPIN:Duncan 63

McBRIDE:Capt.93

McCALL:Albert 3;Dr.J.S.
124;Euella 78;Lena 85.

McCALLAM:M.C.74;

McCALLUM:J.L.74;John D.75
Annie A.75.

McCAMERON:Sarah M.63

McCANN:Jas.122

McCARROLL:Green L.146.

McCAUGHAN:J.J.63

MCCAUSLAND:Mary 126.

McCHAIN:Mr.96

McCLAUD:Saml.12

McCLENAN:Amelia 77

McCLENNAN:Rev.Jas.111;
Emma 111

McCOMB:M.A.4

McCONNELL:Jas.77;Mrs.
Eliza A.147;Robt.P.147.

McCORD:M.R.114;W.J.113,114.

MCCORMICK:Andrew 143;W.B.23

McCOWN:12

McCOY:Dora 76

McCOYAN:Walter 12,15,5;

McCRACKEN:Rev.88

McCRASKEN:Arthur 63

McCUE:D.H.47.

McCULLOUGH:Addie 89;Rich.
121;Robt.143,147;

McCUTCHEON:J.H.2,105,111.

McCUTCHEON:Fannie E.103;
John M.103;Maggie 103;R.B.
118;

McDANIEL:E.B.84;E.B.Jr.
85;Jos.63;Wm.64.

McDONALD:A.50;J.A.12,50;
John 12,44;Jos.73;Mrs.Sarah
75;

McDOWELL:E.P.99;

McDUFFIE:Angus 64;Murdock 64.

McEVERS:H.K. 73

McEWEN:Campbell 139.

McFADDEN:Frances 143; John 64,147;Wm.143.

McFARLAND:J.M.75

McGARR:Owen 58

McGEHEE:Saml.12

McGINTY:Delia 66

McGRATH:Bettie 83,85; Caldwell 114;Julia 79; Mamie 85,90;

McGRAW:Chas.117;Jos.72;

McGREGOR:John C.72

McHATTON:Chas.G.148; Fenelon 148;Jas.A.146, 148;

McILWAIN:H.R.71

McINTOSH:Caroline M.20; David 20;David S.26.

McINTYRE:Hugh 64;John 64

McKAY:John P.35;Robt.64

McKINNEY:Jas.P.43;44; K.W.2.

McLARAN:Jas.64

McLAUGHLIN:Andrew 131; J.B.29.

McLAURIN:John 2,5,6,12, 27;Sarah G.6;

McLEAN:Jas.123;Thos.122

McLEMORE:John C.4

McMEEKIN:Lawrence 95;Mrs. 98;Mrs.Lucy 95;

McMILLAN:Ceasar 75;Danl 26;Sally 20;Sarah 20.

McMURRAY:J.J.97;Mrs.89; Mrs.E.B.114.

McNAIRY:A.D.18;Eliz.P. 8,18.

McNEILY:J.S.82,131;J.T. 128;May Percy 98;

McQUAID(McQUIDE,McQUAIDE) Jas.M.12,52;Dorcas 52; Mary C.52.

McQUILLAN:A.P.25;Cynthia Jane 25;Cynthia P.25;Jos. 25,38;Jos.R.12,25,26;

McQUILLAN:(cont.)Martha A.12,25,37;Melissa A.5, 12,25;Melissa J.5,25;Wm. B.3,5,25,26,39;Jas.M.12;

McRAVEN:Lucy D.88;Robt. D.50;Thos.85.

McWHIRTER:Josie 51

McYOUNG:John 12

MEACHAM:Orville 12;

MEADE: Mary 75

MEARES: Dr.John L.94,117; Mrs.Bettie A.94.

MEDLEY:Geo.B.98

MEECHAM:Jas.M.139;C.C.139.

MEISNER:C.F.96,124;

MELCHOIR:Emeline T.129; Henry 98;Henry H.73;L.A. 72;Sarah J.71.

MENDELSOHN:Herman 118.

MENNFIELD:Caleb 100

MERCHANT:Mary 74;Roxana 68;Ulysses 68.

MERCLKELD:Geo.148;Jos.C. 148;Mary Ann 148.

MERRICK:P.F.66

MERRIL:N.96

MERRILL:Saml.12.

MESSINGER:Bacon 27;G.W.B. 12,27;Geo.27;Sophia 27; Sybelia A.27.

METCALF:F.A.70,107,146; P.Evie 93.

MIALE:Rev.Father 76

MIEURE:Mrs.S.J.115.

MILES: Thos.W.7

MILLENS:Ann Jane 43;Belle 43;Wm.43.

MILLER:Benj.M.67;Georgie M.80;Harvey 111,144;Henry 72;Henry H.94;Horace 44; J.R.1;J.W.36;Jane H.144; Jas.M.71;John 12;John A. 150;John B.19;John C.144; John W.4;Laura 144;Lewis 12,27;Maggie J.111;Polly Ann 66;Sallie 71;T.Marshall 47;W.C.87;

MILLS:B.B.60;W.5;Wm.L. 143.

MILLSAPS:Barton 7,12,28; Wm.66.

MINOR:Polly 12;Robt.12.

MINZIES:Jas.122

MITCHEL:Mrs.124

Mitchell: R.W.C.79.

MIZZELL:Mary E.25.

MOBLEY:I.Hosea 21;Lizzie 21;Pleasant M.146.

MOBRAY:(girl)121

MOCK:Celestine 89

MOLLISON:Robt.12,53.

MONTAGUE:Annie 152

MONTAIGUE:Mrs.Annie de 80

MONTGOMERY:C.P.133;Chas. 99;D.C.68;Della 83;Dr.D.C. 80,85,86,99,104,130;Eliza B.103;Eugene 99;Heddins 133;J.M.72,77,80,103,133; Jane 144;Julia 72;Kate 100;Louisa 67;M.A.40,100; Mary C.72;Mrs.Frances S. 104;Russel 67,148;S.W. 100;Sallie 80;W.P.69,94, 98,100;Alex 144.

MOON:Rev.E.H.82,83.

MOORAN:Abe 12

MOORE:Abe 12;C.12;Capt. Wm.W.48;E.40;Emmet N.28; Ernestine 48;F.W.12;E.N. 12;Franklin W.28;Harry 12; J.H.85;Jas.C.105;Jesse 12 45;John 103,105,133;John H.77,130,133;John M.88; Josephine 73;Maggie M.67; Martha 133;Mary 103,133; Mary E.28;Michael 66;Minerva M.12;Mrs.M.F.133;Mrs. Mary E.51;Mrs.Rachel 28; Nancy G.74;Oliver P.28; Rachel 5,12;S.S.5;Saml. L.1,12;Saml.S.5,28;Thos. A.28;W.H.102,130;W.N.86; Wm.F.5;Wm.S.28.

MOOREHEAD:Saml.J.22

MOORMAN:Meta 134,135.

MOREHEAD:Chas.S.94

MORGAN:Col.C.E.121;J.H. 75;Jane P.73;Julia 78; L.E.124;M.L.90;Mrs.100; Oliver T.68,71;

MORRIS:D.124;D.L.12;Dave 123;Henry 146;Henry N.145; M.103,123;Mary 145,146; Mrs.D.121;Mrs.M.121; Sol 78;W.J.12.

MORRISON:Geo.Jr.19;Geo. L.19;John 12;Marg.Maude 19;Mary Collins 51;Wm.A.50.

MORRISS:Henry T.66;Jane 66

MORRISSY:John 99

MORSON:Arthur A.79;Dr.78; May 91.

MORTON:(blank)41;Eliza 29;G.W.29;Jos.29;Mrs. Wash.41;Wash.12.

MORZINSKI:M.I.76

MOSBY:Carrie 77;Eudora 87;G.148;John B.98;L.H. 29

MOSELEY:Alfred W.29;Burrel 29;Burwell 55;Cath.29; Eugenia 12,29,55;J.M.29; John H.12,29,55;Lucy 12, 29,55;Mrs.Sallie A.57.

MOSELY:A.W.55,60;Lutie 83; Carrie 77;Cath.Ann 55.

MOTT:A.B.74;Albert M.74

MOULTRI:Ed.12

MOUNGER:H.C.139

MOWBRAY:Mrs.Thos.121

MOYSE:Harriet 97;Leon 97;Levi 127.

MULHOLLEN:A.M.39;John M. 39;Nathl.39;Thos.J.39.

MULLER:Annie 92

MULLINS:Rev.E.F.68;E.J.67.

MUNDELL:Cath.125;Jos.H. 125;W.125.

MURCHISON:Amelia 12

MURDOCK:Alfred 143

MURFF:J.Dudley 74;Mrs.M.A.131

MURPHREE:John 93;

MURPHY:E.28;J.W.69;
Sarah A.73.

MURRAY: 12;Alfred 53;
Gov.Eli 117.

MURRELL:Saml.12,44;

MUSE:Henry M.95

MYERS:F.C.12,20,25,26,
37,38;Henrietta F.20,
26,37;Henry C.59;John
125;W.G.78;Wm.2,4,18,
20,26,33,37,38,39,124;

MYRICK:Mary 35,36,37;

N

NAIL:Jas.36;Mary 36;

NANCE:A.B.85

NAPPER:John 56

NASH:Hagan 12;Wm.Rich.68

NEAL:Jas.12;T.L.56;

NEDLEY:Geo.B.46

NEELY:Mary 66

NEFF:John 77

NEGUS:Jas.E.Jr.77

NEIBERT:Jos.12,43;Sarah 43.

NEILY:J.S.131

NELMS:Mrs.Nancy 103;W.J. 103.

NELSON:Alice 74;Bessie
Howe94;E.R.12;Emma 7;
Emma H.12;Eunice 7;
Eunice Ann 7;Francis L.
7;Howard J.12;J.T.73;
Jas.7;Jesse 94;John 7;
John H.68,75,94,124;
John L.148;John N.7;John
S.68,70;John Sharp 101;
Julia L.7;Laura 83,84;
Marg.D.51;Mary L.7;Mary
L.L.4;Mary L.S.12;Mrs.
Bessie 94;N.J.70,123;
NathanThos.7,73,94;Pett-
way 7;Rev.Walker 80;
Robt.53;S.S.12,51;Sam J.
12;Saml.4,7,12,28,31,53;
Thos.7;Thos.C.4,7;

NEWCOMB:H.D.133

NEWHILL: Rev.Mr.79

NEWMAN:Ben F.66;I.A.118;
J.A.74;S.B.17.

NEWPORT:A.P.20;A.R.26;
Albert G.37;Carsand 20;
Sarah C.37;

NEWSOM:E.L.88;Jos.D.87

NEWTON:Emma 72,74;Fannie
M.78.

NICHALS:Marecy 12;

NICHOLS:Mrs.Eleanor 142
Wm.142;

NICHOLSON:I.E.28;Mrs.
Martha 28.

NOBLE:Allen 12

NOLAND:Hal 83;Mary H.83

NORCORN:Frederick 40;
Wm.R.40.

NORFLEET:W.B.39

NORMAN: Lula Van 91;

NORMENT:Wm.T.72

NORTH: Elisha 2,5,6,8,
28,38;

NORTHAM:Thos.M. 2

NORWOOD:John 68,151;N.L.53

NUGENT:Aimee 109;Col.W.L.
109;Mary Cath.94;Nellie 83
87;W.L.87,94,153;W.S.67;
Wm.L.68,69,72;

NUNNALLA:H.H.12

Nurse:Polly 92

NUTT:Mary 138;Miss 86

O'BANNON: Columbus 117;
D.B.82,114,117,135;Mrs.
Mary F.114;Wm.P.103;

O'CONNER:Mrs.90;Kinnie
107;Mrs.Josephine 107;
Tim 107.

O'HEA:Maj.112.

O'NEAL:Jas.57,58;Kitty 12;
Mrs.Caroline 108;R.T.108.

OAKLEY:Rev.J.T.78;,76.

OBANION:D.B.74
ODOM:W.F.17
OFTEEN:M.66
OLIN:Albert 82
OLIVER:Saml.C.66
ORFUT:Maria 134
ORGLER:Gussie 92
ORR:Marg.67
OSBORN:Benj.29;Wm.29.
OSSTERNS:Joel 60
OSTEENS:Simon 66
OSWALD:Jas.W.71
OUSLEY:Harriet B.108; Thos.66
OVERALL:Cath.134
OVERBY:J.A.132;Mr.87
OVERTON:Thos.B.95
OWEN:Jacob 29;Mollie E. 139;Rev.J.A.91Will S.29.
OZBURN: C.M.91

P

PACE:A.D.79,86,106;E.J. 67;Fanny Percy 106.
PADDLEFORD:C.E.46;Louella 46;Wm.B.12,46;
PAGE:Mary L.85;Rev.T. 77,78,124;
PAINE:Rev.Robt.70
PARKER:A.K.90;Benj.64; Jas.B.41;Jas.P.40,41; John M.41,53,139;Mary D.41;Mary I.40;Mary J. 41;Mrs.John M.138;N.B. 45,46;Rich.64;W.L.V. 64;Wm.41.
PARKS:Amanda 30;Geo.10, 12,143;Geo.C.45;Geo.N. 1,6,12,30,45,142;Geo.N. Jr.30;Geo.P.4,45;Geo.V. 4;Geo.W.30;Jas.M.12,45; King P.45;Marg.E.30; Rebecca 35;S.G.35,60,149; Susan 142;Susan E.30; Thos.30,142;Thos.G.45;

PASSINC:Edna W.12
PASSMORE:Emma 134
PATTERSON:H.W.26
PAUL:Lucy 93
PAXTON:A.G.83,139;A.J. 79,80,86,93,94,109,110, 137;A.J.Jr.81,137;Andrew 139;Cornelia 93;Elisha 94;H.M.94,110;Hannah 86; John G.64;Lucy 80;R.E.111; Wm.74;Wm.F.110.
PAYNE:I.S.7;John F.143; R.T.146;
PEACE:Frances A.1;Marinda L.1;Willis 1;Wm.H.13,31;
PEACOCK:Wm.64
PEAK:Emma 88;Jas.Ann 128; Mrs. 106.
PEARCE:Geo.82;Rev.81.
PEARSON:B.T.131;Bascom T. 69.
PECK:A.H.64;G.H.64.
PEELER:Ezra 139;Richmond 51
PEINE:Charley 44
PENDING:(Est.of)12
PENDLETON:B.151
PENICK:Rev.E.A.83
PENNINGTON:Edw.38.
PENNY:B.F.70,106;Carrie 106;Dr.Alex 132;Mrs.A.C. 106;W,T.69.
PENRICE:Francis 64;John H.75;John S.101;John J. 149;Jos.B.143;Susan E. 142;Wm.38,64,144,147;
PEPPER:Daniel G.120; Freida 116;S.116.
PEPPERMAN:S.85,119;
PERCY:C.B.142,145;Eleanor N.142;Ellis W.142;Fanny 79;Fanny E.142;Harry 102; Henrietta 142;J.W.142;Lady 87;Leroy 83,85,128,135,138; Leroy P.106,142;Maria 142; (cont.)

PERCY:(cont.)Nannie I.
135;Robt.H.142;Sam F.
102;Thos.G.142;W.A.
79,106,128,129,135,142;
W.A.Jr.87,135;Walker 92;

PERKINS:Capt.J.L.118;
Mrs.Jennie S.118;Sarah
44;Thos.132.

PERRICE:John S.101

PERROTTE:Mary 77

PERRY:(boy)121;(child)
123;Frances G.137;Fred
121;Jas.121;Matilda E.
69;Mrs.Jas.121;Mrs.T.P.
122;Nellie 80;Sidney L.
137;T.P.77,123;Thos.H.137

PETERS:Bettie J.100,120;
D.G.100;Dr.Matt.L.97,120;
Julia H.83;Minnie 89,120;
Mrs.89;

PETIT:John J.83,120.

PETTWAY:Ida 31;Julia I.
31;Laura Danks 31;R.W.1,
2,5,8,12,16,24,28,31;
Sallie Gwin 31;Thos.R.31;

PETTY:A.J.70

PEYTON:L.M.13;A.13;Mrs.
Malvina F.51;

PHARR:(Also sp.Farr)
Albertus 30;Cicero 19;
Elias 2,3,5,8,12,18,19,30;
Eliz.31;Eliza A.12;Esther
19;Eunice M.30;Hampton 31;
Hampton H.30;Henry 5,19;
Henry A.31;Henry N.5,18;
Hester 5;Jas.5;John N.30;
Marg.18;Marg.B.5;Marg.S.
30;Mary 5;Mary E.8,30;
Robt.5,18;S.Albertus 31;
Saml.A.5;Sarah 5,18;Sarah
Ann 19;Sarah E.30;Teresa
5;Ursilla 30;Ursilla M.8,
30;Walter 18;Walter N.5;
Walter S.19;

PHEISFAS:R.B.12

PHELAN:Kate O.80;Sen.80.

PHELPS:Alonzo J.140;Sol.
144;V.S.137;Va.T.140;W.G.
137,140;

PHILLIPS:B.E.66;J.L.69;
J.W.143;S.F.139;S.J.131;
Sallie J.139;Wm.H.69,139;

PICKENS:W.H.31

PIERCE:Granville S.66;J.O.
73;Mattie O.73;

PILCHER;Fred F.111;
Mason 111.

PILCHERS:Anna C.78

PINKNEY:Ned 13

PINKSTON:T.E.13.

PINTARD:Estelle 83

PITTMAN:G.W.22

PLACE:Harriet 138

PLANT: Fred.P.141

PLANTATIONS:Aldemar 113;
Andalusa 33;Ashland 112,
115;Auburn 97;Baconhorn
27;Bavarian 47;Bear Garden 21;Bear Lake 56;Belle
Aire 95,152;Ben Lomand 30,
45,47,48;Buckland 138;
Burleigh 52;Burnlea 40,
46,52;Burtonia 140;Cammack 48;Chicovea 35;Choctaw Bend39;Clover Hill
52;Cottonwood 30,56;
Council Bend 46;Danover
46;Dunbarton 17,27;Duncansby 57,58;Egypt Ridge
115;Eldorado 30,47;Esperanza 42,57,58;Eustasia
22;Farland 53;Forkland
126;Glenmary 105;Glenn
Annie 18;Hollywood 119;
Ingomar 51;Keystone 101;
LaGrange 96;Lammermoor
146;Linden 99,114;Live
Oak 132;London 102;Loughborough 77,100;Maeklenberg 129;Mills 48;Mosswoo
111;Mound Pleasant 149;
Mulberry 94;Muscadine 48;
Oakland 99,103,127;Oakley
54;Omega 21;Onward 44,126
Otterburn 52;Pace 116;
Palmetto 152;Panola 77,10
Reality 138;Redleaf 139;
Richland 141;Riverside 12
Roach's 153;Rosalie 55;
Valewood 51;Walnut Ridge

PLANTATIONS:(cont.)23;
Wayside 105,139;Whitehall
93;Wildwood 95,102,126;
Willow Grove 41;Windsor
138;Woodland 43;Woodstock 96;

PLATT:Anna123;Geo.W.
128;Mrs.S.A.122;

POGEL:Andrew 74;Eliza
G.96;F.A.74,96;JUlia
A.96,122;

POHL:Florence 119;Theodore 117,119;

POLLE:Minnie 84

POLLO:Mrs.L.123

POLLOCK:W.A.128,134;

POND:T.E.119

POPE:Wm.H.145

PORTER:Ben 40;C.12;J.N.
31;Nettie 91;W.L.123.

POWELL:A.H.6;Becky 134;
Emily M.15,147;Fannie A.
84;G.P.68;Ira M.68;Mattie
81;Mordecai 1,3,5,6,15,
39,60,147;Mrs.T.W.84;
Thos.81;Thos.W.70;W.B.88.

POWER:Callie H.76;Stephen
H.76.

PRENTICE:Geo.D.95.

PRESCOTT:J.W.16,17,21,24,
25,32,31,35;Wm.66.

PRESTON:Caroline M.130;
Lynas 12;Marg.23;Susanna
44;

PRIBATSCH:Max 52

PRICE:Ann E.132;Anna 56;
Eliz.132;H.V.132;Jacob12,
53,54,56;Jas.56;12;Annie
12;John 56;Lucy 13;Rev.
J.W.85;

PRINCE:Alex.38;Cynthia
38;Eliz.38;Jane 38;John
G.T.38,142;Myra Jane 38;
Polly Berry 38;Robt.38;
Sally 38;Wm.Berry 38.

PRITCHARD:Jas.69.

PRYOR:(blank)124;Fred 122;
Girl 121;Mrs.F.123;Wm.B.66

PUCKETT:Walter 66

PURCELL:Rev.J.B.153

PURLOCK:Anne 48

PURNELL:Wm.12

PURSER:Harriet B.134

PUTNAM:C.F.74;Fannie A.
79;H.B.72,79,122;Hiram
121;Julia R.74.

Q

QUELAR:Rev.Father 77,78.

QUICK:Walter 77,122;

QUINLAN:J.L.97

QUINN:Dr.88;Maggie 88;

QUITMAN:Eliz.151;F.Henry
151;Fredericka 151;Gov.
John A.151;M.Rosalie 151.

R

RABB:E.M.133;L.H.133.

RACHELMAN:Morris 84

RADJESKY:Louis 122;R.122;
Rachel 124.

RAFFINGTON:Jennie G.71

RAILY:Emma Laws 85

RAINES:Sam 139

RALPH:John 123

RAMSEY:D.B.83;Rev.D.B.84,85

RANDOLPH:Eliz.Landon 96;
Mary T.102;Nannie B.96,102;
W.F.73,96,102;

RANEY:Marg.J.129

RATCHLITZ:Julius 121

RATH:Fred 92

RAWITZER:Rev.Chas.78,79;

RAWLINGS:J.W.131

RAWLS:Rich.4

RAWORTH:H.P.83

REDDIN:Mollie E.73

REDWOOD:Thos.17

REED:Geo.131;Wm.B.146.

REESE:Thos.133

REEVES:Mrs. Jas.101

REGIONS:Jos.66

REOCHE:Robt.91

REYNOLD: J.6

REYNOLDS:Chas.C.52; G.W.66.

RHEA:Willie T.136

RICH:O.H.T. 60

RICHARDSON:Col.E.117; Edm.58;Marg.E.117;Mary E.20,37;Mrs.Patton 117; R.R.20,26;37;W.W.91;

RIDDLE:Alfred J.131

RIGGS:Frank119;Miss 119

RILEY:Nancy 13

RING:C.F.45

RITTER:Ida P.13

RIVES:Annie M.131;John O.131;Mary 131;Mary B. 73;Mary L.131;Mrs.O.C. 109;O.C.101;Orville C. Sr.100;Mattie A.74;

ROACH:Benj.153;H.Eliz. 58;M.J.44;Mahala P.H. 58;Martha 44.

ROBARDS:Alice 76;Chas. L.152.

ROBB:Carrie E.107;Ellen 134;Eugene A107;Fannie G.107;G.W.149;J.H.73, 106,136,138,109;Jos.H. 75;Jos.H.Jr.109;Mary A. 149;Mattie B.109;Mattie T.106.

ROBERTS:John C.66;Percy 69;Rebecca 72

ROBERTSHAW:Adele 107; Jas.107,128.

ROBERTSON:Alta C.13,32; Eliz.M.145;Ella C.13,32; Geo.54;Geo.R.17;J.H.13; J.M.142;J.W.35;Jas.W.1; Jos.W.2,32,142;Leanah 13, 32;Lula C.13;Lula V.32; Olive V.32;Thos.W.5;W.4; W.M.145;

ROBINSON:Cam M.97;Dr. 43,44;Dr.Henry 82;Geo. 13;J.W.40,143;Jeremiah S.153;Lucy 83;Mrs.Lucy 114;N.E.19;Talee 13;

ROCHE:C.W.89

RODEN:Geo.74

RODMAN:Mrs.116

ROGELLIO:Emanuel 20

ROGERS:Henrietta 43; Mrs.Mollie119;W.B.119.

ROGHERS:Ida R.75

ROOT:J.L.43,54;

ROSENSTOCK:Clara L.120; Minnie P.120;Morris 89, 120.

ROSS:J.J.67;Lizzie 90; Matilda 138;

ROW:M.134

ROWE:Jas.H.114;Wm.J.60

ROWELLS:John A.85

ROY:Belle 86

ROYALL:T.F.151

ROYSTER:Milton 53

RUCKS:Lewis T.145;Arthur 111;B.N.86,137;Hal 87; Henrietta 145;J.T.109; Jas.145;Jas.T.100,147,152 Judge 91,116;L.T.101,110 Lee 137;Louise 91;Louise V.145;Maggie 109;Maria L 145;Marian 68;Marion 119 145;Mary 81;Mrs.S.J.97; S.T.92;Sadie M.137;Salli 82;Sallie B.109,152;Sam T.87,119;Mrs.M.M.111;

RUDY:B.F.13;W.H.13

RUISOLD:Miss 131

RUNNELS:Hiram G.65

RUSHING:Henry 13,32;Jas. Monroe 35;Mary 31;T.J.75 Wm.3,4,8,13,31,32;

RUSHTON:Thos.H.131

RUSSELL:Kate A.71;Wm.65

RUTHERFORD:Eliz.V.136; Madge 136;

RUTLAND:N.60

RYALLS:Lucy 93;Mrs.93

RYALS:R.C.74,77

RYAN:Katie 86

S

SAGER:John 81

SAIDEN:Hy 137

SALE:Mrs.Jane A.117

SALIZIGER:Anna C.129; Henry G.129;Louisa T.129

SALMON:Mamie 115

SAMFIELD:Rev.Dr.84

SAMUEL:A.M.143;Sallie 138

SANDERS:Carrie J.97;A.H. 2,33;G.W.71;H.33;H.H.13; Isom 71;M.R.75,94,104; Mrs.M.A.94;Norman 112; Stephen 33;T.B.33;Walter L.90;Ward 146.

SANFORD:C.C.13;Mrs.Geo. 122.

SANSOM:Rev.Dr.85

SATTERFIELD:Dr.W.E.83, 107;E.Y.131;Emma K.128, 131;Emma Y.128;Milling M.128;Mrs.E.R.111;V.J. 128;Wm.E.128;

SATTERWHITE:Annie F.72

SAUNDERS:A.H.2;John 143; W.R.74;

SAVAGE:Dolly 65;Rowland 65.

SCHALL: Jos.A.78

SCHERER:Yetta 80

SCHLESINGER:H.98;Isadore 98;Leo.98,84;Rachel 98.

SCHMALHOLZ:F.X.99

SCHMIDT:Fred.W.65

SCHULTE:John Ber.90;H.27.

SCHURZ:Carl 79

SCOTT:Abr.M.65;Abraham 116;Chas.74,103;Dr.W.A. 103;Edw.W.83;Evi 129; Fannie 116;Garrett 124; Geo.Y.72,103;Girl 121; H.P.13,50;Horace 129;I.S. 15;J.M.140;J.W.84,108; Jacob 84,85;Jane 144;Jeff. 108;John 5,13;John A.65; John F.65;Lilly B.91;Luey 129;Mamie 84;Marg.129; Mary 60;Mary A.129;Mattie 129;Miss Willie 121;Mrs. C.S.120;Neville B.92;P. 54;Perry 65;Sallie E.72; Sarah J.68;Wm.144;Wm.P.68.

SCRUGG:Rev.86

SCRUGGS:Lula 13

SCUDDER:E.N.22;Marie G.13

SCURLOCK:Josie F.89

SEAY:Dr.83;Lenore 93; May 83.

SEIVERS: Mrs.M.123.

SELLERS:Alice G.34;Amelia A.34;B.M.2,13,3,6,33,147; Cornelia 147;David 33;E.R. 3,13,33,34,147;Edw.B.34; Elbert A.34;Emily147;Emily C.33,34,147;Henry C.13,34; Isaac 3,12,13,33,34,142,147; Isaac F.13,34;Jas.F.34; Silas 33;Susan A.34;T.W.3, 13,33,34,43;Thos.33,142; Thos.Wm.147;W.B.3,33,147;

SELSER:Elisha 65

SESSFORD:Emma 84

SESSIMS:John G.21

SESSIONS:Rich.13

SESSUMS:Davis 91;Rev.David 89

SEXTON:Jennie 119

SHACKLEFORD:John 2

SHALL:Euella M.112;J.A. 112,138;Mrs.M.C.112;

SHANNAHAN:Annie 78;D.M.72;112 Marg.T.85;Dan 123;Mrs.M.O.112.

SHANKS:Geo.65;Jas.D.75;

SHANNON:W.F.95

SHARKEY:Wm.T.65

SHARP:Abs.65

SHARPLIN:Wm.65

SHAW:Helen 124;J.L.69,70;Maurice W.89,93;Mrs.T.B.123;T.B.82;Zilph.88

SHEARER:Letitia 142;W.B.142.

SHEFFNER:Chas.77

SHELBY:Albert 34;Albert C.35;Annie 76;Bayliss P.65;Bettie 82;Creath 39;E.W.2,5,7,8,4,20,25,26,28,34;Ella P.103;Evan 3,22,24,39;Evan B.35;G.B.109;Hattie 134;Isaac 103,151;Isaac Jr.103;Janie P.109;Janora 109;Kate 134;Mary 65;Mollie Kate 35;Mrs.Bettie 134;Mrs.Evan W.6;R.P.2,8,17,20,34,35,39,50,65,143;T.J.39,60;T.J.Jr.40;Thos.5,38,39,65;Thos.J.2,24,34,35;

SHELL:Julia A.71

SHELLIS:Melvin H.3,34

SHERIDAN: Thos.65;Victoria 65.

SHERMAN:Jacob 84,86.

SHIELDS:A.Hunt 116;John W.106,111;Mr.106;W.B.13;Willie 106.

SHINES:Sallie E.90

SHIRLEY:Jas.151

SHOAF:Eliz.34;Emeline M.34;Henry 34;Jacob 13,34;

SHONGUT:AAron 119

SHOREY:Mrs.121,122;S.O.79,108;

SHORT:Rev.88

SHULTZ:H.27.

SHUMAKER:Rev.J.H.93

SHUTE:Anna E.102;Blanchard 102;J.D.102.

SIBLEY:W.L.19,21,43,48,51;

SIGLER:Eliza 75

SILLER:Walter 90

SILVERBERG:Mrs.Eva 86

SIMMONS:G.W.65;Jimmie 13;Phillip 48;Saml.65;Wm.5;

SIMPENDORFER:John 123

SIMPSON:John 121;M.J.73;O.P.13;Sarah 65;

SIMS:Capt.R.G.100,104,113;John Hampton 100;Mrs.104;Mrs. Mamie 85;R.L.76,100;Robt.B.93;W.H.65.

SINK:Geo.B.13,44;

SINSABAUGH:John 75

SKINE:Ben 65;Vergil 65

SKINNER:C.B.40;Caroline M.137;Caroline R.137;Dr.N.C.85;J.S.13;John S.40;Joshua 80,132,137;Louisa 13,40;Maria F.137;N.C.69,137;Theodorick R.40;Tristin L.88,137;Tristrim 78.

SKIPWITH:Thos.56

SKIPWORTH:Virginia 69

SLATER:Green F.78;Mrs.Laura M.110;Mrs.Vastine C.110;

SLEATOR:Thos.M.93

SLEDGE:Sidney S.144

SLOAN:A.D.46

SMALL:Helen B.77;Jas.S.28,147;John 96;Mrs.John 123;Sarah Ann 78;Wm.H.97.

SMALLOW:Emeline M.34;Steven D.34

SMART:David 141

SMEDES:Lovey 91;W.C.30;Gen.Chas.91

SMILEY:Alfred 42

SMITH:A.F.68,144,150;Abe 122;Benj.65;Cath.13;Chas.E.51;Mrs.Chas.E.51;Chas.H.80;Clark W.113;Dr.Geo.107,132;Dr.Jas.M.65,71,81,

SMITH:(cont.)110,116, 132;Eleanor F.68; Eunice W.13;Evie H.72; Fannie Harriet 132; Fannie K.116;Fillar 126; Francis P.65;Frank E.74; Frank P.123;G.W.N.4;Geo. G.132;Georgia 91;Georgiana 132;H.45;Harry 132;Henry 126,148;J.D.87,110,116; J.T.70;Jane 68;Jane Pryor 132;Jas.D.113;John B.133; John J.152;Jos.65;Lawrence 13;Lovena 13;Lawrence W. 52,51;Lee 13;Lee A.13,51, 52;Lou 52;Lovena 51;M.C. 51;Marg.S.30,51;Martha R. 132;Mary E.G.132;Minerva B.4,35;Mollie 135;Mrs.F. P.122;Mrs.Myra 95,116; Myra 144;O.B.36;P.H.13, 51;Preston 13,52;R.M.3, 6,8,13,19,30,51,59;R.W. 21,48;Robt.2,77;Robt.M. 31,52;Robt.Jr.52;Sarah 1; Stephen 13;W.F.148;Walter J.51;Wm.126;Wm.Chew,M.D. 13,42;Wm.F.152;Wm.L.148.

SMYLIE:Mat 65

SMYTHE:M.S.140

SNOEBERGER:H.M.78

SNOWDEN:M.H.133;Mrs.Rosa 133.

SOLOMAN:Bertha 79,119; M.119.

SOMERVILLE:Robt.87,116.

SOMMERS:H.54

SOUTHWORTH:Susie 80

SOWERS:Chas.M.108

SPEAKES:T.B.124

SPELL:Jos.G.65

SPELLS:David 70,71; M.F.71

SPENCER:Jas.G.52;Marshall 105;Rose 105;S.M.47,52; Selden 13,52;

SPICER:Robt.M.40

SPIERS:R.H.138

SPIKES:Wm.66

SPURLOCK:Ned 48

ST.CLAIR:A.M.80

STAFFORD:Chancellor 77; Dr.W.S.122;Edw.81;Mrs. E.124;

STAMPLEY:D.Y.152

STAMPS:John 65;Volney 65

STANDARD:Chas.W.73;J.M.126

STANDEFORD:Virginia 89

STANDIFER:Rev.R.M.86,87,92.

STANLEY:Mrs.Cath.M.52,53; Wright 53.

STANTON;Annie 22;Fred.20.

STAPLES:Walter R.146

STARK:W.W.103

STARKE:Sallie S.82;T.O.65

STARLING:Chas.H.134,138; Georgia 92;

STARNES:Macklin 13

STARNS:Lucy 44

STEADMAN:J.H.75

STEFFGEN:C.84

STEIF:STEIFF:Jos.5,13,35

STEINBERG:Mr.81;E.122;

STENNIS:John 2

STEPHENSON:John 65;Mary 65;Wm.66;

STERLING:Bowman 102;Bowman Jr.126;Corrine 93;J.B.126; Penelope I.126;W.H.116; Wm.F.126.

STERN:Cicie 13;Henry 13; Jos.13;

STEVENS:J.O.45;Joel 50; Thos.T.143;

STEWART:H.T.131;W.B.131

STICKNEY:Lillian H.77; Rev.G.W.75,77;

STIESS:Julia 70

STILE:John 65

STINSON:J.A.126;Wm.75;

STOCKARD:Dr.R.R.79

STOCKET:Thos.G.152;

STOCKMAN:Anna Bell 91

STOCKWELL:Geo.H.137;Mrs. 94

STOKES:Macklin 13;

STONE:Alfred H.110;Carlile 102;Clarence 111;Corrine 110;D.L.73;Daisy 102;Dr. 111;Dr.O.W.82,110;Ella 110; J.71;J.C.102;Jas.70,115; Mary H.110;Mary W.115;Mrs. Jas.105;Mrs.Kate H.116,117; Thos.102;W.A.41;W.W.102,110;

STORM:Edw.81

STOUT:Mary Ellen 13;W.F.13

STOWE:John 142

STOWELL:Lyman 121

STRACHAN:D.53

STRAUSS:Ferdinand 87

STREAM: Geo.122

STRECHIN:David 13

STRETCH:I.11

STRINGER:Drusilla 65

STRONG:Eliz.A.M.50;Isaac 50

STROTHERS:J.B.74

STROUECKER:Geo.Fearn 95; Lucy 95;P.A.95;

STRUM:Jos.78

SUBILEAU:Rev.J.85

SUBLER:Rev.Mr.80

SULLIVAN:Ann 35;Cath.35; E.C.13;J.J.5,8,13,4,24,35; L.S.13,35;M.A.13;Martha K.13,35;Mary J.35;Nancy Y.141;Oliver Goldsmith 1, 141;Saml.N.35;Saml.W.141; Susan A.1,13,15,35,141; Victoria O.67;W.B.130.

SUMMERS:Max 59;Wm.126.

SUTTON:Benj.130;Eliza 94;J.M.97;Jas.M.94,109, 129,130;Kate 69;Mrs.Laura 97;Steve 122;Thos.86; Thos.J.71,130;W.W.5; Wilsey 82.

SWAIN:Jennie O.88;Mollie 90;Nettie 86;S.R.117.

SWAN:Pamelia B.153

SWANSON:Cataline 35,36; Jas.4,13,35,36,37,38;Jas. Jr.4,35,36;Mary 36;Minerva B.4,35,36,37;Monroe 35,36;

SWITZER:J.T.70;Minnie 88; Mrs.81;Mrs.Nannette 109;

SYKES:Willie E.87

SYLVESTER:Tom 123

T

TALBUTT:Chas.B.71

TALIAFERRO:Benj.A.151; Judith 151;

TAMPLIN:Eugenia 84;Pricilla 69;Z.69,71;

TAPLEY:C.S.145

TATE:Jas.W.127

TAYLOR:Alvin 66;Benj.B. 13;Bettie 41,73;David D. 19;J.D.78,122;Lytton L. 70;Mary C.19;Mary H.21; Mollie L.72;Polydore 117; Sadie 91;Saml.T.71;Wm. 3,13;Wm.H.142,145;

TEATS:Mrs.C.K.79

TEDO:Agnes 56;Lucy 56; Jinny 56;Wm.56

TEIDAMON:Mrs.Rebecca 109

TELFER:Wm.121

THEOBALD:Alice 134;Annie 134;Harriet B.133,134; Minerva B.36;Mrs.H.B.94; Thos.S.144;Wm.B.36;

THERELKERD:D.H.65

THERREL:Benj.76

THOMAS:Baxter 90;Bessie 92;J.J.151;M.66;Nellie 128;O.D.74;E.N.140;

THOMELY:J.E.13.

THOMPKINS:Jas.142

THOMPSON:Emory B.127; Herbert 109,134,135;J.W. 89;Jas.75;Julius 109, 134,135;Laval 138;Lewis W.39,134,135;Lucius 134; Martha Ellen 135;Mrs. Sarah 137;Nancy 48;Peter 48;S.A.78;Sallie 134,135.

THRELKELD:D.H.143

THURSTON:F.P.131

TIBBETTS:H.B.40;Louisana 40.

TIDWELL:Edm.3,5,13;Rich. 65;Wm.65.

TILFORD:Mrs.Robt.105;

TILLEY:W.Jr.124.

TILLMAN:Ann Maria 13,56, 57;Annie B.129;Dr.108; Ella 74;F.M.74;Hardin 65;J.T.129;Jas.A.129; Jeff.111;Junius P.56,57; Laura A.56;Lewis 13,56, 57;Louis 28;Malachi 65; Mattie M.56;Sallie A.56.

TILMAN:S.6

TOBIN:Capt.118;

TOMLINSON:W.E.66

TOMPKINS:Geo.M.142;Georgiana 142;John M.143.

TONEY:Jas.C.65

TOOLEY: Mary 65

TOOMBS:R.S.135

TOOMER:FranCIS G.77

TORREY:Eugenia 134,135;

TOUCHSTONE:Dempsey 65; Wm.H.65.

TOY:E.P.50;H.P.13;W.W. 136;Wm.J.47.

TRAMBLE:(blank)123

TRAMMEL:Mrs. 122

TRAVIS:Ella 13

TRAYTON:M.65

TRIGG:Judge 96;A.B.123; Davis B.97;Nancy 94; Sallie 94;W.R.71,72,94, 97,69.

TUCKER:John 65

TULL:Wm.G.127

TUNSTALL:John 65;Lynch 65;Thos.65.

TURNBULL:Andrew 57,58, 59,65,69;Andrew Jr.55, 69;Ann 57;C.F.58,59,69; Cath.57;Chas.141,143; Chas.F.13,152;Claudia 58,59;Cornelia 57;Dr. R.J.13,57,58,59;E.H. Bay 58,59;Fred.65;Fred. G.144;Gracia M.67;H.Eliz. R.58;Lewis 13,57,59;Lewis A.K.58;Mary R.13,58,59; Matthena 57;R.J.6,57,58, 60,69;Rosa K.58;Rose S. 152;Sinclair 57;Wm.67;

TURNER:Alice 93;Celly 135; Clara 55;Henry 46;John 55; Marshall 55;Rev.T.W.90; Sarah 135;Wm.135.

TUTT:W.G.102,126;

TWILFORD:R.W.83

TYLER:Nancy 60

U

UNDERWOOD:R.66

URQUHART:Eloise 89;Mrs. 80;Sadie 83;

UZNAY:Mamie 78

V

Valentine;R.8

VALLIANT:F.127,128,130; Fanny 87,88,91;Frank 68, 88;L.B.68,69,106;Leroy 88,125;Leroy B.128;Mayor 81;Mrs.116;Mrs.F.101; Tenie 128.

VAN OS:Maurice 48; Morris 51;

VANCE:Bettie 135;Eliz.136; Guy P.135;Letitia H.135; Lula V.135,136;Sue 136;Va. 135;Will 136;Geo.T.135; Hamilton M.22;Mrs.Ida M. 118;Otey 136;Rev.A.M.120; Robt.68;Wm.L.135,136;Wm. L.Jr.136.

VANCLIVE:Thos.65

VANDAVENDER:Mary A.14.

VANMETER:Amanda S.68.

VANNERSON:Judge 104;Wm. 20.

VANOMAN:Jas.129;Mary W. 129;Silas 129.

VARNER:Jas.7;John 7;Jos. 7;Mahaley 7;Saml.7;

VAUGHN:Cora Lee 87;David C.113;Harry 123;J.E.89; John 113;Louis 76;Minnie 90;Mrs.C.A.73;

VAUGHT:G.C.77;114;N.G.115

VERNEN:Saml.7

VERNON:Chas.152

VICK:Henry W.66;N.H.2

VILEY:John 148

VINING:Jeptha 65

VINSON:Stokey 65

VIOLET:(no other name)1

VOOHIES:F.F.70

VORMUS:Albert 87;Louis 89

W

WACHSMAN:Mrs.M.92

WADDELL:A.W.131;Alberta C.35;Geo.35,39;Mary B. 17,35,39;

WADDILL:Geo.C.35;Geo. Jr.35.

WADE:Geo.81;Jas.M.146; L.T.19,21,14,43,92;

WAGNER:Frank 122

WAKEFIELD:M.S.14,47; Melissa 47.

WALCOTT:Mrs.T.G.106;Robt. H.129;T.G.113,129;

WALDAUER:Bertha 84; Emma 88

WALKER:C.L.20;Doswell 84;Dr.J.S.79,102,110; E.V.Jr.41;Ellen 14;Eliz. 58,59;F.W.14;Fannie 14; FREEMAN 148;Jas.S.148; John 59;Laura 57;Letitia 60;Marg.H.153;Mrs.Ann 59; N.S.139;Orville B.110; Peter M.153;R.J.65;Rosa K.T.58,59;Sarah F.148.

WALKIN:Mary S.L.7;Wm. S.7.

WALL:Abe 123;Geo.A.116; Joe 116

WALLACE:Jos.65,143,147; Wm.44;

WALLIS:E.68;E.S.67;T.A. 74;T.R.72;

WALLS:Jake 46;Millie 46

WALTEN:Gray 14

WALTERS:Wiley A.28

WALTON:Claudia 83;J.G.67

WALWORTH:H.F.65

WARBURTON:Rich.14;

WARD:A.G.30,45,47,52; Adelia 148;Amy 148;Aurelia 23;Carroll 23;Emily M.126;Evermont 148;G.V. 86,108;Geo.W.66,143;Jas. 86;Jeremiah S.65;148; John W.145;Junius R.108; Marg.E.30;Mrs.A.124;R.J. 65,126;Thos.66;

WARDEN:Nellie 123

WARE:Nathan A.145;Nathl. 65

WARFIELD:Dr.L.105;E.R. 105;Florence 90;Mrs.Carneal 100;Thos.B.65;

WARING:Jas.A.132

WARTCHE:WARTSKI:WASTCKI:
Minna 120,137

WARTHUR:Isaac 66

WASHINGTON:Geo.137;
Minnie 137.

WATERS:J.F.72;J.T.F.
70;S.E.90;

WATKINS: Leigh 20

WATSON:A.P.88,112;Anna
24;B.E.48;Benj.B.33;
Georgia 24;H.C.140;Harriet 14;Hattie S.112;J.J.
28,45,52,53,60;Jeremiah
24;John 65;L.C.46;L.C.Jr.
48;L.W.48,50;Louis C.48,
14;Martha Eleanor 73;
Mrs.E.D.112;Mrs.Louis W.
48;Olivia 24,48;Pompey
14;Thos.29;Virginia 82;
Willis 73.

WATT:Mary Bell 89

WATTS:Rebecca 72;Robt.
85;

WEATHERBEE:C.F.113

WEBB:Joe G.87;John 65;
Mary 65;Lommie 87;

WEBBER:A.W.130

WEDLEY:G.B.MD 14,46;
Mary 46;

WEEMS:L.B.73

WEESE:Henry 65

WEIGHTMAN:Minnie V.14

WEILENMAN:Addie 87;
Mary C.90

WEISENFELDT:Mrs.L.124

WEISS:Hannah132;Ludwig
132;Emeline 77;Jacob
132;John 73;Malinda 84,
132;Morris 77,114,132;

WEITZENFELDT:L.123

WELCH:Chas.65

WELEIG:WELLING:Antram
14,57;Henry 57,

WELLS:Carson 26;Cath.26;
Frances 20;Frances Foster
25;Henrietta F.26;J.J.14,
25,26,37;Martha A.Chaney
8,25,26,37;Martha J.26;
Mary 109;Mary E.26;Saml.
1;2,55;Saml.W.8,14,16,20,
25,26,37;Sarah Frances 20,
26;Willie B.109;Wm.73;
Wm.C.66.

WESCOTT:Mrs.C.E.54;Wm.
F.54.

WESLEY:Aaron E.14;Chas.
14;Indiana 14;Robt.Jr.
14;Robt.Sr.14;Steven 14;

WEST:A.C.73;Aemilius C.
103;Lizzie Mauray 72;
Mary 35;Sallie B.78;Steph.
35;W.E.72,79.

WESTBROOK:E.C.17

WETHERBEE:Eva122;H.E.76,
119,130;L.P.123;Mable 124;
Mrs.Belle V.82;Mrs.L.P.
122;Wes.124;Wesley O.75.

WHEATLEY:Mary Louise 138;
W.B.73;Mrs.E.N.86.

WHEELER:Albert 123;John
14,46;Julia 46;Mark 65;
Mary E.132;Wash.14

WHEELESS:Henry S.127

WHITBY:WHITELY:M.J.V.7

WHITE:C.S.82;Chas.S.105;
Dr.Stuart 102;Ellen 38;
Emily 152;Franklin 152;
H.6;Henrietta 1,38;J.J.
2;Jas.48;Jesse 152;John
66;Lucy 152;Martha E.67;
Mary 38;Mrs.Amanda B.105;
Mrs.Mary L.76;Octavia 38;
Stuart 70;Van Dyke 152;
Willie B.123;Wm.1,38;Wm.E.
14,38;

WHITEHEAD:Arthur 84;(blank)
41;Mr.107;Rennah 107;S.Y.
14,38;

WHITEWAY:Albert 134,137;
Ed.80;Ellen 137;

WHITFIELD:Ben 66.;

WHITTEN:Martha 16

WHITUS:James Monroe 36, 37.

WICKLIFFE:A.W.83,94.

WIGGINS:H.R.92

WILBURN:Adelia 148; Amanda 148;Joel 148;M. Alice 148;Wm.H.148.

WILCOX:Jas.O.68

WILEZINSKI:J.128,130;

WILHAM:Chas.59

WILKERSON:J.F.73;Jeff. 65;M.L.92;Mrs.Mary E.53

WILKINS:G.M.57;Wm.W.142

WILKINSKI:Flora 132

WILKINSON:D.M.66;I.S. 65;Jane 65;Peter 65;

WILLBORN:S.J.134

WILLHITE:Penelope 144

WILLIAM:R.2

WILLIAMS:Eliz.138;Aaron 14;Anna 107;Chas.123; Chas.E.14;Chas.P.107; D.G.8;D.T.2,5,14,24; Daniel 91;Frank 70; Ginney 126;Grant 97; H.R.72,74;J.M.148;J.R. 149;Jas.14,75;John 14, 112;Lizzie 55;Louisa 14,77;M.C.14;Marg.A.15; Martha A.72;Melissa 46; Merritt 107;Mrs.E.1.35; R.14;Sampson 15,29,27; Smith 14,46;Sylvia 46; T.J.139;C.P.107.

WILLIAMSON:Russell M. 143

WILLINGHAM:John W.7

WILLIS:Fannie 82

WILLS:J.D.98

WILMOT:Anna L.71;Bowman 116;J.L.71;Lena 81.

WILNE:Geo.P.99

WILSHIRE:R.A.74

WILSON:Anne 50;A.G.139; A.L.66;Adelia 129;Bettie A.70;Capt.J.W.104;Eugene 129;Gilmore 50;J.S.72, 73;Jack 50;Jas.74;John 129;K.R.73,78,104;Rachel 50;Sam 14;Saml.A.139; Sarah 129;Stephen 50; Susan 14,50;Thos.W.68; Victor F.151.

WILZINSKI:H.137;N.137

WINEBERG:Lena 84

WINFIELD:Amelia 14;

WING:C.R.92;

WINGATE:E.F.66

WINGFIELD:A.P.79;Bowdrie 100;Mrs.Mattie 137

WINGPEGLER:John W.73,71

WINN:Aramus 151;Emaline S.151;J.B.129;Orsames 129;S.B.139;Saphrona 129

WINSLOW:E.M.14;O.135; R.P.14

WINSTON:Jos.88;Robt.L.14

WINTER:Maria 121;W.S.75

WISE:Isidore 82

WITKOWSKI:Mrs.A.V.117; Gustave 43,107;

WOLFE:Chas.W.119

WOLFENSTEIN:Minnie 78

WOOD:Ethan A.26;L.H.129; Leonorah 135;M.92;Nancy A.20;Wm.129;Wm.N.101; W.S.22

WOODBURN: John 152;John R.68,152.

WOODS:Alfred 14;Henrietta 85;Lena F.74

WOODWARD:Alfred 60; Thomtom 60.

WOOLF:Lulu 87

WOOLFOLK:Dr.J.P.17;J.E. 14,24;J.H.2;J.P.29,39; Jas.B.14,24,35;Leannah 24;P.P.24;V.T.14;Verl.32

WORTHINGTON Amanda 70, 94;Annie 88;Ben 128; Benj.T.73,106;Carrie 83,85,87;Chas.138;Dr. W.W.114;E.P.138;E.T. 138;Edw.138;Elisha 138; Elly 125;G.P.68,94,130; Geo.T.153;Isaac 106,128; Josephine 130,153;Lydia 88;Mark 100;Mary B.71, 83;Mary M.67;Mrs.Amanda 105;Mrs.Ann 67,106,128; Mrs.Geo.P.103;Mrs.B.T. 100;S.105,115; Saml.83,105;Theod.69, 128;Thos.85,106,128,138; Thos.M.67;W.M.102,105, 115;Wm.128,138;Wm.W.138

WRAY:Elijah 91

WREN:Wm.B.143

WRIGHT: Abraham 66;C.J. 74;G.M.105;J.Price 90; Martina 76;Mrs.105; Myrthe E.149;Robt.R.75; W.E.149;W.S.138;Wm.3

WRIGLEY:Caroline 131; Edw.W.130,131;Geo.130 131;Henry 130,131;John Lees 130,131;Sarah J.131

WYATT:Ed 104

WYNENS:Allen 143

Y

YAGER:Andras 134;Andw. 97;Geo.134;Goodie 134; Leroy 134;Lula 134; Lula C.97;Marg.97;Marg. R.134;Maurey 134;Mr.A. 118;Wm.134;

YANDALL:Wm.W.3

YEAGLE: Geo.L.147

YEISER:Chas.R.128;Emma 131;Katie 128;

YERGER:Alex 74;Amanda V.68;Anna Hunter 95;Arth. R.123;Bettie 138;Col. Alex 101;Hal 115;Harry 71;Harvey 138;Jas.R.117; Jennie 137;Judge Shall 115;L.P.80;Malvina 74; Mary A.127;Mary H.138; May 74;Mildred H.111; Mrs.Mary 115;Mrs.Shall 109;Mrs.E.B.101;Mrs.Hal

YERGER:(cont.)111;Mrs. Henrietta 116;Mrs.W.G.95; Orville 136;Shall 138; W.G.95;W.Y.135;Will 120; Wm.111,138;Wm.G.71,74,128, 137,138;Wm.Jr.120;

YOCUM:Sophia 124.

YOUNG:Dr.J.L.86;Grant 14; Martha 44;Mrs.121;Mrs.G.A. 78;Mrs.J.H.97;N.14;R.A.67;

Z

ZUNTS:Jas.E.149.

www.ingramcontent.com/pod-product-compliance
Lightning Source LLC
Chambersburg PA
CBHW030552080526
44585CB00012B/345